Reinventing the Republic

Reinventing the Republic

GENDER, MIGRATION, AND CITIZENSHIP IN FRANCE

Catherine Raissiguier

Stanford University Press
Stanford, California

Stanford University Press
Stanford, California

Printed in the United States of America on acid-free, archival-quality paper

Library of Congress Cataloging-in-Publication Data

Raissiguier, Catherine, 1957-
 Reinventing the Republic : gender, migration, and citizenship in France / Catherine
Raissiguier.
     p. cm.
 Includes bibliographical references and index.
 ISBN 978-0-8047-5761-4 (cloth : alk. paper)--ISBN 978-0-8047-5762-1 (pbk. : alk. paper)
 1. Women illegal aliens--Political activity--France. 2. Women illegal aliens--Legal
status, laws, etc.--France. 3. Women immigrants--Political activity--France. 4. Women
immigrants--Legal status, laws, etc.--France. 5. France--Emigration and immigration-
-Political aspects. 6. France--Emigration and immigration--Social aspects. 7. France--
Emigration and immigration--Government policy. I. Title.
 JV7984.R35 2010
 305.48'96912--dc22   2010004866

Typeset by Bruce Lundquist in 10/14 Minion

To Selam, Jacqueline, and Jean

CONTENTS

LIST OF FIGURES

PREFACE

My work on *Reiventing the Republic* started in the mid-nineties as I watched, from a distance, a group of undocumented immigrants come out of their legal and social obscurity to challenge the French state and its immigration policies. I did not know then what the book would be about or, for that matter, if it would be a book at all, but I immediately sensed that what these immigrants were doing was worth my political and scholarly attention.

The story that ignited this project began in 1996 in the sanctuary of a Parisian church suddenly disrupted by an early-morning police raid. The *sans-papiers*, literally "without papers," occupying the church were undocumented immigrants and refugees under threat of deportation. They were demanding that France legalize their status. They argued that it was the French state and its increasingly restrictive immigration policies that had created them. Insisting that they were not *clandestins*—a French word connoting both the illegal and the hidden—but simply without papers (and hence without rights), they managed to highlight and pry open fissures and contradictions within the dominant narratives and practices of the French state and its civil society.

As I planned a research trip in 2002 to analyze *sans-papiers* organizing in France, I thought my research would lead to a straightforward qualitative study of the struggle and generate a much-needed feminist analysis of the *sans-papiers* movement. I wanted to trace undocumented immigrants in one of the Paris *banlieues* and in the southern city of Marseilles, where I knew groups of *sans-papiers* had been agitating for change since the early-morning raid that had set this study in motion.[1] The research trip was productive and successful. I gathered enough materials to produce a nicely layered analysis of the struggle. I also gathered something else, though: a nagging sense that in order to understand fully the political import of the *sans-papiers'* intervention into the French political arena, I would have to connect their struggle to that of other groups also fighting for inclusion and fair treatment in France. *Reinventing the Republic* is the result of this lingering sense. Although the book offers a unique feminist reading of the *sans-papiers* movement, it moves beyond it and looks at the ways in which France has helped produce undocumented immigrants (and others) as impossible subjects of the French Republic, and at how these subjects, in turn, might help us imagine different forms of inclusion and belonging.

My investigation of the *sans-papiers* is based on in-depth semidirected interviews of undocumented immigrants, their French allies, and other political and social actors involved with and around the movement. It also draws on detailed observations of the organizational meetings of *sans-papiers* collectives, of the internal structure of those collectives, and of the particular dynamics of the movement.[2] Finally, it builds from close readings of the legal, political, and cultural texts that have constructed the *sans-papiers*. I focus on the laws that created the legal impasse in which many of the *sans-papiers* find themselves. I also scrutinize popular representations of the *sans-papiers* in the French media and its coverage of the movement. I pay particular attention to the vast array of visual imagery (graffiti, photos, and cartoons) that has been produced about and around the *sans-papiers*. More specifically, I analyze these images for their gendered meanings and for the ways in which they intersect with discursive processes of racialization and othering.[3]

Besides the tangible success of the actual legalization of thousands of *sans-papiers,* the movement also challenges existing notions of citizenship and political participation in a modern Western democracy. By coming out and voicing their grievances, and by refusing to be represented by good-willed French citizens, the *sans-papiers* have defied business as usual in the traditional arenas of the have-nots. Women—especially in the early stages of the movement—refused to remain silent. Though often unnoticed, they challenged dominant representations of immigrant women in France. Through its careful analysis of women in the *sans-papiers* movement, *Reinventing the Republic* builds on a growing body of scholarship that has begun to point out the invisibility of women in studies of population movements, and to uncover the presence and role of women within French immigration.[4] However, these studies tend to isolate gender from other forms of domination and do not always capture the less tangible ideological, cultural, and personal aspects of immigration.[5] Building and expanding on this body of knowledge, I propose an approach that focuses on a local site of resistance and foregrounds the narratives of undocumented women, known as *sans-papières*.[6]

The *sans-papiers* movement offers a unique opportunity to study the complex gendered and transnational processes that have produced the *sans-papiers*. They allow us to focus on a specific group of immigrants who, in spite of their heterogeneity, share common experiences and have developed a politics based not on (national or gender) identity but rather on the commonality of their social locations. Finally, because of the unique strategies they use, the *sans-papiers* offer an ideal case study of how, in France, anti-colonial and antiracist struggles, feminist and queer activism, labor organizing, and cultural movements can (or fail to) intersect to produce innovative social and political interventions.

The *sans-papiers*, needless to say, have generated many studies in France. However, with only a few exceptions—the work of Madjiguène Cissé, Claudie Lesselier, and Jane Freedman stand out—most of these studies do not focus on women within the *sans-papiers* struggles, let alone explore the ways in which gender intersects with other forms of exclusion and domination in France.[7] Analyzing the multiple meanings of the *sans-papiers* story demanded that I borrow from a broad spectrum of fields and analytical approaches, including history, sociology, and cultural studies. It also reignited an early hunch that in order to understand its impact fully I would have to place the *sans-papiers* struggle in relation to other sites of contestation.

In the past decade, a variety of social movements leveled interesting critiques of the French republican tradition and brought renewed scholarly attention to the topic. The parity (*parité*) movement that established equal representation of men and women among candidates for elective office in 2000, the gay and lesbian movement that won civil unions—*Pacte Civil de Solidarité (PaCS)*—for both heterosexual and homosexual couples in 1999, and the *sans-papiers* movement that has been demanding the collective regularization of undocumented immigrants since the mid-nineties emerged as fruitful sites to explore and better understand the French political tradition and the major challenges it faces in the twenty-first century. Joan Wallach Scott's *Parité! Sexual Equality and the Crisis of French Universalism* and Enda McCaffrey's *The Gay Republic: Sexuality, Citizenship and Subversion in France*, for instance, offer timely analyses of political movements that engage and challenge France's republican political tradition.[8] Both authors analyze how recent debates about gender and sexual orientation are transforming traditional constructions of citizenship in France, and they point out the contradictions and limits of a system rooted in abstract universal equality. These two texts allude to immigration and its attendant racial politics, but fail to explore seriously their complex and underscrutinized relation to gender and sexual politics. As a result, neither fully documents the complexity of the crisis that is troubling the French republic. Neither captures the creative and resistive possibilities that exist where different groups and their politics meet.

Reinventing the Republic focuses primarily on undocumented immigrants and their political and cultural interventions within universalist France. However, the analysis spans other sites of contestation as well. By connecting activist struggles that may ignore each other and that too often are studied separately, the book highlights the ways in which different forms of exclusion and discrimination operate and modulate each other in France. Indeed, it is these insights into three different social movements (*sans-papiers*, *Parité*, and *PaCS*) that enable *Reinventing the Republic* to question and challenge the dominant narrative of a "French exception." Although the book offers a solid cultural analysis of the *sans-papiers* and their movement, and foregrounds the crucial role played by women within the struggle, its major contribution in fact lies in its critique of the French republican tradition. Ultimately, with undocumented immigrants, queers, feminists, and other outsiders-within, *Reinventing the Republic* strongly asserts the need for and possibility of different ways of being in and of France.

ACKNOWLEDGMENTS

This book has been a long time in the making, and writing it has often felt like a lonely affair. Yet it would not have been possible without the help of the many activists, friends, colleagues, students, and family members with whom I have been sharing its arguments for over a decade.

My first thanks go to the undocumented immigrants whose story lies at the heart of this project. My heartfelt gratitude goes to Madjiguène Cissé, whom I never had the privilege to meet because she was no longer in France when I conducted my fieldwork; still, her actions, thoughts, and writings have had a great impact on the ideas I present in the book. In Paris, Saint-Denis, Marseilles, and Lille I was met with exceptional generosity and help from a variety of *sans-papiers* and *sans-papières* and their French allies. In particular, I thank Aminata Diane, Aminata Diouf, and Beija Benkouka for their commitment to the struggle and their willingness to help me understand the internal dynamics of the movement.

I also thank the many other scholar-activists who shared their work and ideas with me while I was conducting my research for this project. I am immensely grateful to Claudie Lesselier, who shared her activist insights, opened her archives, and generously provided me with the documents that she and the RAJFIRE had collected over the years. Claudie introduced me to other activists in the field and rigorously commented on an early essay that has made its way into the book. I thank Saïd Bouamama, Mogniss H. Abdallah, Marianne Wolff, Roland Djane, Judith Martin, Agnès Clusel, Claude Goislot, Roseline Tiset, Nadia Châabane, Isabelle de St. Saens, and Béa Verri, who also shared their ideas, resources, and activist contacts.

The research phase of this book was aided by grants from the University of Cincinnati Taft Memorial Fund. New Jersey City University also partially supported this project through its Separately Budgeted Research funds. I thank the College of Arts and Sciences and the Office of the Vice President for Academic Affairs at New Jersey City University for their continued support.

I am indebted to my students, who generated interesting and provocative questions about the arguments generated in the book. More specifically, I thank the graduate students at the University of Cincinnati who took my Gender, Immigration, and Citizenship seminar and asked the difficult questions. I also thank several colleagues in Cincinnati who read early versions of the work. I have especially gained from my discussions with Karla Goldman, Joanne Meyerowitz, Katharina Gerstenberger, and Maura O'Connor. At Jersey City University, Hilary Englert, Chris Cunningham, Mary Loving Blanchard, Jacqueline Ellis, and Mirtha Quintanales helped me think about the women's narratives and how I would integrate them into the text.

I presented parts of this research to a number of audiences from a variety of fields. They all helped to strengthen the interdisciplinary reach of the text. In particular, I thank the Feminist Theory and Gender Studies Section of the International Studies Association for providing a challenging and supportive environment in which to present and discuss pieces of this research. During the academic year 2005-2006, I had the privilege to participate in the interdisciplinary seminar Diasporas and Migrations organized by the Institute for Research on Women at Rutgers University. I thank all of the colloquium participants; they pushed my thinking in interesting and productive ways. I also thank the Institute's director, Nancy Hewitt, and its associate director, Beth Hutchison, for their warm welcome and their continued support. My gratitude goes to Kayo Denda, who read my paper and provided insightful comments. In 2006 I presented an early version of Chapter 5 at the Women and Society Seminar at Columbia University. I thank all of the seminar's participants for their ideas and their questions. I especially credit Robyn Rodriguez for offering a smart and challenging response to the paper and for her ongoing support. I thank Susan Fischer for inviting me to share my work and for introducing me to the Women and Society Seminar community.

I thank Melissa Ragona, Henrietta Gunkel, Steve Edwin, and the late Claude Zaidman, who gave parts of this project a careful read and gave me confidence that it was indeed worth publishing. I also thank Obiama Nnaemeka, Anne Sisson Runyan, Cynthia Enloe, Judy Scales-Trent, Signe Arnfred, Liz

Kennedy, and Patricia Catrillo for the many ways they have helped and supported me and my work. My heartfelt gratitude goes to Mireille Rosello and the Stanford University Press's anonymous readers who read the manuscript in its entirety and provided invaluable feedback.

This project is a much better one because of the many friends who have given me their time and support over the years. In particular, I thank Chris Cuomo, Karla Goldman, Ursula Roma, Karen Schlanger, Laurie Fuller, Erica Meiners, Junko Kanamura, Nadine Audibert, Danièle Borgeon, and Kowsar Chowdhury.

Many people at Stanford University Press helped make this a better book. In particular, I thank Kate Wahl for taking interest and believing in this project from the start. I thank Jennifer Helé, who during her short stay at the press helped in many ways as I navigated the revision process. I also thank Mariana Raykov, who managed the production process; Joa Suorez, who helped greatly with formatting and other technical questions; and Alice Rowan, for her careful copyediting.

My family in France and in England asked candid questions about the content and the unusual length (in their mind) of the project. In their own way they helped it along. I would not have been able to finish this book if it had not been for the support, love, and infallible help of Lycette Nelson, with whom I share my life. She read the manuscript in its various renditions many times; her editorial savvy helped the readability of the text tremendously. Finally, I thank my daughter, Selamawit Rose Nelson. I would be remiss if I did not mention here that I received great help from the staff of Selam's day care. In particular, I thank Shakeea Rodriguez for taking such good care of Selam while I was at work on this project. Selam's inner beauty, her kind spirit, and her strategic interruptions of the writing with giggles, scribbles, and play requests have certainly helped me get to the end line.

Reinventing the Republic

INTRODUCTION: TAKING ON THE REPUBLIC

France's open door is closing.
Christian Science Monitor, September 18, 2007

It is not yet fortress France, but the welcome mat is vanishing for immigrants.
San Francisco Chronicle and Washington Times, June 16, 2008

The issue at stake is the unfinished condition of democracy, and that issue obtains the world over: there is no such thing as the "French exception."
Yann Moulier Boutang, November 27, 2005

I BEGIN THIS ANALYSIS by exploring the ways in which France has managed to hold on to and successfully export the idea of a "French exception" while aligning itself with a broad European Union. trend of immigration control and border closure for third-country nationals.[1] As this chapter's opening quotes suggest, the "French exception" narrative is indeed one of the most successful, enduring, and contradictory aspects of French political culture.[2] In *Reinventing the Republic*, I argue that the "exceptional" nature of the French political tradition resides rather in its ability to foreground a strong discourse of universal inclusion and equality along with its unique resistance to acknowledging exclusionary and discriminatory discourses and practices both in its past and in its present. The former has fueled productive forms of resistance and contestation within France. The latter has certainly limited their liberatory potentials.

Adrian Favell, in his comparative study of France and Britain, documents how French ruling elites, through the sheer reiteration of the "French exception" narrative, participate in the "reaffirmation of a particular national myth." Favell importantly points to the myth of French republican citizenship as a public theory "at pains to mask the recentness and artificiality of its construction and the incompleteness of the questions it focuses on."[3] Belying the dominant "French exception" narrative, Favell points to the growing influence that supranational forces have (and the related declining role of national intellectual elites) on immigration policies in France. Interestingly, in the preface to the second edition of *Philosophies of Integration*, Favell also acknowledges the unique role played by the *sans-papiers* movement in challenging the republican myth of citizenship and, in the process, generating a growing awareness of the "racially-inflected" position of "black African migrants" in France: "The outcome of the grassroots *sans-papiers* movement also revealed a new edge to French immigration politics, introducing critical arguments about human rights and 'personhood' in a French debate normally dominated by nationally-bounded normative considerations."[4] Indeed, by disrupting business as usual and inserting "critical arguments" into immigration discussions in France, the *sans-papiers* movement invites us to rethink Franco-French understandings of citizenship, national belonging, and equality. Throughout *Reinventing the Republic*, I document the various challenges leveled by the *sans-papiers* and the *sans-papières* (the women in the movement) at dominant French political narratives and their attendant administrative practices.

IMPOSSIBLE SUBJECTS, IMPOSSIBLE POLITICS

Increasingly restrictive immigration policies in France have turned large numbers of immigrants, among them many women, into *clandestins* (a label they strongly reject). By increasing police scrutiny and symbolically constructing certain immigrants as criminals and outsiders, recent immigration laws have in fact intensified the forms of civil and economic *précarité* many of them experience.[5] Throughout the book I argue that—against the backdrop of global economic transformations, the construction of Europe, and increased national anxieties—hegemonic discursive and material practices construct certain immigrants as impossible subjects of the Republic. I borrow the term *impossible* from a small group of scholars who use the concept of *impossibility* to analyze related but different mechanisms of belonging and exclusion.[6] In France, discursive constructions of foreigners as "impossible citizens" date back to the beginnings of the French Republic. Sophie Wahnich, in her work on hospitality and national belonging in the context of the French Revolution, documents how the foreigner takes shape (*prend forme*) through a series of discourses and practices that posit him as a potential traitor to the budding nation-state (1789–1794).[7] Wahnich documents, among other things, the emergence of a new administrative apparatus that singles out foreigners and in the process creates different types of subjects within the Republic: "The dyad foreigner/national is constructed during the revolution on these bases, the nation can only be one and indivisible[. . . .] In a revolution where the stranger remains a paradox of announced universality, the territorialization of identities is the avowal of an accepted closure of the revolutionary project."[8] In the ongoing tension between dreams of hospitality and needs for security of the first years of the Republic, Wahnich argues, the stated formal rights of foreigners are sharply weakened by their increased surveillance.[9]

Mae N. Ngai charts a history of immigration restriction in the United States that began after World War I, to uncover the dual and related production of illegal aliens as impossible subjects of the United States as a modern nation. Restriction, Ngai argues,

> invariably generated illegal immigration and introduced that problem into the internal spaces of the nation. Immigration restriction produced the illegal alien as a new legal and political subject, whose inclusion within the nation was simultaneously a social reality and a legal impossibility—a subject barred from citizenship and without rights[. . . .] The illegal alien is thus an "impossible subject," a person who cannot be and a problem that cannot be solved.[10]

By focusing on South Asian queer politics in the United States, Gayatri Gopinah analyzes and challenges the various processes that elide the possibility of certain subjectivities within dominant nationalist and diasporic discourses. She argues:

> Given the illegibility and unrepresentability of a non-heteronormative female subject within patriarchal and heterosexual configurations of both nation and diaspora, the project of locating a "queer South Asian diasporic subject"—and a queer female subject in particular—may begin to challenge the dominance of such configurations. Revealing the mechanisms by which a queer female diasporic positionality is rendered impossible strikes at the very foundation of these ideological structures.[11]

In this book, I use the concept of impossibility to conjure up the complex mechanisms (both material and discursive) that establish impossible subject positions within the French nation. These mechanisms include discursive practices that turn certain immigrants into unthinkable members of the national body, as well as material and legal practices that locate them in spaces of impossibility. In addition, I deploy the term *impossible* to suggest the unnerving and "unruly" forms of political intervention that these mechanisms elicit. Here I draw on the work of Monisha Das Gupta on South Asian politics in the United States, in order to evoke the ways in which immigrants are involved in political practices that question nation-based understandings of civil membership, and to show how they invent new ways to stake their claims and stage their battles.[12] In particular, like Das Gupta, I am interested in exploring the various ways in which certain immigrants "fight against multiple techniques of subordination through claims that do not rely on citizenship."[13] Within a "complex of rights" that draws on local, national, and transnational laws, these immigrants creatively engage the political system that has put them under erasure.[14]

REINVENTING CITIZENSHIP

French republicanism is often described as a unique system that has generously opened the door to political refugees, established equal rights for individual immigrants settled within the national territory, and conceptualized nationality in terms of political membership rather than ethnic descent. The French republican model of immigration is said to have successfully integrated several waves of immigrants into the national community and socialized them into the French republican culture.[15] Feminist scholars, however, have forcefully argued, on the basis of the doctrine of abstract individualism and the strict division between a public (male) sphere and a private (female) sphere, that the hegemonic rhetoric of "the Republic" and "universal citizenship" is in fact based on the exclusion of women.[16] Gender discrimination, they argue, is constitutive of the republican tradition. Scholars of colonialism, immigration, and race relations have also demonstrated that the republican tradition is filled with contradictions that have shaped France's relationship toward foreigners and colonial subjects and delineated the contours of its politics of immigration. These scholars highlight the presence of processes of exclusion and racialization within the republican model of immigration and integration.[17] These processes, according to French historian Gérard Noiriel, tend to be deemphasized because "the French model" is traditionally opposed to the German one and found "generous" in comparison.[18] To date, however, there has been little discussion of the ways in which dynamics of racial and gender exclusion intersect to produce multiple and interrelated processes of exclusion and domination in France.

The racially inflected forms of exclusion that have resulted from the immigration and nationality laws discussed in this book are still being described by many within France as extraneous to its republican tradition. Indeed, such mechanisms are often presented as anomalies that have developed on the fertile terrain of an international economic crisis and because of the growing and perverse influence of a radical Right squarely positioned outside the republican consensus.

In *Reinventing the Republic*, I build on and depart from this interpretation in two ways. First, I argue that processes of exclusion and racialization have indeed changed over time, and increased at moments of economic and political crisis, but far from being anomalies within the French republican tradition, they are in fact *constitutive* of that tradition.[19] Second, I suggest that these mechanisms, which affect entire migrant communities, must also be understood as *gendered* and *classed* processes. As a whole, *Reinventing the Republic* can be read as one intervention within recent French conversations that contest deeply entrenched understandings of the French republican tradition as uniquely inclusive and egalitarian. Recent organizing efforts in France by feminists and queers have challenged such understandings. For instance, activists involved in the parity movement and those who agitated to obtain civil unions in France, albeit in different ways, have questioned traditional constructions of citizenship in France and generated a greater public awareness of the contradictions and limits of a system rooted in abstract universal equality.

The basic goal of the parity movement was to ensure French women equal access to elective office and, more important, to enable them to represent the nation.[20] French parity activists (*paritaristes*) established a direct link between gender disparity within elected bodies and the lack of actual democracy in France. "By accepting the routine exclusion of women within popular representative bodies," *paritaristes* declared, "the French republic, which claims to be democratic, ranks at the tail-end of European nations in terms of female representation in parliament."[21] To remedy the situation and begin a much needed process of democratization in France, gender parity would have to be codified into law, and voting mechanisms would have to be transformed to allow for its application.

Rejecting a politics of quotas that would point to minority rights and an American-style multiculturalism, *paritaristes* demanded that political power be equally divided between men and women.[22] The inclusion of women in the political process, they insisted, would not happen on the grounds of their ability to better represent the interests of other women but rather on the grounds of their given ability (just like men) to represent the collective interests of the nation. To render parity intelligible within the dominant idiom of the Republic, early formulations of parity were indeed strictly universalist.

Building on her early historical work on the French revolution in *Parité!* Joan Wallach Scott once again exposes the limits of a political and discursive model that produces excluded groups and categories of people who are then left to invoke their particular status (their difference) in order to make rights claims. Scott reminds us that focusing on difference is always a flawed strategy within the logic of the Republic, which historically has seen difference as not amenable to abstraction and therefore not intelligible within French universalism. By figuring the abstract individual as always already sexed, Scott tells us, the *paritaristes* managed to write women into the logic and the reach of universalism. Also, by insisting that the abstract individual is always male or female (an invocation of universal anatomical dualism), they succeeded in erasing sexual difference from the list of meaningful categories within French politics. "In a strikingly original and paradoxical move," Scott writes, "the paritaristes sought to *unsex* the national representation by *sexing* the individual."[23] In other words, *paritaristes* were able to subvert the mechanisms that have long positioned women as impossible subjects of the Republic.

Detractors of the parity movement, however, have pointed out its essentialist and elitist impulses, its naive reliance on legal remedies, and its lack of attention to other forms of inequality.[24] Others have critiqued the movement for its wholehearted embrace of republican models of political inclusion and representation. In particular, the *paritaristes*' insistence that "sex is a universal difference produced, in the context of the *Pacte Civil de Solidarité* (PaCS) debate, a serious backlash.[25] Even Scott, who takes issue with most of these criticisms for their reductive and ahistorical stance, does concede that it is precisely the "essentialist possibilities" connected to the sexual dualism at the core of *parité* that allowed later-day *paritaristes* to reframe parity within a dangerous understanding of sexual difference (and its related normative heterosexuality) as a law of nature and therefore as the basis for modern democratic representation.[26]

The insistence of activists on the universality of sex difference made discussions of parity possible in France and ensured the passage of the constitutional amendment that successfully concluded the campaign for parity. It also posited women (but not other groups) as worthy of representing the nation.

Here I would like to suggest that French *paritaristes* accomplished two contradictory things at the same time. On the one hand, they managed to shatter the hypocrisy of "formal" equality and highlight the ways in which, in France, men have used the very concept of abstract universalism to snatch political power and keep it. On the other hand, in the process they ignored other social hierarchies and blocked the possibility of alliances with groups that might have a shared interest in questioning the conditions of political and social inclusion within the French republican tradition. Indeed, by prioritizing sex and gender over other forms of discrimination and exploitation, the *paritaristes* and their supporters failed, in the end, to articulate the many ways in which sexual difference inflects and is inflected by other sites of difference.

As is discussed at greater length in Chapter 6, proponents of civil unions in France also worked within the boundaries of French republicanism. Indeed, the PaCS legislation provides rights and privileges to all couples regardless of their sexual orientation. In spite of its universal dressing, the agitation that led to the PaCS law was meant to address sexual inequality and the specific situation of lesbian and gay couples in France. By highlighting and politicizing some of the prerequisites of republican citizenship, such as the relegation of sexuality to the private sphere, queer activists (like *paritaristes* and *sans-papiers*) point to the various mechanisms that construct impossible subjectivities within the French Republic. Moreover, and in spite of the limitations of the PaCS legislation, it has been suggested that the very inclusion of lesbian and gay couples in French law—like the inclusion of gender parity—represents a radical challenge to the Republic and opens up a discursive and political breach for future transformations.[27]

Reinventing the Republic foregrounds the *sans-papiers* movement and points out ways in which it might help us imagine and effect such transformations. Like Eric Fassin, French scholar and author of the manifesto *Pour l'égalité sexuelle* (For sexual equality), *sans-papiers* believe in the possibility of a radical universalism in France.[28] In the manifesto, Fassin invites us to imagine a republic founded on the absolute and principled rejection of any form of inequality and discrimination within its bounds. This is not a republic, however, based on abstract universal principles. Rather, it is a republic that looks hard at how it has created impossible subjects, and at how it responds, because it must, to the political challenges leveled by them.

In *Reinventing the Republic*, I read the *sans-papiers* movement as a unique political and cultural intervention. In particular, I am attentive to the creative ways in which the *sans-papiers*—as modern French products—appropriate and transform notions of democracy, citizenship, and republican belonging. At the same time, I point out the many ways in which they have been turned into impossible subjects of the Republic.

The *sans-papiers* also alert us to the dual and contradictory mechanism that lies at the heart of the institution of citizenship. As Linda Bosniak demonstrates in *The Citizen and the Alien*, for liberal democratic societies, citizenship is always dual and contradictory. On the one hand, and within a particular nation-state, citizenship functions as the basic framework for inclusion and democratic belonging (universal citizenship). On the other hand, citizenship presupposes the existence of a limited and bounded national community based on the exclusion of nonmembers (bounded citizenship). Bosniak highlights how in many conventional accounts these two meanings get conflated. This confusion not only reduces the usefulness of the concept but also obscures the very production of stratified others embedded in the institution of citizenship. Pointing to the "romanticism" inherent in hegemonic understandings of universal citizenship, Bosniak poses a crucial question: "*who*" is it "that rightfully constitutes the subjects of the citizenship that we champion"?[29]

Figure I.1 Two *sans-papières* at the megaphone. Photo by C. Raissiguier.

Societies committed to egalitarian democratic principles often attempt to solve this tension by promoting a politics of immigration control and regulation (a hardening of the border) while asserting and protecting the rights of immigrants residing within the national territory (a softening of the interior). This compromise has certainly been the hallmark of the French politics of immigration since the 1970s. Political and legal theoretical models that build on this inside/outside dichotomy and rely on the insularity of the nation-state are flawed, Bosniak contends. They ignore the increasingly porous quality of borders and cannot address the ways in which rules of citizenship, which include the terms of entry and residency at the border and the rights afforded to aliens on the inside, shape and construct one another.

Notwithstanding the political and analytical usefulness of Bosniak's study and her acknowledgment that "identity" is indeed one of the core elements of citizenship, *The Citizen and the Alien* falls within a broad body of scholarship that treats citizenship primarily as a legal and political concept. By analyzing different technologies of power that construct impossible subject positions within the Republic, as well as the resistive strategies that those who inhabit these positions are bound to deploy, my analysis treats citizenship as a mechanism of subject formation. Here I draw from the work of Aihwa Ong, who conceptualizes citizenship as subject-making and calls for analyses that focus on "the everyday processes whereby people, especially immigrants, are made into subjects of a particular nation-state."[30] *Reinventing the Republic* analyzes these processes by looking simultaneously at the ways in which *sans-papiers* are being made and at the ways in which they are making themselves within the confines of the French political tradition. In particular, it argues that the *sans-papiers* draw on the foundational discourse of the Republic to insert themselves into its civil community and, in the process, transform the very terms of its belonging.

Reinventing the Republic documents the ways in which *sans-papiers* fight over political representation and explores the meanings attached to their presence in France. The book discusses the innovative strategies deployed by the *sans-papiers*. In particular, it highlights how they have rendered visible their impossible social location and the various processes that have positioned them there. My analysis underscores the unruly practices deployed by the *sans-papiers*. Indeed, by insisting that they must come out "in broad daylight," and by taking charge of their own movement, they refuse the dominant logic that would rather keep them hidden and silent. In a similar way, by resisting the multiple forces that make them unintelligible both within and outside the movement, undocumented women, *sans-papières*, have inserted themselves within the French political sphere and have claimed their right to participate in the matters of the Republic. In many ways, then, the *sans-papiers* enact and demand what Bosniak proposes as a bold and logical—if paradoxical—possibility: the citizenship of (undocumented) aliens.

As I discuss in Chapter 2, one of the most innovative moves made by the *sans-papiers* is their organization around an identity of lack, which has enabled them to focus on the structural forces that shape their everyday lives and to collaborate politically with other groups that share this constructed lack. Within the confines of French political culture, this is indeed a brilliant move. Focusing on a shared social location makes it possible for the *sans-papiers* to stake claims based on the principled rejection of the structural and systemic production of stratified others. By avoiding the language of "difference" and focusing on the universal dignity of the person, they render these claims audible within the French Republic and open up the possibility for coalition politics both within France and beyond its borders. The *sans-papiers* are not staking their claims on the basis of belonging to a national community or on the basis of status citizenship but rather on the rights that "being here" affords them.[31] The *sans-papiers* draw on a variety of legal discourses that offer them different rights at the local, national, and supranational levels. By unlinking citizenship from national belonging, the *sans-papiers* align themselves with current discussions that challenge the hegemony of the national-citizen coupling within liberal democratic societies.[32] Finally, by focusing on the concrete ways in which discursive and material practices undermine the basic rights to which they are entitled, the *sans-papiers* help disrupt notions of abstract universalism that dominate French political parlance.

Taking *sans-papières'* narratives seriously and focusing on the gender underpinnings of the local and global forces that locate them in spaces of impossibility illustrates how the intersection of multiple social forces shapes French politics of immigration and immigrant women's everyday lives. The interviews included in this book shed light on the ways in which economic forces and gender stratification, for instance, have contributed to the "clandestinization" and "precarization" of certain immigrant women in the context of the restrictive turn in immigration policies in France. *Reinventing the Republic* documents the many ways in which immigrant women are locked within tradition and the domestic sphere. I argue throughout that this is one of the key mechanisms by which women are located within zones of impossibility. The book also demonstrates that *sans-papières* critically engage French laws and administrative practices that continue to place them in zones of impossibility. In particular, they demand that they be granted rights as individuals and not as members of families.

Like other immigrant women before them, then, *sans-papières* understand and advocate for women's legal autonomy and the individuation of immigration rights. These claims, however, never became central within the *sans-papiers* movement. Throughout I document the myriad and complex ways in which women are linked to the family. By juxtaposing parallel but different processes that place certain immigrants and queers outside conventional and normative understandings of family and nation, *Reinventing the Republic* suggests that extending the "impossible subject" label to other stratified "others" such as women and queers could help activists articulate stronger connections between different struggles and draw political leverage from these linkages. It would also help avoid the pitfalls and blind spots of political analyses that focus on single axes of subjugation.

CHAPTER OUTLINE

The book begins with a brief introduction to the movement, its actors, and the political and theoretical challenges they raise for political and academic observers. Chapter 1 follows the *sans-papiers* during the first two years of the struggle. By using the published writings of Madjiguène Cissé, a spokesperson for the *sans-papiers*, the chapter highlights the central presence of women in the early stages of the movement. It also begins to analyze how gender relations helped shape the contours of this social movement.

Chapter 2 analyzes in greater depth these undocumented immigrant women and their relationship to the movement and to French civil society. It opens with a discussion of the particular framing of the *sans-papières* and other immigrant women in France. The ideas introduced at the beginning of the chapter are then illustrated by a detailed analysis of the media coverage of the *sans-papiers* movement at the time of the Saint-Bernard church occupation. The chapter ends with an analysis of a set of *sans-papières* interviews collected by a feminist organization in the late 1990s in order to contrast these stories with those spun out by the media. The chapter introduces recurring themes within *sans-papières*' narratives. It also presents gender as a key analytical category through which the *sans-papiers*, their movement, and more broadly speaking, French immigration politics must be read and understood.

Concerns about motherhood, families, and demography lie at the core of the French politics of immigration. By focusing on recent constructions of the *sans-papières* as (threatening) mothers, Chapters 3 and 4 highlight a troubling development within the French politics of immigration. Anti-immigrant sentiment, it argues, has increasingly shifted its focus from immigrant men to immigrant women and children. In France this shift occurred along with the transfer from labor migration to family migration in the mid-seventies. Both chapters show how some immigrant women—especially from Africa—are constructed as mothers and wives and locked into "domestic" and "traditional" roles within French society.

Chapter 3 focuses specifically on legal texts and administrative practices, especially those surrounding family reunification policies that have shaped the social location of many immigrant women in France. Chapter 4 analyzes French scholarly production, media constructions, and social service practices to further shed light on the complex ways in which discourses on African motherhood constitute, in part, the material realities of African women in France. Both chapters foreground women's narratives to underscore how African women themselves, especially in the *sans-papiers* movement, critique, resist, and transform the discursive and material processes that make them impossible subjects of the French republic. Taken together, these two chapters illustrate the various ways in which the image of the "African mother" rearticulates old colonial understandings of African people and Africa to racialize certain immigrant communities and the question of immigration in France.

Contrary to popular imaginings, the bulk of the *sans-papières* are working women. Often bringing home ridiculous wages and laboring under terribly precarious and difficult conditions, most of them occupy positions in French sweatshops, work for small family businesses that have flourished in the underground economy, or sell their services as domestics and sex workers. Although many of them provide lucid and complex criticisms of the transnational relations of production and exploitation that are shaping their work experiences, none of them express the desire to give up wage labor and its attendant but varying levels of economic independence. Chapter 5 links the emergence of personal identities to the larger phenomena of economic restructuring, national and transnational politics, and population movements.

Borrowing the cadence of French militant chants ("Chicks, fags, migrants: solidarity!"), Chapter 6 analyzes the PaCS law and the parliamentary debates that led to its passage. My analysis sheds light on little-studied links between racism, homophobia, and sexism in France. By analyzing the connections between anti-immigrant and antigay rhetoric, the chapter illustrates some of the ways in which hegemonic discourses that construct certain people as impossible subjects borrow from and articulate with one another.

· · ·

The *sans-papiers* regularly invoke and criticize the language of the Republic; their manifestoes, public speeches, and political slogans speak that language but also demand that it translate into actual gains for them and their loved ones. Through a feminist analysis of the movement, its actors, and their rhetorical strategies, *Reinventing the Republic* uncovers at one and the same time the radical possibilities as well as the limits of the discourse of the French republic. Throughout I argue that in spite of its deep contradictions, French republicanism does offer powerful resistive tools to the *sans-papiers* and others *sans* rights in France. By insisting on both the usefulness and the limits of the French republican tradition, this book offers an analysis that refuses simple either-or solutions to one of most complex political issues facing France today.

1 *SANS-PAPIERS*: PEOPLE AND MOVEMENTS

Like all undocumented immigrants, we are regular people. Most
of us have lived among you for many years. We migrated to
France with the willingness to work and because we had been
told that it was "the fatherland of men's [sic] rights." We could
no longer stand the poverty and oppression that reigned in our
countries. We wanted full bellies for our children. We were
dreaming of liberty.

Sans-Papiers Manifesto[1]

IN THE SPRING OF 1996, postcolonial immigrants launched a resistance movement that has redrawn the boundaries of grassroots immigrant politics in
France.[2] The *sans-papiers* organized early as collectives and demanded that
the French state legalize their status.[3] The movement gained national and
international attention when, in August of 1996, in Paris, the police forcibly
removed three hundred *sans-papiers* from the Saint-Bernard church, which
they had occupied for two months.[4] The movement soon extended to the
whole country, and *sans-papiers* collectives have since appeared throughout
the European Union.

My aim in this chapter is twofold. First, I introduce the *sans-papiers* who
launched the movement and frame their struggle within immigrant politics
in France. Then I examine the participation of women in the first two years
of the movement (March 1996 to June 1997). By analyzing the writings and
speeches of Madjiguène Cissé, the coverage of the conflict by the French
media, and secondary sources on the *sans-papiers*, I explore the ways in
which gender relations played an important but undocumented role in the
emergence of this social movement. I also begin to highlight the presence
and impact of immigrant women within the French politics of immigration.

Figure 1.1 *Sans-papiers* demonstration, Porte St. Martin, Paris. Photo by C. Raissiguier.

WHO ARE THE *SANS-PAPIERS*?

Where do we come from, we Sans-Papiers of Saint-Bernard? It is a question we are often asked, and a pertinent one. We didn't immediately realise ourselves how relevant this question was. But as soon as we tried to carry out a "site inspection," the answer was very illuminating: We are all from former French colonies, most of us from West-African countries: Mali, Senegal, Guinea and Mauritania. But there are also among us several Maghreb people (Tunisians, Moroccans and Algerians); there is one man from Zaïre and a couple who are Haitians.[5]

The *sans-papiers* of Saint-Bernard were refugees and immigrants who for the most part were ushered into the realm of illegality by immigration laws that had become increasingly restrictive since the mid-1970s.[6] In particular, the Pasqua laws contributed to the creation of the *sans-papiers* and gave impulse to their movement.[7] These laws made it impossible for several categories of immigrants to obtain a change of status (*régularisation*) although they were *de facto*, if not *de jure*, nondeportable primarily because of their attachment to France through family linkages. As a result, thousands of legal residents in France were structurally located in a social and civil underground with no access to legal work or to social and civil protections: "Most of us entered the French territory legally. We have been thrown into illegality through the tightening of [French] laws[. . . .] Without papers we are without rights."[8]

Among these three hundred *sans-papiers* one could find asylum seekers whose case files (*dossiers*) had previously been rejected (*déboutés du droit d'asile*), spouses or children of legal immigrants, parents of children born in France, and parents of French children.[9] Most of them had entered the country between 1980 and 1990. The vast majority of the Saint-Bernard's *sans-papiers* were from sub-Saharan Africa—most of them from Mali. More than half were women and children (eighty women and one hundred children, to be specific). All of the *sans-papiers* from the Saint-Bernard collective were members of France's former colonies. The composition of the *sans-papiers* population has changed over time. Today, for instance, one might find immigrants from Eastern Europe as well as from China in *sans-papiers* collectives.

For obvious reasons, it is impossible to draw an accurate sociological portrait of undocumented immigrants in France. However, we can assume that undocumented immigrants share some of the characteristics and some of the trajectories of other recent "legal" immigrants. I use French census figures to delineate these characteristics and trajectories, and draw from official reports on the exceptional *régularisation* procedures of 1981 to 1982 and 1997 to 1998 to expose the complex and changing sociological realities of the French *sans-papiers*.[10] Capturing the sociological contours of the *sans-papières* experience is even more difficult, because French statistical reports recurrently fail to provide gender-specific figures.[11]

Immigrants from sub-Saharan Africa arrived in France fairly recently. In 1962, immigrants from the African continent constituted almost 15 percent of the total immigrant population in France. However, the vast majority of these immigrants originated from the Maghreb, with 11.6 percent from Algeria, 1.1 percent from Morocco, 1.5 percent from Tunisia, and a mere 0.7 percent from all other African countries. Their numbers remained fairly low until 1975: they were 1.4 percent of the total immigrant population in 1968 and 2.4 percent in 1975. This proportion reached 4.3 percent in 1982 and 6.6 percent in 1990. This is also the period in which women from these communities began to enter massively into France.

Two exceptional regularization procedures implemented under socialist leadership in 1981 and 1997 provide interesting data on the social location of undocumented immigrants in France. In each case, the French state created an exceptional mechanism through which undocumented immigrants could obtain a change of status according to a specific set of criteria. Official reports investigating a sample of the successful candidates for each procedure provide useful if somewhat incomplete information on the *sans-papiers*. In 1981, 142,000 of the 150,000 case files deposited were granted a change of status. Although the numbers given for the 1997 procedure differ greatly, most official reports state that 80,000 of the 144,000 case files deposited between November 1997 and December 1998 received a positive response.[12] Background information on successful applicants for both procedures document that the vast majority of them had migrated to France from the Maghreb and sub-Saharan Africa. Chinese immigrants began to appear in sizeable numbers only in the 1997 procedure, where they represented almost 10 percent of all successful case files.

By comparing the two procedures, we can highlight major differences between the two groups of immigrants. The 1981 procedure granted a change of status to undocumented immigrants who were mostly men (83.5 percent), had not resided in France for very long (only 10 percent had been there for more than six years), and were almost all employed at the time of the procedure (95.3 percent). In contrast, women represented almost half (49.3 percent) of those who obtained a change of status in 1997; 61 percent of these undocumented immigrants had resided in France for more than six years, and only 31.3 percent of them declared having a job at the time of the procedure.

What data gathered from the 1981 and 1997 procedures also tell us is that, beyond a certain shared *précarité*, undocumented immigrants who obtained a change of status came from a wide range of social backgrounds and countries of origin. They also presented a broad and diverse spectrum of personal circumstances before and after arriving in France. Finally, the data also tell us that undocumented immigrants are not the most desperate and deprived of all the candidates for international migration. The educational attainment of the undocumented immigrants who obtained a change of status in 1997 to 1998, for instance, was fairly high. Indeed, around 60 percent of them had between six and ten years of schooling, with the highest educational attainment levels found among nationals from China and the lowest found among nationals from Mali. One in ten of the successful candidates declared having had some tertiary education.

Most of them were employed prior to leaving their country. Indeed, 60 percent of them were engaged in some form of labor, while others were either students (20 percent) or not engaged in any labor activity (20 percent). Here gender differences are striking: 40 percent of the women stated that they were not engaged in work or education prior to coming to France, whereas only 6 percent of the men fell into the same category. The proportion of students in secondary or tertiary education, however, was roughly the same for men and women. The lower rate of labor participation for women, the authors of one report suggest, is partially due to the fact that women often work in a family farm or business where they are typically not perceived (even by themselves) as actual workers.

Finally, these reports corroborate national census figures on the increased presence of "families" and children among immigrants from certain communities in the 1980s and the 1990s. Undocumented immigrants granted a change of status in 1997 were more likely than those granted one in 1981 to be accompanied by a spouse and children. In 1981 the vast majority of the successful candidates (62 percent) were single. In 1997 only 30 percent of the case files fell into that category. Differences between national groups were also noted, with more families found among the Chinese and more isolated men among the Africans. In 1997, 60 percent of the case files were those of individuals who had children living with them in France at the time of the procedure.

The women and children photographed (but unseen) by French journalists in the summer of 1996 were newcomers to the French immigration scene. In many ways, these women and children are the disturbing reminders that immigrants from sub-Saharan Africa, like other immigrants before them, are here to stay. What seems different about these children and women is that they are at the very heart of a social movement that is engaging the very foundation of the French Republic. This is not to say, of course, that immigrant women before the Saint-Bernard *sans-papières* were not involved in political struggles. In *La cause des sans-papiers*, which charts the history of the *sans-papiers* and their particular forms of political organizing, Johanna Siméant documents that women have regularly been involved within *sans-papiers* struggles, including participating in hunger strikes.[13] Siméant highlights the decentralized nature of these struggles and suggests that, because they are less controlled by men than the struggles organized within traditional immigrant organizations, women might find it easier to invest themselves within *sans-papiers* mobilizations.[14]

The Saint-Bernard struggle, however, was exceptional in that it was the first time that family units including mothers and children were part and parcel of

Figure 1.2 *Sans-papières* with their children at national demonstration. Photo by C. Raissiguier.

the direct actions generated by the movement. Different also were the tactics and strategies deployed by these *sans-papiers*. Current *sans-papiers* struggles have emerged from a long history of immigrant organizing in France, having borrowed and transformed its strategies in new and interesting ways.

THE MOVEMENT AND ITS STRATEGIES

We have always thought that we had the right to demand papers. Bereft of fundamental human rights, turned into illegal aliens (clandestins) by the constant modifications of French laws [. . .] we had to question France—its institutions and its public opinion.[15]

The *sans-papiers* I analyze here initiated their struggle on March 18, 1996, by occupying the church of Saint-Ambroise in Paris. During the four days that preceded their expulsion from the church, the group constituted a case file for each *sans-papiers*, around which to organize the demand for a collective change of status.[16] Between March 22 and June 28, 1996, three hundred *sans-papiers* moved out into the street and occupied numerous public spaces, including two churches, a theater, a leftist bookstore, a union local, and an unused railway site.[17]

The *sans-papiers'* choice of a public and collective display of their presence on French territory is the first, and probably most important, element of the movement's strategy. The *sans-papiers* creatively appropriated, transformed, and politicized the (in)visible, precarious, and nomadic character of their lived experiences. Through a series of performative iterations of the impossible social location in which they find themselves (many of them can be neither regularized nor deported), the *sans-papiers* have produced what I call a politics of the impossible. I use the term *impossible* here to mean that it is the very social conditions of impossibility that have helped produce the movement's political strategies. *Impossible* also suggests the unruly quality of the movement. Finally, it accounts for the built-in dangers of a politics that borrows (because it has to) the language and grammar of the French Republic.

The Saint-Bernard *sans-papiers*, in a collective form of street theater, enacted their refusal to be turned into outlaws and illegal immigrants (*clandestins*) by the French authorities. In the process, they were able to do two contradictory things: bring themselves back into and unsettle the logic of the human rights discourse at the core of the French republican model, and position themselves as subjects under French law while critiquing the inner workings of the law itself.[18] "We are not illegal immigrants. We appear in broad daylight."[19]

A collective "coming out" of the closet of their state-created and forced clandestine status, then, is at the heart of the *sans-papiers'* tactics. By making their presence visible, they are forcing the French state to address a situation that it would much rather sweep under the rug. As long as the *sans-papiers* remain dispersed, hidden, and silent, they can fill the positions that eagerly await them in the underground economy. They can be brandished as symbols of France's economic and social woes. They can be dramatically carded, singled out, and deported in order to appease anti-immigrant feelings in the general population and, more specifically, among the followers of neo-fascist Jean-Marie LePen.[20] Although successful on many levels—the movement did force the French state to address the *sans-papiers* and to redress some of the legal nightmares it had created—such a strategy is not without risk: "We, *sans-papiers* of France, have decided, by signing this manifesto, to come out of the shadows. From now on, in spite of the risks it creates for us, it is not only our faces, but also our names that will be revealed."[21] By putting their names on the line, the *sans-papiers* have also become more vulnerable to tracking and forced deportation. The *sans-papiers'* insistence that they are not illegal but rather assigned a location that makes it impossible for them to participate fully in French society is a contradictory move. On the one hand, it brilliantly points to the discursive and material processes that construct impossible subjects of the French Republic. On the other hand, because the *sans-papiers* do borrow the language of the Republic to make their claims, they at once are bound by and reinscribe its binary and exclusionary grammar. For instance, by pointing out that most *sans-papiers* are not *clandestins*, they end up reinforcing distinctions between "good" immigrants (those who entered France legally) and "bad" ones (those who did not).

Looking at the various locales that the *sans-papiers* inhabited during the spring of 1996 helps us trace the kinds of linkages they established with segments of French civil society. After their expulsion from Saint-Ambroise, the *sans-papiers* received a wide range of (mixed) support from antiracist, labor, and humanitarian organizations; progressive clergy; leftist groups; and French intellectuals and artists. The second strategy used by the *sans-papiers*, then, is their reliance on allies from a variety of organized and unorganized sources and their claim to autonomy and self-determination.

Indeed, the *sans-papiers* have been incredibly successful at securing support from large segments of France's public opinion. They have managed to pull people into the streets for large demonstrations in the middle of the summer, when political interest (even in France) and activism are weak. They have had people come and support them in their direct actions and act as neutral observers. *Sans-papiers*' allies have revived the practice of the republican "sponsorship" (*parrainage/marrainage républicain*). This ritual was created during the French revolution when two citizens could sponsor a third one by welcoming her or him into the Republic. In the context of the *sans-papiers* movement, these rituals are celebrated in French town halls where progressive mayors give some formality to these symbolic rituals. Sponsors agree to serve as mentors and to help the *sans-papiers* in their dealings with the French authorities. Beyond the symbolic gesture and the practical help they have generated, the *parrainages/marrainages* have also created dialogues among elected officials, French citizens, and the *sans-papiers*.[22]

At the end of March 1996, while the *sans-papiers* had found refuge in the *Cartoucherie* theatre in Vincennes, under the leadership of acclaimed French director Ariane Mnouchkine, some one hundred French intellectuals launched a civil disobedience campaign. They called for the repeal of the Pasqua laws and invited French citizens to offer foreigners the asylum "denied [to them] by the state" and to "disobey by all means necessary these unjust and immoral laws that transformed denunciation and discrimination" into the duties of citizens.[23] Around this dynamic emerged a group of respected French citizens who were willing to serve as mediators between the *sans-papiers* and the state:

> We are, at the moment, invested with no mandate [from the state]. We are not yet mediators. There are 25 of us. In the next few weeks, we want all case files to be examined with goodwill each time—if possible—within the boundaries of the French law. When not possible, we want to see how we can humanely find solutions to the most difficult cases.[24]

In collaboration with the *sans-papiers* themselves, a group of mediators (*collège des médiateurs*) generated a list of ten criteria for the change of status of *sans-papiers*.[25] The mediators were successful in convincing the government to look globally at the three hundred case files. On June 26, the French authorities announced that only forty-eight *sans-papiers* (among whom twenty-two were involved in the Saint-Ambroise occupation) would be legalized; all others would be deported. Two days later the *sans-papiers* moved into the Saint-Bernard church and hardened their position. On July 5, ten of them started a hunger strike.

Although the *sans-papiers* have been very savvy at tapping into all sources of support for their struggle, they have also made it very clear that they and they alone should determine the direction of the movement.[26]

> The struggle has taught us many, many things. It has taught us first of all to be autonomous. That has not always been easy. There were organizations which came to support us and which were used to helping immigrants in struggle. They were also used to acting as the relay between immigrants in struggle and the authorities, and therefore more or less to manage the struggle. They would tell us, "Right, we the organizations have made an appointment to explain this or that" and we had to say, "But we can explain it very well ourselves." Their automatic response is not to get people to be autonomous, but to speak for them. If we had not taken our autonomy, we would not be here today. Because there really have been many organizations telling us that we could never win, that we could not win over public opinion because people were not ready to hear what we had to say.[27]

The *sans-papiers'* adamant demand for autonomy and self-determination generated the structure of allies' collectives working in conjunction with and under the leadership of the *sans-papiers* themselves. This structure, however, did take several French political actors by surprise. Indeed, French antiracist and humanitarian organizations, political parties, and other supportive groups have had to adapt to the redefined nature of the French allies' role:

> It's quite extraordinary to see how the [antiracist] organizations—mine included—were taken aback by the fact that foreigners were taking the liberty to actually speak about their own issues and to organize their own fight[....] Foreigners gained power in their relationship to the allies. Before, they used to be allied to those who *defended* them [...] by troubling business as usual they troubled the nature of that relationship.[28]

Several French political actors and organizations found the *sans-papiers'* agenda too radical, wrongheaded, and bound to fail. Many urged them to tone down their demands. Commenting on this dynamic, Jean-Pierre Allaux—a long time member of the Network for the Information and Support to Immigrants (*Groupe d'information et de solidarité aux travailleurs immigrés*, or GISTI)—explains that some organizations did attempt to discourage the *sans-papiers* and then backed away from offering political support by simply providing humanitarian help when needed.[29]

In *La cause des sans-papiers*, Johanna Siméant provides a thorough analysis of the mobilization of French allies in support of the struggles of the *sans-papiers* since the 1970s.[30] Siméant clearly documents that antiracist and immigrant support groups, left-wing Christian organizations (*chrétiens de gauche*), and labor unions—in particular the French Democratic Confederation of Labor (*Confédération française démocratique du travail*, or CFDT) have long been mobilized around undocumented worker, refugee, and immigrant struggles. Siméant's analysis traces the emergence of a fluid set of pro–*sans-papiers* organizations and political actors in the aftermath of the 1968 student uprisings and the demise of the French proletarian left. Siméant further highlights the many ways in which French political actors have since then been drawn to the *sans-papiers'* cause. In particular, she argues that French allies invest themselves in immigrant struggles, which they both perceive and render more radical—more "heretical" to use Siméant's words—than other progressive causes. Since the 1970s, a small but influential intellectual politico-cultural avant-garde has organized around immigrants generally and *sans-papiers* specifically. However, by comparing different kinds and depths of engagement in immigrant struggles, Siméant also cleverly points out that the involvement of French allies is usually greater when a right-wing government is in power and when French allies can rally around more "consensual" claims, as in the massive mobilization against hosting certificates in 1997.[31]

The political boundaries between the *sans-papiers* and their French allies, then, are complex and riddled with fruitful tensions and conflict. It is through these "troubled" bonds, however, that both groups can begin to ask important questions about their relationship to political representation, to France and its republican ideals, and to democratic principles in general:

> We can see the results today: from ACT UP to the Festival of Cinema in Douarnenez, we've won a wide range of support, including in the most remote parts of France. Little by little masses of people have understood that our struggle was raising questions that go beyond the regularization of the *Sans-Papiers*. New questions have gradually emerged: "Do you agree to live in a France where fundamental human rights are trampled on? Do you agree to live in a France where democratic liberties are not respected?" And we have also learned that if we really wanted to be autonomous, we had to learn about democracy. We had to make our own decisions, get them acknowledged as truly representative of us, not allow them to be called into question from the outside, respect them ourselves, and therefore learn to make others respect them, and to implement them ourselves. We have learned that in six months. Without the struggle we would not have learned it in ten years.[32]

The *sans-papiers*' engagement with issues of collective decision making and representative democracy inevitably led them to address the question of women's participation within the movement: "It [democracy] has not been easy. It was not obvious at the beginning that we needed general meetings, it was not obvious that women had to take part in them; it was not obvious that delegates had to be chosen."[33]

SANS-PAPIÈRES ON THE MOVE

The first autonomous action of women in the movement was a demonstration in front of the government building that houses the prime minister, who refused to receive the women's delegation. "On May 11, 1996, the media were not interested in our struggle any longer, our [political] support was weakening. We, the women, left from Pajol in order to march in front of the *Hôtel Matignon*."[34] This action was followed a month later, on Monday, June 24, by the occupation of a Parisian city hall. "[W]hile the movement was looking for ways of renewing itself, we decided—unbeknownst to the men—to occupy the *mairie* of the eighteenth *arrondissement* (municipal district), where for two days we demanded that our case files be reviewed. We thought the interior ministry was biding time, the summer vacations were soon approaching; we felt we had to do something."[35] On November 20, 1996, as a way of marking the international day of children's rights, several women's delegations from *sans-papiers* collectives in Paris and the surrounding areas gathered in front of the city hall of the eleventh *arrondissement* in Paris. The delegation presented a memorandum titled, "In France the rights of foreign children are violated."

However, before women actually started to generate direct actions as women, they had to wage a battle within each collective to gain a voice in the decision-making process. Speaking of the Saint-Bernard collective, Madjiguène Cissé recounts:

> Women have played an extremely important role in this struggle. And it was not obvious that this was going to happen. At the beginning it seemed taken for granted that women would not participate in general meetings: it wasn't necessary, since the husbands were there! Not only did women not have the right to speak; they didn't even have the right to listen to what was being said at general meetings.[36]

Little by little, women began to crash these men-only meetings and insisted that they had something to contribute to the general assemblies. Eventually, women began to meet among themselves. These women's meetings created interesting reactions among the men and launched a women's presence within the movement: "Then the men were really puzzled; they saw us as scheming, plotting, up to no good; they used to hang around our meetings to try to find out what we were saying. In fact these meetings gave great strength to the women, and enabled them to play an important role in the direction of the struggle."[37]

According to Cissé, women have been radicalizing forces in the movement, forcing the men not to give up at difficult turns in the conflict. At one point, for instance, the *sans-papières* looked at the Women's Center (*La maison des femmes*) of Paris—a women-only feminist space—as a possible locale to occupy. Although the occupation did not happen, it forced the men to reconsider their own position on the movement's direction:

> When we were in the 15th *arrondissement*, a Catholic Aid, and the Priest of *SOS-Racisme* (SOS Racism) suggested that we submit our case files to the

Ministry and that we go home, the men were ready to do that, because they trusted the priest. It was the women who did not want to.

They decided that they were not going home and they gave me the job of finding premises. I managed to find an offer of shelter at the Women's Centre but it was not mixed; it was only for women. The women didn't need long to think about it. Since you want to go home, they said to the men, we'll take the belongings, we'll take the children, and we'll move into the women's centre. Then the men told us that meanwhile they had been thinking that we should all stay together and that they would find a place big enough for everybody.[38]

The *sans-papières* ended up not moving to the women's center, but the fact that they thought of it as a possibility speaks to existing linkages—even if tenuous—between their movement and feminist groups in France.[39] On December 13, 1996, the *sans-papières* along with several French feminist groups (*Coordination nationale pour le droit à l'avortement et à la contraception, Collectif féministe de soutien aux sans-papiers*, and so on) organized a meeting to put in place a feminist structure of support for the *sans-papiers* struggle. According to Cissé, in spite of the expressed need to establish such a structure, this effort never fully materialized.[40]

When the *sans-papières* organized their women's march on May 11, 1996, once again the action generated and organized by women enabled the movement to move forward and regain media attention: "In fact each time the movement ran out of steam, the women met and worked out initiatives that relaunched the struggle. Thus there was the women's march on May 11, at the time when we were in Pajol and when the media were no longer reporting about the struggle."[41] The press release for the women's march is one of the few public documents that address the specific issues of the *sans-papières*. The document demands a revision of the criteria for the granting of asylum status so as to take into account gender-based discrimination and gender persecutions. In a similar manner, the press release reiterates a demand that has been made by immigrant women's organizations since the 1970s: that immigrant women be granted autonomous status. These actions strengthened the women's presence in the movement and highlighted the need for a gender-specific reflection on the *sans-papiers*' struggle. Women started to meet independently on a monthly basis. Around one hundred women from all of the collectives gathered and discussed such questions as male domination in meetings and demonstrations.[42]

On January 3, 1997, several *sans-papières* met near the Elysée, the presidential palace, to make their case on their situation and that of their families to Jacques Chirac and his government. Like the *Madres de Mayo* (Mothers of the Plaza de Mayo) in Argentina, the women decided to come back every week until the conflict was resolved. Interestingly, they managed to gather only twice because each time, although many men came in support of the demonstrators, they only managed to render the women's presence invisible. These unauthorized gatherings were also highly policed and therefore difficult to organize on a sustained basis.[43] Around the same time (on December 21, 1996), four women in one of the Paris regional collectives started a hunger strike, which lasted until mid-January 1997. This was the first women-only hunger strike launched within the *sans-papiers* movement.[44] As a result of the strike, all four were legalized.

In September 1997, under the socialist government of Lionel Jospin, then Interior Minister Jean-Pierre Chevènnement issued an administrative memorandum that was supposed to facilitate the change of status of all the *sans-papiers* living in France. The memorandum listed twelve criteria that would justify a change of status. It was quite controversial and was criticized for reproducing some of the legal dead ends that had created the *sans-papiers* in the first place. Such a text would certainly lead to only a partial legalization of all the *sans-papiers*. In the wake of the memorandum, and in spite of the controversies it generated, by November 1997, 150,000 cases had been filed through the French administration. In 1999, three years after the beginning of the struggle, 70,000 *sans-papiers* were successfully legalized and more than 70,000 others were denied a change of status. These individuals, mostly single men, found themselves relegated to the social condition of impossibility that the movement had tried to address. Many were incarcerated in French jails because they lacked legal papers. Many others went back underground.

In the wake of the Chevènnement administrative memorandum and the mixed results it produced, the movement continued and expanded. In 2002, when I was getting ready to conduct my fieldwork in France, occupations, hunger strikes, and public demonstrations were still happening on a regular basis. By then the movement had diversified. The Chinese community, for instance, was very well represented in the Third collective in Paris. *Sans-papiers* collectives and collectives of French allies had emerged throughout France and were spreading within the European Community. Transnational networks of *sans-papiers* were also developing within this new context and were transforming their platform of demands.

Less than ever, though, did we hear about the particular role of women in the movement. Women in fact were much less present when I conducted my field-work than they were during the initial period of the struggle between 1996 and 1998. Madjiguène Cissé explains the absence of women in the later stage of the movement by noting that many of them have been successfully legalized. Those who have not are by and large single or divorced. Women also have the double burden of caring for their families and their children, making it very difficult for them to sustain long periods of strenuous activism and risk-taking activities. Most of them, mothers of French children or children born in France, are now at least temporarily legal residents in France. The question of the legal autonomy of immigrant women has yet to be resolved. What will happen to the women whose status has been temporarily changed because their spouse is French or a legal resident and who find themselves single by the time they need to renew their papers? What will happen to gender issues now that women are less visibly active in the movement? Similarly, questions about violence and harassment di-rected toward women activists within the struggle and from French authorities were not adequately addressed within the movement and stand as a reminder that the *sans-papières'* impossible status is constructed around both the gender dynamics of the movement and those of the French society at large.[45]

CONCLUSION

One of the most interesting features of the *sans-papiers* movement is the highly politicized nature of their agenda. From the very beginning, the Saint-Bernard three hundred (and other collectives that followed in their footsteps) moved their demands to an explicitly political plane by requesting that all racist French immigration laws be overturned and by calling for the legaliza-tion of all undocumented immigrants: "And we want to add that beyond the situation of the Saint-Ambroise families, we ask all our allies to mobilize for the dismantling of the Pasqua laws, and the annulment of the proposed Tou-bon and Debré laws."[46] The French government tried to defeat the movement through sheer force and repression. It also tried to depoliticize the conflict by providing individual responses to what the *sans-papiers* themselves see as a collective problem. By their refusal of this case-by-case logic, the *sans-papiers* demanded that France address the structural location of thousands of undocumented postcolonial immigrants within its national boundaries. The complex analysis that emerged within the *sans-papiers'* struggle looks at the plight of undocumented immigrants in the context of a long history of French colonialism and of a globalizing world economy. The *sans-papiers* have made it very clear that they are here partly because of the growing gap between southern and northern countries, the debt crisis of the 1980s that has plagued their countries, and the structural adjustment policies imposed on them by the International Monetary Fund and the World Bank. They also explain their current situation in light of the construction of a fortress Europe and the emergence of a new politics of immigration within France.[47]

Besides achieving the tangible success of the actual (albeit temporary) legalization of thousands of *sans-papiers*, the movement has also challenged existing notions of citizenship and political participation in a Western democracy. By coming out "in broad daylight," by voicing out loud their grievances, and especially by refusing to be represented by good-willed French citizens, the *sans-papiers* unsettled business-as-usual in the traditional political arenas of the have-nots.[48] In these arenas, privileged political actors and organizations are used to speaking for oppressed constituencies. The *sans-papiers* movement raised many ethical questions for French political actors. Among these concerns is that one of the hardest challenges might be the ability to learn from the other, to let the subaltern narrate herself rather than speak for her.

Figure 1.3 *Sans-papiers* gathering in front of the Bobigny *préfecture*. Photo by C. Raissiguier.

Women in the movement, like the *sans-papiers* at large, have refused to remain silent. They too have come out and challenged dominant representations of immigrant women in France. Women's active participation in the struggle, even when orchestrated around family issues, has produced a double displacement of the French leader and the male head of the family as the privileged speaking subjects of the struggle.[49] This radical displacement, however, has gone, by and large, unnoticed because the *sans-papières* have talked back and acted out in a context where women from new immigrant communities are not seen, let alone heard.

The Network for the Legal Autonomy of Immigrant and Refugee Women (*Réseau pour l'autonomie juridique des femmes réfugiées/immigrées*, or RAJFIRE)—which includes the ASFAD Association for the Support of Democratic Algerian Women (*Association de solidarité avec les femmes algériennes démocrates*), the Women's Center (*La maison des femmes*), the Women of the Sans-Papiers Coordinating Committee (*Les femmes de la coordination des sans-papiers*), and Pluriel-Women in Algeria (*Pluri-elles en Algérie*)—was created in 1998. It has organized around the question of women's derivative rights and called for the legal autonomy of immigrant and refugee women. The RAJFIRE has also sponsored some *marrainages républicains* and organized educational forums on the question of the rights of the *sans-papières*, especially in the case of divorce and separation. The RAJFIRE is the only feminist network in France that has formally coalesced around the *sans-papières* and their struggle. It seems that few French feminist organizations and activists have been active within the network; fewer still have taken up, as a feminist issue, the particularly vulnerable position of immigrant women in general, and that of the *sans-papières* specifically. At a time when the parity movement is engaging the French polity through its radical demand for equal representation for women in all political assemblies and alerting us to critical tensions within French republicanism, it is interesting (and troubling) to note the absence of a large and varied French feminist mobilization around the *sans-papiers* struggle.

By directly confronting the legal impasses that the French law has created for all of them, the *sans-papiers* are forcing France to look at the contradictions embedded in the laws of the Republic. French immigration, nationality, and marital laws have served to ensure that matrimonial and paternal relations almost always determine the legal status of immigrant women. Question about legal, political, economic, and social autonomy for women has long been at the forefront for immigrant women organizing in France. These have yet to be fully addressed in the *sans-papiers'* struggle. Asking such difficult questions in the context of the *sans-papiers* movement forces us to test the limits of single-term analyses. It also invites us to look critically at the ways in which dominant French national narratives (including feminist ones) conveniently and skillfully erase the messy intersections of racial, ethnic, and gender exclusions in its past and present practices.

2 FRAMING THE *SANS-PAPIÈRES*

AS CHAPTER ONE CLEARLY DEMONSTRATES, women were very active in the early stages of the struggle. Indeed, they were present at each of the *sans-papiers'* actions, and one of them, Madjiguène Cissé, was a spokesperson for the Saint-Bernard collective. However, then and ever since, there has been little interest in and coverage of women engaged in the movement and the issues pertaining to them. Although women are graphically evoked when the media reports on the struggle—in fact, one might argue that they have become a visual staple of the *sans-papiers* story—there is a parallel erasure of them as political subjects of the movement. In this chapter, I analyze this dual and contradictory movement of erasure and foregrounding, which, I suggest, positions some immigrant women at the heart of (anti-)immigration discourses in France. My focus here lies on the peculiar framing that renders undocumented women hypervisible and yet unseen.[1] In the next two chapters, I document how some immigrant women have come to represent, in France's social imaginary, the very threat of immigration.[2]

I begin this chapter by pointing out rarely noted connections between different but related discourses that construct immigrant femininities within France. I then move to a brief analysis of the media coverage of the *sans-papiers* movement at the time of the Saint-Bernard church occupation. By reading cartoons and media stories about this crucial moment in the struggle, I begin to flesh out this book's core analytical themes. I end the chapter by discussing a set of *sans-papières* interviews collected by a feminist organization in the late 1990s in order to contrast these stories with those spun out by the media. The narratives presented in these early interviews, like those I later conducted, are highly rehearsed and partially constructed by outside forces. Limited as they are, they demonstrate that the *sans-papières*, like their male counterparts, do talk back. By engaging these interviews as complex, contradictory, and necessarily flawed speech acts, I intend to disrupt the logic that renders the *sans-papière* "unintelligible" and, as a result, outside the bounds of democratic inclusion.

FRAMING IMMIGRANT FEMININITIES

Immigrant women and daughters of immigrants made their entry onto the French political and media scenes in 1989 during an incident that created a national polemic and has been widely referred to as the "headscarf case" (*l'affaire du foulard*). The incident that launched the national debate involved three young women of North African descent who were expelled from a public high school because they refused to remove their Islamic scarves inside the school.[3] Women have remained present within the French politics of immigration and its media coverage around the hotly debated question of the "integration" of North African (male) youths into French society.

The very presence of immigrant women (and their children) within the French national landscape renders visible the settlement and the long-term presence of foreigners who were once thought to be temporary (male) migrant workers (*travailleurs immigrés*).[4] Inside a globalized and Europeanized France in the throes of a deep identity crisis, "the immigrant woman" and her children have indeed emerged as threats to the nation. The wearing of Islamic scarves in French schools, polygamy, arranged marriages, and female genital cutting are important threads within anti-immigrant discourses that present North and sub-Saharan Africans as undesirable immigrants who are unwilling or unable to assimilate into French culture.[5]

Dominant discourses about some immigrants' otherness as rooted in their inability or unwillingness to fit in are dangerous and fuel growing anti-Muslim sentiment in France. Indeed, the "headscarf case" and its discursive ripples established Islam as one of the main roadblocks to the successful integration of postcolonial immigrants in France. Within each of these threads it is women who, though often robbed of any real agency, are conjured up to capture the cultural distance (or proximity) between the French and their postcolonial others. While the fictional construction of the "immigrant woman" stands metonymically for the various ills of immigration, immigrant women (as real historical beings) are erased from the picture.[6]

When cast as mothers of multiple children, these women are perceived as a direct threat to the nation. When cast as wives, sisters, or daughters, they call to mind dangerous and deviant masculinities that imperil the common social fabric. This is particularly true in media coverage, which often portrays immigrant women (or their French daughters) as victimized and oppressed by male relatives or neighbors. Interestingly, the much touted success of young women of North African descent (*les Beurettes*) operates in a similar way.[7] The dominant narrative of the young women's social and professional success upholds at one and the same time the integrative power of the French Republic and the inability of their brothers to yield to that power. Unlike their sisters, these young men, we are told, resist the call of integration. In other words, narratives about the success of the *Beurettes* tell another story as well: that of the failed integration of young Maghrebi men in France. In this typical patriarchal scenario, women are seen as compliant and docile figures. Such deployment of racist and sexist ideas affects not only the women but whole immigrant communities as well. Indeed, it structures an overall narrative of danger and threat wherein women play a central role.

Studies of immigration have only begun to pay serious attention to the presence of women within French immigration flows and the politics they have generated.[8] Here I argue that this double movement of foregrounding and erasure not only obscures the gender underpinnings of immigration but also obfuscates the processes of racial and class formation at play in France today. When fears of foreign invasion and pollution are running wild and when immigration has become so politicized, paying attention to the ways in which "the immigrant woman" figures into the national imaginary and how actual immigrant women participate in the polity is not a luxury. Indeed, the im/material salience of women within polemical nodes of French immigration politics points to the peculiar role that women, gender, and sexuality together play in the construction of racist and nationalist discourses. It also alerts us to the fact that a *sans-papière* subject position is indeed impossible within the Republic (and to a certain extent within the *sans-papiers* movement itself).

THE IMPOSSIBLE LOCATION OF THE *SANS-PAPIÈRES*

In spite of the hypervisibility of the *Sans-Papières* in the media coverage of the Saint-Bernard struggle, I was initially unable to determine the actual number of women involved and their particular stake in the movement. When I clipped articles from the written press, I found that the Saint-Bernard *sans-*

papiers were mostly from Mali but also from Senegal, Cameroon, Guinea, Mauritania, and the Maghreb. I also discovered that among them were some one hundred children and twelve polygamous families. Rarely, however, was mention made of the women, whether single or members of families, who shaped the early developments of the struggle.

Between September 18, 1996, and November 27, 1998, the ADRI (*Agence pour le développement des relations interculturelles*) Resource Center staff collected only fifteen articles on the *sans-papières* per se.[9] Six articles were published in the communist paper *L'Humanité*, five in the progressive *Libération*, three in the Catholic paper *La Croix*, and one in the moderate and well-respected daily *Le Monde*. Although I would not take these numbers as a survey of the French press, they do point to the paucity of articles addressing the specific reality of women in the movement. The content and tone of these articles further suggest that women (and gender issues, when addressed) are seen as affected by the *sans-papiers* crisis but rarely as affecting and shaping its direction and strategies. Nine of the articles focus on one woman and highlight the human interest aspect of her story. The fact that the women are mothers is emphasized in most of the articles. Four pieces use the word *mother* in the title, and all of the articles foreground, more or less, the familial relationships that shape the women and the lives they portray.

This early focus on motherhood and families in *sans-papiers* stories echoes the movement's own decision to organize around the rights of families to stay together.[10] Also, although all of the women featured in these articles are fighting—most of them are active in *sans-papiers* collectives and all of them participate in the collectives' actions—they are framed in the written press within highly individualized narratives of suffering and survival. Even the three articles that document the hunger strike of four women in Colombes are structured around each woman's individual story. Only the *Le Monde* (February 23–24, 1997) and *La Croix* (November 27, 1998) articles underscore the collective nature of the women's struggle and the gendered reality of their specific situations.

We can see, then, that despite the numerical importance of women in early *sans-papiers* collectives (for instance, more than 30 percent of the Saint-Bernard collective's adult members were women) and their continued substantive presence in the movement, dominant media representations of the *sans-papiers* struggle do not take women, or gender, seriously into account. One need only look at the highly respected daily *Le Monde* between August 14 and August 30, 1996, to witness the literal erasure of women (and children) from the struggle. During that period, ten *sans-papiers* who were engaged in a hunger strike for more than forty days were physically at risk. Negotiations between the government and the *sans-papiers* were interrupted, and the French government planned the evacuation of the church but was reluctant to implement such a forced removal in the context of an (inter)national movement of solidarity that was mounting in support of the Saint-Bernard three hundred. During this two-week period, negotiations were at a standstill, and the movement received continuous coverage from the French press. The *sans-papiers* had in fact become so central to the culture that they were also used to illustrate other stories. (See Figure 2.5 later in this chapter.)

In *Le Monde*'s illustration of the crisis, we can see that the movement is conceptualized and presented as a story whose main protagonists are men, especially French men. Indeed, the cartoons published by the newspaper during this period construct the conflict as a narrative that foregrounds French (and white) political actors. In the August 25–26 issue of the paper, two days after the forced removal of the *sans-papiers*, *Le Monde* published a drawing illustrating a story about the challenges facing the French president and his cabinet as they prepared their political agenda for the fall.

Figure 2.1 *MM. Chirac et Juppé préparent la rentrée à Brégançon tandis que s'organisent les expulsions de sans-papiers* [Chirac and Juppé are preparing for the fall in Brégançon as *sans-papiers* deportations are under way]. Cartoon by Plantu. *Le Monde*, August 25–26, 1996. Used by permission.

The cartoon features Jacques Chirac and Prime Minister Alain Juppé against the vacation backdrop of Fort Brégançon, the French presidential retreat on the Côte d'Azur. It is the end of the summer, though, and the title of the front-page story invokes the work that awaits the two men as they prepare for the fall while *sans-papiers* deportations are under way. Both politicians are wearing shorts and print shirts and are strolling on the beach. As a blunt reminder of the early-morning raid on the Saint-Bernard church (where the police used hatchets to break open the doors), Chirac asks his vacation buddy, "Are we going to church on Sunday?" Juppé replies, "Ah? Have you got your hatchet?"

The cartoon is framed by the fort on the left and a church on the right. On the one hand, the fort stands as a highly militarized space used at one time to protect the inside of the nation against outsiders. The fort, of course, also evokes the ongoing construction of "Fortress Europe," whose common goal is to keep non-European immigrants on the outside, if not of the European space itself, at least of its legality. On the other hand, the church offers the promise of a spiritual and political sanctuary to those who do reside inside but lack the human rights protection afforded by legal residency papers. The two politicians, as representatives of the French state, are positioned in the middle of the frame. However, none of the African actors of the Saint-Bernard raid, male or female, are visible in this cartoon. It is almost as if the *sans-papiers* cannot be physically present here or in the imagined space of the Republic. Caught between the raw power of the state, increasingly militarized notions of national borders, and the inflamed rhetoric of foreign invasions, the concrete reality of undocumented immigrants is made to disappear. It is precisely these acts of discursive and material disappearance that the *sans-papiers* resist on a daily basis.

IDENTITY OF LACK AND IMPOSSIBLE POLITICS

Several other drawings represent Chirac lying, like the Saint-Bernard hunger strikers, on a makeshift bed, on the floor of his home, in a church, or in his political headquarters. In these drawings the French president becomes a stand-in for the *sans-papiers*. In one of the cartoons, Chirac is lying on the floor of the Saint-Bernard church itself. A *sans-papiers*, one of the onlookers, stands next to the leaders of the French Socialist and Communist parties.[11] A French policeman is commenting on Chirac's presence in the church: "He is politically homeless" (*c'est un sans-politique fixe*), he says. Plantu's play on words in this cartoon (in France, the homeless are euphemistically named for their lack of stable housing: *sans-domicile fixe*) can be read as a commentary both on the

Figure 2.2 *La Gauche s'unit pour soutenir les sans-papiers de Saint-Bernard* [The Left unites to support the Saint-Bernard *sans-papiers*]. Cartoon by Plantu. *Le Monde*, August 22, 1996, *Sélection hebdomadaire*. Used by permission.

president's political choices and on the emergence of new social movements in France, movements organized around what I call here an identity of "lack."

There is no place, literally no home, for the Saint-Bernard debacle (characterized by excessive force, racism, human rights abuse, and so on) in the Republic, the French civil servant seems to suggest. This idea, which is one of the foundational myths of the republican tradition, is in fact challenged by the very presence and treatment of the *sans-papiers* in France. The *sans-papiers* have forged strong alliances with other groups who share this collective lack: the homeless, the jobless, and other groups situated at the margins of the Republic. All of them understand very well that the "lack," around which they are constructing identities and launching political actions, is both a result of larger structural forces and what keeps them one step removed from the arena of individual rights and full civil protection.

The various processes that create identities of "lack" for certain people in France are directly connected to the notion of impossibility that I explore throughout this book. If indeed identity, rights, and political actions are usually forged around a shared something (a having or a being), then how can one assert one's rightful presence and state one's claims when such having or being is denied to one? This conundrum has been brilliantly analyzed by feminist historian Joan Scott.[12]

Organizing around an identity of "lack" transforms old notions of identity politics without throwing away the political necessity of "identities" around which to make political claims. What is done away with is an identity that resides in a pre-existing "self." The focus has shifted onto the discursive and material processes that locate individuals and groups within particular social and symbolic spaces of impossibility. Parallels can be drawn between the various (linked but different) dynamics that produce those who lack: the homeless, the jobless, the paperless, and so on. I would argue here that we need to include women and "queers," who in male-dominated, heterosexist, and heteronormative regimes do lack the very recognition that

Figure 2.3 *M. Juppé multiplie les consultations pour régler le conflit des sans-papiers* [Juppé seeks advice from multiple sources to resolve the *sans-papiers* conflict]. Cartoon by Plantu. *Le Monde*, August 22, 1996. Used by permission.

a "normal" and "neutral" gender and sexuality provide. Both women and queers in France are indeed located in an "impossible" political space. Those who "lack" have to state their claims on the basis of their difference within a political system that vigorously rejects such demands on the basis of abstract universalism.

Organizing around "lack," then, is a creative, adaptive strategy that makes good sense in a culture that resists political claims based on difference and minority status. Indeed, minority policies that focus on the shared experience and social location of particular groups are routinely rejected in France. Claims such as that of French scholar Dominique Schnapper that such policies "would break with a long tradition of national integration in France and weaken (and perhaps even dissolve) the social fabric" are common.[13]

The only female presence in the cartoons is French actress Emanuelle Béart, who in one of them is semi-hidden by the altar but attracting much of

Figure 2.4 *Les sans-papiers attendant une réponse sur leur sort après l'évacuation par la force de l'église Saint-Bernard* [The *sans-papiers* are waiting for a determination of their fate after their forced removal from the Saint-Bernard Church]. Cartoon by Plantu. *Le Monde*, August 29, 1996. Used by permission.

the attention of the photographers covering the forced removal of the *sans-papiers* (see Figure 2.2). Béart was an active supporter of the *sans-papiers* and had just joined them in the occupation of the church. Ironically, as is astutely conveyed in this drawing, the French actress alone received more press coverage than all of the *sans-papiéres* present in the church during the entire occupation. The cartoons also evoke the racist slippery slope in which the Republic is engaged in its brutal handling of the *sans-papiers*. This is best captured in a drawing published in the August 29 international edition of *Le Monde*.

In this drawing, two unarmed African men are being savagely beaten by two French policemen in full riot gear while a nonrepentant Jacques Chirac is kneeling at the confessional: "What? Confess what, Father?" he replies to an invisible priest. The cartoon reminds readers that segments of the Catholic Church have been supportive of the *sans-papiers* struggle. In particular, Father Coindé, the priest who offered shelter to three hundred of them in the Saint-Bernard church, stood out in his unequivocal support for the undocumented immigrants who had sought refuge in his church. It is also clear here that Plantu draws from existing racist imagery to represent the brutalized *sans-papiers*. Africans are caricatured in ways that are reminiscent of colonial representations of African "natives." The cartoons, no doubt, are meant to accentuate the racist overtone of the Saint-Bernard's evacuation and the politics of immigration that led to it. The inability of the French president, whether feigned or real, to recognize his wrongdoings here echoes the Republic's inability to face its own colonial and racist ghosts.[14] Unfortunately, the cartoons also deemphasize the *sans-papiers*' agency and resistance throughout the crisis.

In this cartoon, as in all the others discussed here, immigrant women are nowhere to be found. It is interesting to note that photographic representations of the *sans-papiers*' struggle cannot help but capture the presence of women. Women are indeed present at all the movement's actions, as is often documented in photographs of the many demonstrations organized by the *sans-papiers*. Photos are less likely than drawings to eradicate the presence of women. In the cartoons, at least in Plantu's in *Le Monde*, women are literally eviscerated from the image.

A front-page story of the August 14, 1996, issue of *Le Monde* is about the decline in vacation-time road accidents in France. Next to it one can also read a story about the *sans-papiers* and the help they are increasingly receiving from leftist and humanitarian organizations.

A cartoon (see Figure 2.5) in which a French policeman is driving a whole African family back to the border is cleverly used to illustrate both stories. One of the black backseat passengers says, "The French are driving better and better!" The white policeman, as the driver, is at the center of the image. In the backseat, one adult male is surrounded by a "slew" of children and one woman—presumably his wife and the mother of all the children. This representation of an African woman in relation to the *sans-papiers'* struggle is both exceptional and typical. It is exceptional in that usually women are not present in these cartoons, and typical in the sense that she is the quintessential African woman who gets conjured up when the African presence in France is in need of a trope. Tellingly, she is silent in the cartoon and half-hidden by the car's window frame.

This visual narrative, however, belies the more complicated story unfolding in the Saint-Bernard church. Indeed, the reader need only turn to page 6 of the paper to discover the story of Marianne Camara. The twenty-seven-year-old Malian mother of two is angry and determined. She has just joined the four other women involved in the hunger strike in protest of the forced hospitalization of the strikers: "Babies were crying, perhaps the riot police were trying to scare us so that we'd abandon the struggle. But we will not give up. We are not afraid of a church evacuation."[15] Camara, then, is a mother who,

Figure 2.5 *Les soutiens aux Africains sans-papiers se multiplient* [Support for undocumented Africans is mounting]. Cartoon by Plantu. *Le Monde,* August 14, 1996. Used by permission.

unlike the woman in the cartoon, is speaking and acting. Burying Camara's story in the back pages of the paper is another way of erasing the active presence of women within the struggle. Camara's story is the kind of counternarrative that I foreground in *Reinventing the Republic*. This is a narrative that resituates immigrant women at the center of the story and looks at the ways they participate in and transform the discursive and social practices that shaped the French politics of immigration at the turn of the millennium.

By engaging this counternarrative, my aim is to complicate and disrupt hegemonic representations of postcolonial immigrant women in France. In the next section, I turn to a series of interviews collected by French feminists in 1998. Together, these RAJFIRE interviews constitute a unique portrait of the *sans-papières* involved in the early stages of the movement. As early iterations of the *sans-papières* story, they also give us a glimpse of the narrative strategies used by the women to locate themselves against (and sometimes within) dominant representations of foreigners, women, and immigrants in France. Finally, they allow us to look at a different frame—one that posits the women as agents and as part of a collective struggle. Framed differently (but framed nevertheless), the *sans-papières* tell stories that help us flesh out their im/material presence in the dominant narrative about the *sans-papiers* movement in France.

COUNTERNARRATIVES: THE RAJFIRE INTERVIEWS

These interviews were collected in the Paris region by radical feminist activists between July and December 1998 and aired on the feminist radio show *Femmes libres* (free women) on Radio Libertaire.[16] They were also published in the RAJFIRE Brochure No. 2 in March 2000. The RAJFIRE interviews are the only available collected body of *sans-papières'* voices from that period of the struggle. As such, they stand as a unique document that sharply contrasts with mainstream analyses and representations of the *sans-papiers* movement. The RAJFIRE activists have been remarkable in their sustained efforts at collecting, preserving, and making available documents that trace the role and place of women within *sans-papiers* struggles.[17] Among the many groups involved in immigrant struggles in France, the feminist network stands out for its multifaceted and long-standing engagement in the *sans-papiers* cause. The RAJFIRE has been providing a space for undocumented immigrant women to speak out, has generated a gendered analysis of the French state and its immigration law apparatus, and has constructed a rich archive of *sans-papières'* experiences and political interventions. It has also made this archive available through a variety of media, including brochures, radio programs, a documentary, and a Web site.[18] As a researcher, I was generously given access to all of the RAJFIRE's documents and invited to attend and observe some of their meetings.

The RAJFIRE Brochure No. 2 highlights the purpose of the network and the aims of its publications:

> The RAJFIRE (Network for the Legal Autonomy of Migrant and Refugee Women) is a network of organizations and individuals that was constituted in May 1997 and, among other things, publishes this brochure.

> The intent of this publication is to create a forum for undocumented women to speak out. We want to document how women are confronted with the French laws that restrict the rights of foreigners, to bring to light their role within the movement and the obstacles they encounter, and to maintain a trace of their trajectories, their struggles, and their lives.[19]

By placing the interviews in a brochure that also offers its readers a feminist analysis of French immigration laws; various articles, petitions, and flyers documenting women's participation in the struggle (March 1998–December 1999); as well as listings of useful addresses and resources, the RAJFIRE activists, unlike the mainstream press, see the women's individual narratives as part of a larger story. The RAJFIRE frame uses gender as a key category of analysis and highlights the unique role women have played in the *sans-papiers* movement in France:

> I belong to the Coordination 93 [a *sans-papiers* collective] and the RAJFIRE [. . . .] We'd like to also produce a brochure with these various women's testimonies in order to let people know the specific realities of undocumented women, because they are often nonexistent in other [social] movements while the *sans-papiers* movement in France started because of women.[20]

Taken as a whole, these interviews offer a unique window into the lived experiences of *sans-papières* in France and address a set of interrelated themes that help us understand the various layers that create what I call here *social conditions of impossibility*. These themes range from papers and legal status, familial linkages, work relations, health issues and social coverage, spatial mobility and freedom, to fear, anxiety, and activism. Most of the themes discussed in the rest of the chapter are also present in the interviews I personally conducted in 2002 and are explored at greater length later in the book.

By connecting my own interviews and analyses to those of the RAJFIRE activists, my aim is threefold. First, I mean to recognize the tremendous work the RAJFIRE has accomplished in the context of the *sans-papiers* movement. I also want to present the *sans-papières'* stories I collected as reiterations of stories told by other women before them. Finally, in doing so, I mean to attend to the changing backdrop against which the stories are being told and to the constructed (framed) nature of the telling itself.

> I am from Ivory Coast. My nationality is Ivoirian. I am an artist, a song writer, and a singer.
>
> I entered France on September 26, 1990.
>
> I do not have papers. In 1991, I filed for my regularization. They asked for a ton of papers. I presented them. They gave me a receipt [that entitles one to legal residency for a period of three months]. It was renewed every three months up to nine months. Then, all of a sudden, I was sent, via mail, my deportation notice.

Maîmouna is an African woman who migrated to France in the early 1990s. She entered French territory alone. At thirty-eight, she is a widow (her husband died in 1986) and a mother of six children whom, except for one, she left behind in Africa. I open with Maîmouna's interview because it illustrates a common and somewhat new migratory pattern: women who migrate alone or before other family members. Most of the women interviewed by the RAJFIRE activists entered France legally—often with short-term tourist visas—and for a variety of reasons (the most common being that they have overstayed) have become undocumented. Most, like Maîmouna, have filed petitions to obtain a change of status, and many were, at the time of the interviews, under threat of deportation.

Maîmouna's interview is also typical in that it tells a story organized around specific dates, conditions of entry, and immigration status: "I entered France on September 26, 1990. I do not have papers. In 1991, I filed for my sojourn papers." The precise and cursory quality of the telling reminds us that these stories have been told many a time to social workers, lawyers, allies, and civil servants. They follow a narrative structure shaped by French immigration laws, by the ways in which they are implemented at any given moment (in any given office), and by the localized political choices of *sans-*

papiers collectives and other nongovernmental organizations providing support to undocumented immigrants. In many collectives, for instance, allies "help" undocumented immigrants construct life stories that will then be part of their case files. These life stories, although based on facts provided by the *sans-papiers* themselves, are structured in ways that emphasize what the ally thinks is going to appeal to the civil servant or servants in charge of reading the case file.

Beyond the rehearsed and, at times, formulaic quality of their narratives, the interviews often offer interesting critiques of the material and discursive processes that have rendered many of these women undocumented. Maîmouna, for instance, states that she is being denied a change of status because she entered the country with a short visa. Refusing the logic of the French administration and pointing out the disingenuous reason invoked for its refusal, Maîmouna explains that it is virtually impossible for women like her to obtain anything but short-stay visas: "They told me that I did not have a long-stay visa. But from Africa, when you go to France, that's not possible, if you're not a civil servant, if you're not rich. A poor woman like me cannot obtain a long-stay visa; that's not possible."

Like many women interviewed by the RAJFIRE and myself, Maîmouna challenges the logic and exposes the contradictions of the French republic. She reminds us that the French administration is requesting entry papers that are by and large denied to poor and nonelite women from African countries. Indeed, France started requiring visas from tourists interested in visiting the country in the mid-1980s after a wave of terrorist attacks. Moreover, since September 1986, consular authorities have not had to justify their refusal to grant a visa. In part because of these changes, the percentage of denied requests (even for short-term visas) drastically increased in the mid 1990s.[21]

Maîmouna's interview illustrates that changes in the conditions of entry and sojourn have created new spaces of impossibility for immigrants desiring to enter the country. Her emphasis that it is only certain women (women who are not part of the civil servant elite and women who lack the financial tools to weather the long waits and the cost now connected to obtaining a tourist visa) who are denied is worth noting here. Indeed, it is the intersection of several forces that restricts some women's mobility. Another recurring motif in the RAJFIRE interviews is the notion that women who are single and who do not have children born in France have not been able to obtain a change of status.

Nathalie, for instance, who has lived in France for ten years without papers, links her inability to obtain papers to her single and childless status: "Because I am single, I don't have children. I am not entitled [to papers]."

The interviewers, however, do point out that other women who are married and have children have not been able to obtain papers either. Familial links to a legal resident or a French person certainly help, but they are not the only elements taken into account by the French administration. In fact, one of the recurring criticisms voiced by *sans-papiers* activists and their allies is that, for the most part, administrative decisions are completely arbitrary. The *sans-papiers* manifesto, which opens Chapter 1, makes this point loud and clear. The arbitrariness of the decision-making process denies, in all practical matters, the due process that would provide undocumented immigrants a certain level of protection expected in democratic societies. Such arbitrary processes pave the way for all forms of discriminatory practices, increase the *sans-papiers'* vulnerability, and locate them in social spaces where they are not entitled to full civil rights protection.

It is important to note, however, the few things that are likely to generate a positive decision from the administration and a successful change of status. Fatima's interview, for instance, corroborates the fact that one's ability to document a union with a French person (even when that relationship is with a person of the same gender) can tip one's petition in the right direction:

Fatima: I filed my petition for a change of status after the 1997 administrative memorandum came out, and I received a negative response from the *préfecture*.[22] I appealed twice—and was still denied. In the meantime, I had contacted the collective of undocumented gays and filed another petition—directly to the Ministry [of the Interior]—that this time included proof of my union with Véronique.

Claudie Lesselier: Do you think that these elements determined the decision?

F: Yes for sure! It was thanks to that!

CL: But same-sex couples are not recognized under French law. . . .

F: They are not recognized officially, but in practice they are. I filed this petition in July and I received a positive response within two months. I had included a letter from Véronique stating that we had been living together since 1990; letters from friends who know us; testimonies; we photocopied photos that included the date of the shot.

As we will see later, connection with (and activism within) a *sans-papiers* collective is also a determinant in Fatima's successful outcome and in the outcomes of other women interviewed by the RAJFIRE activists. The notion of familial links is important to explore further and is fully developed in the next two chapters. Khadidja, who has lived in France for thirteen and a half years, has not been able to obtain a change of status because of lack of familial linkages in France. She recounts that "in the negative decision I was sent [it says that] I am single, I don't have any dependents [in France] and my familial links are back home; they are referring to my parents, in other words. I have uncles here with whom I lived and I was adopted by my grandmother [who lived in France]. Unfortunately, my grandmother passed away four years ago, I became dependent on my uncles as a result."

What is important to note is that Khadidja (like many other women) is being penalized not simply because she does not have familial links in France, but also because she still has familial ties "back home." Whether these ties are meaningful to Khadidja herself is unfortunately of no importance to the French administration. Khadidja, however, stresses that, due to her personal trajectory, her familial ties in France are now stronger than those in Morocco: "I was adopted here by my grandmother so I did not belong any longer to the family that was back home. I belonged to my mother's family, my uncles, my aunts; since I was eleven it's them who took care of me. They are all married, they have children; they are all documented, naturalized even."

Khadidja's testimony, like many others, illustrates the discrepancy between real-life situations and the rigidity of administrative categories. It also points to the complex reality of transnational familial ties that have been produced by France's colonial project and anchored by globalization. Although her ascendants are indeed based in Morocco and are now part of her extended family, the family members who actually care for and support Khadidja—her closest relatives—are all located in France. As I discuss at length in the next two chapters, the material and discursive processes that lock women into familial (and traditional) spaces also create social conditions of impossibility. When the interviewer asks her if she intends to go back to Morocco if she is unsuccessful in obtaining a change of status (thus evoking Khadidja's difficulty in adapting to the Moroccan tradition), Khadidja replies, "It's not even the tradition. It's Moroccan life. No, I could not stand it. Let's start with the lack of employment; here I have everything I need. All right, I do not have papers, [but] I have a job. It's true that I cannot take a vacation and go see my family[. . . .] I am independent, I have my own money."

Khadidja's rejection of the interviewer's interpretation (that she would not want to go back because of the Moroccan "tradition") is interesting in itself. Indeed, what Khadidja focuses on is the material and life-quality gains that staying in France affords her. So, instead of invoking the amorphous notion of tradition, the *sans-papière* astutely refocuses the interview on the material autonomy she enjoys in France in spite of her undocumented status: "I am independent" here, "I have my own money."[23] As we will see in the stories I collected myself, this self-sufficiency is of key importance to all the women interviewed for the project. For some of them, supporting themselves is not simply a choice but a sheer necessity.

Maîmouna, for instance, supports herself through her singing. She appears at world music concerts (she has been featured as the opening act for well-known artists such as Angelique Kidjo and Césaria Évora). She sells audio- and videocassettes of her music and performs as a *griotte* (female storyteller, musician, and poet) at weddings and baptismal ceremonies. In addition, she cleans French people's homes. At the time of the interview, Maîmouna was working on her second album. She had a contract with a record company, which she hoped would entitle her to sojourn and residency papers. Her interview highlights the specific challenges of working without papers, addresses the difficulties of paying for medical care without social coverage, and discusses a recurring theme in all the Radio Libertaire interviews: that of the unscrupulous lawyer willing to take her money but ineffective in securing a change of status. However, like the other women interviewed here, Maîmouna does not entertain going back as a real possibility: "No. I cannot leave for Africa like this. Whatever little money I make, I send it all to my children, each month. If I go back to Ivory Coast, how will I feed them? Their father is dead, I cannot."

Maîmouna also points to the global processes that have transformed the country from which she emigrated and made it impossible for her to return. These global processes, as is discussed throughout the book, shape the social conditions of impossibility.

Overall, the RAJFIRE interviews demonstrate that undocumented migrant women have little difficulty finding work. Some types of employment are not available to them, of course, because they might require papers, but none of the women talked about the difficulty of finding work. Nathalie, for instance, discusses her live-in maid job at the house of two French medical doctors:

> *Nathalie*: Both of them are doctors but they don't pay enough, because I don't have papers.
>
> *Interviewer*: How much do you make?
>
> *N*: FF 4700 [roughly $800 at the time of the interview].
>
> *I*: Per month?
>
> *N*: Yes.
>
> *I*: For how many hours of work?
>
> *N*: From 8:30 AM until 7 PM.
>
> *I*: Every day?
>
> *N*: Yes, even on Saturday.
>
> *I*: Even on Saturday. Saturday afternoon and Sunday?
>
> *N*: Yes.

Nathalie's interview also documents that her employers refused to offer her a work contract (*une promesse d'embauche*), which might have enabled her to obtain a change of status: "But he told me that they could not afford it, that they did not have the money because it was too expensive. They are paying me half [of what they're supposed to]. That's why they cannot hire me legally." Her employers refuse because they would have to meet French work and pay regulations and pay social security taxes that would provide Nathalie with health coverage and other benefits. Her testimony illustrates how falling ill within these illegal forms of employment leads to loss of income and, in some cases, the denial of basic health care.[24] Nathalie, who cut herself on the job, had to be hospitalized because the cut got infected: "I stayed two weeks in the hospital. I just came out. Today she called me to go back to work the day after tomorrow. If not, I'll lose my job."

Caroline's interview illustrates the lack of migrant women's legal autonomy—an issue that has been at the core of migrant women's organizing since the mid-seventies. She entered the country in 1993 with a six-month visa to join her husband, who had lived in France for twenty years and was a legal resident. An actress, Caroline immediately registered at the conservatory for a course in filmmaking and editing. When she and her husband inquired about a change of status, they were told she would not get it. Under the Pasqua laws, Caroline had to go back to the Central African Republic to obtain the legal right to enter France for family reunification. Her husband was afraid and insisted she go back to Africa. Caroline refused: "I said I can't go back because to start I am registered at the conservatory, I have to finish my studies, and on top of that I don't have anybody there. Two months after I arrived my mother passed away. My big brother is here; he has the French nationality. My little sister is here; she has been living here for ten years already. Both are legal residents." Eventually the stress proved to be too much for their relationship and Caroline and her husband separated, leaving her undocumented and with absolutely no claim to residency and sojourn papers: "And they replied, like, we cannot grant you the right to stay because you are no longer living with your husband."

Even if Caroline had managed to obtain a change of status, a separation would have meant that she would not have been able to renew her sojourn or residency card. (Upon a change of status, immigrants are usually issued a temporary card for one year). Interestingly, several of the interviews oppose two characters: *l'avocat verreux* (the unscrupulous lawyer—literally "wormy"—who can be male or female) and *la marraine* (the republican godmother) or the good and helpful French ally. Nathalie, who has never worked with a lawyer, has sought help from a *marraine* from *la maison des femmes*. Afraid that she could not successfully advocate for herself, she decided to seek help from a French ally: "Yes, I felt that alone I wasn't getting anywhere." Prodded by the interviewer, who forcefully suggested "you are intimidated and scared?" Nathalie replied, "Yes, I am a little shy, but not afraid at all." Other women, however, do talk about the constant state of fear that their undocumented status has created for them. Yamina and Dalila, for instance, shared their fears during their collective interview:

> *Yamina*: Yes, it is a little tough as far as work goes. I am taking care of my employers' child and I also clean their home; the bosses are fine, but the subway, that's far, and without papers I am afraid; yes, I am always afraid of a police check and I take the subway morning and night!
>
> [. . .]
>
> *Dalila*: Me, from 5 on I am at home and I stay there.

Besides undocumented migrant women having different levels of fear and anxiety, another recurring theme is the lack of spatial mobility they experience. For many, this lack of mobility is particularly painful because it makes it impossible for them to maintain "normal" relationships with members of their family. Most of them talk about their inability to visit aging or ailing parents in their country of origin. Dalila, who never leaves home after 5 PM, explains how she also cannot go back to Algeria because she would not be able to reenter the country: "No, if I go back I am stuck. I have my mother who is very ill and you know very well what's going on in Algeria. As long as I don't have my papers, I cannot go there; I am stuck here."

CONCLUSION

Except for Fatima, all the women interviewed by the RAJFIRE activists were unable (at the time of their interview) to secure a change of status for themselves. All of them are "regular" women who are simply fighting to obtain a right to stay in France and ameliorate their social condition. These women, like the ones I met in 2002, are not (and do not think of themselves as) heroic activists. Most of them, in fact, happened upon collective action after having tried a variety of individual approaches to solving their situation. Most tried to work alone or with a private lawyer before reaching out to an NGO or a *sans-papiers* collective. By becoming active in a social movement, the *sans-papières* forge alliances with individuals and groups that they might not have encountered outside of their social action.

The unique analytical power, the potential coalitional work, and the impossible (unruly) politics that these alliances can generate are exciting. Nacira Guénif-Souilamas and Eric Massé speak to this potential when they write about the various processes that scapegoat young immigrant males of North African origin in France. By seeing the "immigrant," her children, queers, and women all as products of French modernity, Guénif-Souilamas and Massé help us think of the *sans-papière* as a subject constructed at the intersection of multiple discourses and social forces. They also invite us to imagine solutions that engage such intersections:

> We are also saying that the struggle against sexist discriminations is inseparable from the struggle against racist discriminations and differential "ethnic" assignments. *This is why we have to see, in the trio formed by the figures of the queer, the Arab boy, and the veiled girl, not the enemies of modernity but rather the incandescent actors of a contemporary democratic hypermodernity.*[25]

In the process of trying to improve their lives and of testing out a variety of strategies, most *sans-papières* do develop a keen critique of the symbolic and structural forces that shape their everyday realities. They do see that collective efforts are often fruitful, even if not revolutionary and if somewhat limited. Through their everyday practices, they reinvent old notions of citizenship and, in the process, invite us to redraw the boundaries of the Republic and re-define the terms of national belonging in France. As Fatima says, "Of course I am going to continue [to fight within the collective for undocumented gays]. I have a lot of hope; we received quite a few positive responses lately. For couples it is getting better; for single individuals, I don't know." And according to Khadidja, "No, there is no reason I should hide. I've been living in France for thirteen and a half years; I totally have the right [to stay][. . . .] I have been living in France for thirteen years and it entitles me to certain rights."

3 THE LEGAL CONSTRUCTION OF IMMIGRANT WOMEN IN FRANCE

KARINA, A YOUNG ALGERIAN MOTHER OF TWO, has a long-standing connection with France and especially with the city of Marseilles.[1] Although born in Algeria, she has spent most of her life on the north side of the Mediterranean. After several moves back and forth between the two countries, Karina finally reentered France in 2000 with a tourist visa. Three months later, when the visa expired, she found herself without papers. Her story illustrates how legal texts and administrative practices have shaped the social spaces within which postcolonial immigrants move and the relations they build therein. More specifically, it gives us a glimpse of the various processes that have contributed to the formation of transnational lives and families within the juridico-administrative context of immigration in France. It also gives substance to the ways in which immigrants' lives and families have been transformed by the restrictive turn in French immigration policies since the 1970s. Finally, it reveals how gender hierarchies, at play on both sides of the Mediterranean, have shaped Karina's own trajectory. Karina's story reminds us that we need to pay attention to these hierarchies (and how they intersect with other hierarchies) in order to understand fully why she, unlike her brothers, finds herself without papers in a country where she grew up and went to school and where a large part of her family resides legally.

In 1962, when Algeria won its independence, Karina's father left his country to look for work in France.[2] Karina's grandfather had done the same thing in 1915 and the rest of his life had been split between the two countries. He lived and worked in Marseilles for eleven months of each year and spent one month in Algeria with his wife and young children. While in Marseilles he managed several restaurants, employed his sons in his business, and over the years had several French companions who bore him eleven children. Throughout the years he also brought over several of his Algerian sons to France to work in the family restaurants. Karina's father was one of them.

Like his father before him, Karina's father began a life split between France and Algeria. But unlike his father, after a few years of one-month summer visits to Algeria, he finally sent for his family. Karina, her mother, and her brothers arrived in France in the late 1960s through the procedure of family reunification. Three more children were born to the family in France. When Karina was four she was sent back to Algeria to keep her grandmother company. However, when she turned six, her parents brought her back to Marseilles so she could start school in the French public education system. Karina stayed, grew up, and attended French schools until 1987. At that time, her parents decided they wanted to return home, retire, and live in the villa they had had built for them. Karina made the conscious (but with hindsight, problematic) decision to follow them:

> My father wanted to get closer to his mother. I followed along with the younger children. I thought that I would go to Algeria. . . . France is not so welcoming to foreigners. I thought I would go back to Algeria and teach. I [thought I] was not losing much by going back to Algeria. We used to go every year. We did not realize it was a developing country when we were there on vacations. . . . I studied education for two years [at the normal school] and I became a teacher of French. That's where I met my husband—he too was a former immigrant [and he too is now *sans-papiers* in Marseilles].

In 1989, Karina's mother decided to bring the whole family back to Marseilles to flee the civil war that was tearing Algeria apart. Karina and two of her brothers decided to stay in Algeria. Karina explains that she was bound by a contract to the Algerian state whereby she had agreed to teach for a number of years after finishing her state-sponsored teacher's training. Karina also explains that her parents had failed to protect her rights by making sure she maintained a legal connection to France in case she decided to return: "My rights were not put forward. If you fail to come back to France after a six-month absence, you lose your [residency] papers. The boys kept going back and forth so they would not lose their legal standing. I didn't."

In the rest of the interview Karina explains that she and her husband felt in danger in a country where fundamentalists targeted teachers and civil servants. After several years of frugal living and careful planning, in 2000 Karina, her husband, and their two children arrived in France on a short-term visa with approximately $30,000 in savings. When I met Karina in 2002, most of the money was gone, both she and her husband were working in the underground economy, and both were active in the Marseilles *sans-papiers* collective. Karina was hopeful for her family's future, and saw her participation in this struggle as a way to take charge of that future and transform the gender relations that contributed to turning her into a *sans-papière*. At the end of the interview, she concludes, "Now that I feel like my head is above water. I want to continue [the struggle] for other women. [When I tell women,] 'There is a march on Saturday' [and they reply,] 'Wait, I have to talk it over with my husband'—that has got to stop!"

I open this chapter with Karina's interview because it places the *sans-papiers* and *sans-papières* experience against three sets of realities that have helped to create it. Indeed, France's colonial past, its complex and contradictory immigration policies, and the centrality of family and familial ties in the lives of women subtly organize her narrative. At their intersection we see emerge a dynamic that places Karina, and other women like her, in a particularly precarious social location. Here and in the next chapter I focus specifically on the role of the family (and familial discourses) in the shaping of that location. Families, and what constitutes them, are constructed and shaped by a variety of discourses and material practices. In this chapter I turn my attention to both by looking at family reunification policies. Immigrants, according to French law, are entitled to have family members join them. The procedure, called *family reunification*, entitles any foreigner to bring in a spouse and children (under the age of eighteen) as long as the foreigner is legally present in France and can show proof of "adequate" lodging and income resources.[3] Family reunification policies have changed over time, shaping both the size and the composition of immigration in France.[4]

FAMILY REUNIFICATION: HISTORICAL CONTEXT

Family reunification, like the rest of French immigration policies, has emerged from the country's economic and demographic needs and been shaped further by its unique political culture. Since the beginning of massive migration into the country, in the middle of the nineteenth century, French politicians and administrators have designed complex immigration plans to meet the country's contradictory needs and adhere to its republican principles. France has addressed its periodic labor shortages by actively recruiting single men as temporary and dispensable migrant workers (*travailleurs immigrés*), but has also compensated for its historic low birthrate and attendant demographic decline by facilitating family immigration and promoting the permanent settlement of foreign populations.[5]

The juridico-administrative matrix for the regulation of immigration in France was established by the Order of November 2, 1945. It has been amended many times and was last modified in 2005. The civil code (nationality and marriage laws), the penal code (deportation and *interdiction du territoire* (denial of entry and residence), the health insurance code, the work code, and asylum and refugee laws also inform the status and rights of foreigners and immigrants. Myriad bilateral agreements affect how immigration policies are actually applied. Finally, international law, supranational treaties, and the high political stakes of immigration in France have produced the conditions for the constant fine-tuning of the November 2, 1945, matrix.

Ethnic ranking of would-be immigrants was seriously considered during the crafting of the 1945 Order but was not retained in its final version.[6] The favoring of European immigration, however, did find its way into, and has lingered, within the structures of immigration recruitment and regulation

Figure 3.1 *Sans-papiers* demonstration, Porte St. Denis, Paris. Photo by C. Raissiguier.

in France.[7] Resting on unspeakable (within the Republic) prejudices about "us" and "them" and about the assimilability (or lack thereof) of certain immigrants, this ethnocultural trend is central to and constitutive of the French politics of immigration.

After World War II, during three decades of unprecedented economic growth, French governments facilitated the entry and settlement of European immigrants (first from Germany and Italy and later from Spain and Portugal) and their families.[8] During the first few years after the war, for instance, European immigrants were entitled to financial help when they settled with their families.[9] In spite of the National Office of Immigration's efforts, (legal) family settlement was hampered by serious postwar housing shortages and by sharp discrepancies between official immigration policies and on-the-ground recruitment practices.[10]

The number of entries through formal family reunification procedures stayed low until 1957.[11] It is only after 1960, with the implementation of the procedure of *régularisation sur place*, which allowed family members to change their status after the fact, even when they had entered the country illegally, that family reunification numbers began to swell.[12] In 1971 the number of such entries peaked, reaching a total of 81,500 individuals brought in through the procedure. Since then, however, the number has steadily decreased, hovering below 20,000 after 1994. In 1997, at the height of the *sans-papiers* crisis, only 15,535 individuals were allowed entry through the procedure of family reunification.[13]

Family reunification policies have been created with a women-and-children-will-follow scenario in mind. In turn, they have affected women and children in specific and unique ways. Later in this chapter I analyze both the gender underpinnings and the gendered effects of French immigration laws. More specifically, I focus on some of the changes in family reunification policies in the past three decades to analyze the legal mechanisms that locate the *sans-papières* in social spaces of impossibility. I argue that laws, discourses, and practices that link a woman's residence, ability to work, and chance of obtaining residency papers to those of her husband endanger immigrant women's legal autonomy, increase their dependence on men, and intensify their overall *précarité* and vulnerability. I end the chapter by discussing the situation of the undocumented immigrant women I interviewed in 2002. The interviews illustrate some of the gendered effects of immigration law discussed here. They also demonstrate that *sans-papières* critically engage French laws and administrative practices that continue to place them in zones of impossibility. By interspersing *sans-papières*' narratives throughout my analysis, my aim is to document how the women themselves understand and negotiate the impossible social locations they have come to inhabit.

In July 1974 France closed its borders to work immigration. Since then, increasingly restrictive laws have been implemented to contain and regulate non-European and family immigration. Successive French governments, regardless of their political locations—whether "left" or "right"—have deployed a dual approach to immigration. On the one hand, they have tried to curb legal immigration by tightening policies, and to stop illegal immigration by cracking down on undocumented immigrants. On the other hand, they have worked to establish and protect the rights of legal immigrants and to ensure the integration of those already present in the national territory.[14] This dual process has been quite uneven, in part because of the continued disjuncture between stated immigration goals and actual immigration practices.[15] The unevenness of the process must also be analyzed as an effect of gendering and racializing discourses and practices. Women and immigrants from France's former colonies, in particular, have been imagined as presenting unique characteristics and challenges. As a result, they have been affected differently by the dual process just described. Ideas about "race" and "gender" and the way they intersect have had interesting (and yet little studied) effects on the development and deployment of France's politics of immigration. Here I turn my attention to these effects, with a particular focus on family reunification policies.

CHANGES IN FAMILY REUNIFICATION (1974–1998)

Although French law is gender neutral (it refers to "spouses" rather than to "wives" and "husbands"), institutions, cultural norms, and social interactions are not.[16] As a result, "gender-neutral" policies can and do have gendered effects. It has been amply demonstrated, for instance, that the so-called end of legal work immigration in 1974 hastened and deepened an already existing momentum toward the feminization of immigration in France. Indeed, in the mid-1970s family reunification became the predominant form of immigration and, to a lesser degree, of regularizing the status of undocumented spouses and children already present in France. Since then, the vast majority of legal entries have occurred through the procedure of family reunification. In the 1990s, family immigration (all procedures included) accounted for 60 to 70 percent of all entries from non-European Union countries. In 2002 it accounted for

73.5 percent of all such entries.[17] Although family reunification is open to all, it is mostly women and children who enter the country through these channels.[18] In 1996, for instance, 41.5 percent of family reunification immigrants were adult women, 10.7 percent were men, and 47.8 percent were children.[19]

Because most immigrant women entered the French territory through the process of family reunification, their immigration, citizenship, income-generating power, and social benefits are connected to the status of a male family member. In other words, it is the legal status of a spouse (or father) that determines the legal status given to a woman. The severing of familial and marital relationships can put immigrant women and their daughters in a legal bind vis-à-vis the French state, and in the worst-case scenarios it ushers them into the realm of illegality. Legal scholars, grassroots immigrant women's organizations, and international agencies have underscored and deplored this constructed legal vulnerability of immigrant women in France. Many of their rights have been defined as derivative rights.[20]

In the mid-1970s, in the wake of the first oil crisis of 1973, and in an ideological climate that linked immigration with the growing problem of unemployment among French nationals, France tinkered with family reunification legislation in a spate of contradictory decrees, administrative memoranda, and laws. During that time, family immigration was in turn suspended, reauthorized, recognized as a basic human right, curtailed, and allowed again under certain conditions. On September 27, 1977, for instance, Lionel Stoléru announced the suspension of family immigration for the following three years. Public outcry was so strong that the state secretary modified the policy to allow family reunification as long as rejoining members agreed not to seek paid employment.[21] The *Conseil d'État*, in 1978, declared the decree illegal and reiterated that the right to live with one's family was one of the core rights of French law.[22] In spite of the decision, and repeated public statements that support it, successive administrations have tried to curtail this fundamental principle in France.

Legal barriers to immigrant women's access to paid employment, in particular, have emerged as a key element within the history of family reunification legislation in France. Indeed, by letting women in but denying them the right to be gainfully employed, French immigration laws have reinforced immigrant women's lack of autonomy. Short-term measures restricting the employment of foreign workers' wives and children, which had cropped up in the mid-1970s, continued until the election of socialist François Mitterrand in 1981. About this process, Catherine Wihtol de Wenden and Margo Corona DeLey write: "Access to the labor market was permitted for women during most of the period up to May 1981. But it was linked to their spouses' legal and socio-economic status and women were allowed to enter the employment market only in those occupations and localities where it would not be regarded as displacing native workers."[23]

These restrictions allowed French authorities to select preferred national groups and allow them into particular sectors of the labor force. Andrea Caspari and Winona Giles clearly document, for instance, that members of the Portuguese community—and Portuguese women in particular—were allowed entry, given permission to work, and regularized at a time when this was much more restricted for non-European nationals.[24] Wihtol de Wenden and Corona DeLey further argue that these measures, in the context of a global economic recession, worked to increase certain immigrant women's dependence on men, further weaken their already precarious economic position, and boost illegal work for immigrant women.[25] Historically, then, legal texts on family reunification and the ways in which they were applied have created a framework in which immigrant women lack legal autonomy. This problem lingers today in spite of fundamental changes to the law of 1984.

Before 1984, spouses and children introduced through the procedure of family reunification were granted a residency card that mentioned their status as "family members" and did not include the right to seek employment. Residency and work permits were separate documents. Those family members who wished to work for a wage needed to request a work permit once they could document that they had secured a job. The law of July 17, 1984, established two types of sojourn or work cards: a temporary sojourn card (for varied amounts of time that cannot exceed one year) and the residency card, which is valid for ten years. Both cards entitle the recipient to legal work. Since 1984, family members who enter the country through the procedure of family reunification obtain the same card as the resident member; renewal is automatic for those who obtain a ten-year residency card. For those who receive a temporary card, renewal is tied to their ability to provide for themselves should the familial link be severed. This particular change in the law of 1984 marks the end of strict "derivative" rights for immigrant women in French immigration law.

However, women are still rendered legally vulnerable by the common administrative practice of the nonimmediate issuance of residency and temporary cards and the handing out of application receipts (*récipicés*), which are valid for only three months and must be renewed repeatedly to ensure the person legal protection.[26] Moreover, the decree of December 4, 1984, abolished the regularization procedure, which allowed an *a posteriori* change of status (*régularisation sur place*) for individuals who had joined a family member outside the legal boundaries of family reunification. Until then, families could choose the type of procedure applicable to their situation: family reunification through either *introduction* or *régularisation*.[27] Since January 1985, family reunification can be initiated only by the immigrant already legally residing in France and while family members are still in the home country. The conditions to initiate the procedure include the following:

1. The person requesting family reunification must have resided legally in France for one year.
2. The person requesting family reunification must demonstrate a stable income (equivalent to minimum wage) and a full-time job (a departure from the 1976 legislation that did not exclude scholarship recipients, interns, and workers with part-time employment).
3. The person requesting family reunification must demonstrate adequate housing arrangements for the size of the rejoining family.
4. Rejoining family members cannot have a medical condition that would prevent them from entering the country.
5. Rejoining family members must obtain (when necessary) a visa.[28]

In March 1993, a conservative government, with Charles Pasqua as prime minister, developed and implemented a stringent politics of immigration control. It introduced three legal reforms that amended the nationality code, modified the conditions of entry and sojourn of immigrants, and transformed the practice of identity controls.[29] These laws are not one and the same, but they are often linked and associated with the name of Charles Pasqua, who orchestrated these legal transformations and gave the tone to the political campaign surrounding them.

The immigration law of August 24, 1993, restricted the conditions of entry and sojourn for immigrants and further tightened the conditions for family reunification. Since the passage of this law, accessing the right to family reunification has become a long and complex affair and, for many, no longer a possibility. Immigrants who file a family reunification request on behalf of family members now need to document at least two years (instead of one) of legal sojourn in France, and their ability to meet appropriate *personal* housing and resources requirements.[30] The 1993 immigration law demands that family reunification happen in one unique step. No longer can immigrants bring family members incrementally over time as their social standing improves and they are better able to meet the necessary housing and income requirements. The Pasqua laws of 1993 also prohibited the entry of polygamous families into France through the process of family reunification (only one wife and her children can be brought into the country through the procedure). It also prohibited the renewal of residency permits of foreigners in polygamous situations.[31]

There is no doubt that the 1993 law increased the legal vulnerability of immigrant women. As we have seen, it made legal family reunification harder to achieve. It also stipulated that, in the case of divorce or estrangement within a year after the issuance of residency papers, these papers could be taken away from or not renewed for the foreign spouse. When in breach of legal status, women can be deported to their country of origin. Mothers of French children are protected from such deportations under French law, but they find themselves undocumented and therefore unable to work legally or to claim and receive certain social and health benefits.

Overall, the Pasqua laws have been criticized for destabilizing the immigrant community in France by increasing police scrutiny and by symbolically constructing the immigrant as a criminal and a threatening subject. They target non-European immigrants and, most particularly, immigrants from France's former colonies. Finally, the vagueness of some of the provisions and the wide berth created for arbitrary administrative decisions have reduced the overall human rights protection for immigrants and their children. Sami Naïr has described and Danièle Lochack has theorized about the creation of a zone of *infra-droit* (substandard right) for immigrants in which policing and exclusionary practices have replaced the strict application of egalitarian principles and universal human rights.[32] Such restrictive measures created the very conditions that were to produce many undocumented immigrants in France— among them family members who entered the country outside the bounds of legal family reunification—and swell the ranks of the *sans-papiers* movement in the mid-1990s.

In spite of some improvements, the 1998 Chevènnement law did little to diminish the dependence of women on their spouse's legal status. The law did introduce the notion of "familial and private life" as one of the criteria that would be taken into account for legalizing undocumented immigrants. Theo-retically, the law opened up the notion of "family" to include bonds outside those of matrimony, such as common law marriage (*concubinage*) and civil unions of straight and gay couples. However, the notion of "family and private life" is often very narrowly interpreted by the administration.[33] Polygamous family members who entered the country prior to 1993 can have their resi-dency papers renewed as long as they can document that they are no longer bound by a polygamous union and are no longer cohabitating. This specific measure has put some women in extremely vulnerable positions, especially given the limited availability of affordable housing.

A brief analysis of family reunification in France since the mid-1970s underscores that the contradictory circumstances created by French im-migration legislation often put immigrant women and the children who depend on them in vulnerable and precarious situations and work against their long-term integration within French society—a stated goal of French governments for the past twenty years. Along with new restrictions in family reunification came an increase in undocumented immigrant women in the French territory. Catherine Wihtol de Wenden and Margo Corona DeLey describe this process as the "clandestinization" of foreign women in France during that time. According to them, the feminization of the undocumented immigrant population along with the "precarization" of immigrant women is directly connected to the tightening of French immigration laws and poli-cies since the 1970s.[34]

Following their lead, I argue here that legal narratives (as well as popular and scholarly ones, which I analyze in the next chapter) and their attendant administrative practices usher some immigrant women into a dangerous zone of *infra-droit* and precarious living conditions. Located as they are at the bottom of the social ladder, they are rendered even more vulnerable to discrimination, abuse, and exploitation. Migratory profiles changed dra-matically in the 1970s and the 1980s. Indeed, in the second half of the 1970s men began migrating to France after having married a legal immigrant or a young French woman of immigrant descent. Although these changes might be read as interesting reversals of existing gender patterns, it has been noted that these new migratory profiles might anchor (and strengthen) otherwise on-the-wane matrimonial practices. Young women, as a result, find them-selves in difficult situations that sometimes result in profound unhappiness and domestic violence.[35]

FAMILY TIES: THE *SANS-PAPIÈRES* PERSPECTIVES

The interviews I collected in 2002 illustrate three simple facts. First, they show a great variety of personal profiles and life experiences among the *sans-papières*. They also confirm the fact that, for most postcolonial subjects, immigrating legally to France has become quasi-impossible. Finally, they highlight how legal changes have affected the ways in which candidates for immigration understand and negotiate increasingly complex regulations and controls. In addition, they do help us understand some of the gendered effects of these changes and their human impact. The women I interviewed had a variety of reasons for wanting to leave their countries. Some wanted to study abroad, others wanted to live full and independent lives, still others wanted to be closer to family or access better health care, and many wanted to escape increasingly difficult living conditions. Most of these interviews shed light on the near impossibility of obtaining long-term visas and entering France through family reunification procedures. As a whole, they confirm the thesis that there has been a process of "clandestinization" and "precarization" of certain immigrant women due to the restrictive turn in immigration policies in France.

Lisa's story illustrates quite well how the effects of past immigration policies and practices in France affect the present. In her case, the 1960s strategy of placing African male workers in special housing projects (*foyers de célibataires*) to contain family immigration came to haunt her and her husband in the 1990s when they tried to reunite.[36] Indeed when Lisa's husband filed a request to bring his wife under the provision of family reunification, it was rejected because his housing arrangement was not adequate under the law: "Before I came to France I was married already, since 1996. I stayed in Algeria to wait for family reunification but it was not done because my husband was living in a single men housing project, and that's not possible."

Many immigrant men still live in these *foyers*, which offer an alternative to the prohibitive rents in the regular housing market. Lisa's husband would have had to rent a large-enough apartment months ahead of time in order to document adequate housing for his family reunification request. Needless to say, this is not likely to happen for many immigrants, who have a hard time securing low-income housing in large French urban centers. In light of this situation and the difficulty of meeting the requirements for legal reunification, during a family visit Lisa decided to stay: "And in 2000, I got my short-term visa, of course, of thirty days. I came. I told myself: I am going to stay here until I get papers. I will not go. Like that, and I stayed here."

One can say that Lisa, like the other women I interviewed, became un-documented by default when other solutions failed her. Most women talk about the impossibility of securing anything but short-term visas. Lamria, for instance, a natural science teacher in her forties, described how she tried a va-riety of ways of obtaining a long-term visa, to no avail. She decided to move to France when, after a difficult divorce, the stress of living in a civil war began to take its toll: "Then there were the years of terror, there were teachers found with their throat cut in the schools. . . . There was the commute. I had to travel ten miles to go teach. You've got to save yourself!"

Lamria's mother and her two sisters were living in France. Now that she was divorced, she wanted to join them. After several unsuccessful tries, Lamria—like most of the women I interviewed—decided to enter the country with a short-term (tourist) visa. Like most of them, she became undocumented after she overstayed her visa.

> In fact I arrived [in France] at the end of 1998 with a one-month tourist visa. I had tried to obtain a family reunification from there [Algeria], but I could not. I could not obtain the visa. In 1993 I came and stayed three months in France (I had taken a leave of absence back home) and since I saw how dif-ficult it was . . . I wanted to register with the university. . . . I went back with an acceptance letter.
>
> I filed my request with the French consulate in Algeria. But I gave up—in respect to studying and starting something here. In 1993 I filed a request and I did not get an answer. In 1998 I filed again for a long-term visa and the consul-ate sent me a one-month tourist visa. I told myself, I will take this opportunity to stay. . . . My sister put me up. (My sisters are married, have children, and have the French nationality). In 1999 I married a Franco-Algerian with the French nationality, but with Algerian roots like me.

In spite of the fact that her family does reside legally in France and that some of her siblings are French nationals, Lamria clearly falls outside the limits of family reunification policy.[37] She is too old to have her mother file for a reunification procedure, and although she was able to get accepted into a French university, she could not secure the long-term visa that would have enabled her to enter the country as a student. So, in 1998, when the French consulate ignored her request for a long-term visa and sent her papers for a one-month stay, she told herself, "I will take this opportunity to stay." Dis-couraged by her many rejections, Lamria entered the country legally but with the intention to overstay. This step-by-step movement away from legal sojourn (and more rarely, entry) was common among the women I interviewed. Before accepting a future of living without papers, most tried as hard as they could to work within the tight limits of French immigration law. It was only when all legal paths are exhausted that these women embraced more risky strategies. Lamria's testimony is an example of the women's determination and their resourcefulness in the face of the multiple barriers that stood ahead of them.

Louisa, a young activist in the Marseilles collective, recounted her failure also, as a child, to avail herself of the process of family reunification. While waiting to have her sister, who lives in France, become her legal guardian, Louisa entered the country on a tourist visa. Her brother, who is younger, stayed behind but intended to follow when the paperwork was done. In her interview, Louisa recalled the various mechanisms that, in the end, failed both of them in different ways.

> My parents are old, so we filed a request to have my sister become my and my little brother's guardian. At that time my little brother was fifteen and I was seventeen. So I came with a tourist [short-term] visa, because it's impossible to obtain a long-term visa there.
>
> We started the paperwork in 1994. Then we received a notice to come to court. But later, in 1995, we were told that my sister could not become my legal guardian because [by then] I had turned eighteen. The request was granted for my little brother, who had stayed in the Comoros, but we were not able to have him come because he was not granted a visa. So for me, who was here, the request was denied. For my brother, who was there, the request was granted, but he could not come!

The slowness of the review process worked against Louisa. She turned eighteen before the French administration finished reviewing the application; by then she was too old to have her sister become her legal guardian. In her brother's case, although the legal guardianship was granted, he was unable to secure a visa for himself and could not enter the country legally. In any case, for both of them, a family reunification procedure would have to have been initiated by their sister and approved before they could come to France. The level of planning, the technical difficulties in obtaining the required documentation, the slowness of administrative decisions, as well as the arbitrariness of the decision-making process all worked toward the clandestinization of the women I interviewed. Indeed, the combination of more restrictive immigration policies (family reunification included), the generalization of visa requirements, as well as the quasi-impossibility of obtaining long-term ones, have left many of them with the sole options of overstaying a tourist visa or entering the country illegally. Malika's experience illustrates the latter:

> That's right, she [my sister] sent me the papers I needed to show that she would put me up. She sent me everything, but it's Morocco; they did not grant me a visa because I was without a salary and I did not have a bank account—neither I nor my father. I did not have anyone [there]; my whole family is here[. . . .]
>
> What I wanted was a visa, even for two weeks only. But they did not grant me one and then I decided to come in anyway; then I came in like that, without a visa, illegally.

In Malika's case it was the very structure of living and working in the global South that made it impossible for her to make a strong case for her visa request. Indeed, neither she nor her father could demonstrate steady employment (with payment stubs) and sufficient income (with a bank account), which the administration in charge of delivering visas was requesting. Not being able to come through legal means, even for a short time, made Malika consider crossing the borders with someone else's papers. Of all the women I interviewed, however, she was the only one who had entered the country without a visa: "I came through with the papers of someone who looked like me."

Being undocumented, however, creates a layer of vulnerability for women within their own families and in particular within their marital (and domestic) relationships. Aïcha, who was successfully leading a *sans-papiers* collective in Paris when I interviewed her, talked at great length about this aspect of the impact of current immigration laws on women. According to her, women who find themselves undocumented are more vulnerable and experience specific forms of exploitation and precarization due to the fact that they are women— especially women with children: "Undocumented women are more fragile. They sometimes find themselves in dramatic situations; sometimes someone proposes to marry them and later they find themselves on the street. There is also [the problem] of sexual exploitation."

Aïcha gave me two examples of these forms of the gendered effects of French immigration law. In the first case, a young undocumented woman

THE LEGAL CONSTRUCTION OF IMMIGRANT WOMEN IN FRANCE   69

from Madagascar had married a compatriot with the French nationality. They had a child together. However, after her husband abandoned them, she found herself without papers. In addition, her husband's brother had tried to take advantage of the situation and was "protecting" her. "Without papers, she was especially vulnerable," recounts Aïcha. "She was afraid that Children's Protective Services would take her child away from her." Aïcha also recalled the situation of a woman who had three children and was also abandoned by her husband. Her husband had simply left her in France and moved to Austria. No longer attached to her husband's legal status, she became undocumented. Protective Services took her children away but she was able get them back after her regularization.

CONCLUSION

Requests for legal autonomy have been at the center of immigrant women's organizing efforts in France. In a 1984 article in *Hommes et Libertés*—the publication of the leading French human rights organization (*Ligue des droits de l'homme*)—the authors clearly indicate that legal autonomy was at the forefront of immigrant women's organizing in the early 1980s:

> A dossier constituted by the Collective of Immigrant Women [*Collectif des femmes immigrées*] analyzes—and denounces—the politics of family reunification. Composed of twenty-five organizations and various individuals, the Collective, created in 1982, has given itself the goal of defending "the right of immigrant women to exist as persons with the same rights as French women," and of "denouncing any legal or judiciary practices that maintain de facto immigrant women in dependency."[38]

Other immigrant women's groups pointed out the dangers of derivative rights for women and the increased dependency and vulnerability connected to lack of legal autonomy. In 1985 the organizers of *Permanence femmes immigrées femmes sans papiers* (an immigrant and undocumented women's advocacy group), with foresight, alerted the French community to the fact that restrictions in family reunification were bound to create "new categories of undocumented immigrants," especially among women and children.[39]

At the European level, nongovernmental organizations have lobbied to put this issue on the agenda. They have asked the European Community "to ensure migrant women an independent legal status and to recognize, on personal grounds, their right to obtain a work and residency permit, which should reduce their vulnerability in case of divorce, domestic violence, sexual abuse, and rape."[40] As a result of these pressures, the European parliament has begun to turn its attention to the particular situation of immigrant women.

Interestingly, and in spite of what many *sans-papières* think and advocate, the need for women's legal autonomy and the individuation of immigration rights are claims that never became central within the *sans-papiers* movement at large. It is not enough to accept the obvious feminist reading of this situation that it is men and male leaders who determine the common agenda. In addition, it is important to suggest other reasons for the continued nonprioritization of such claims. Undocumented women themselves have often used their status as mothers to seek a change of status. This focus on the family within the movement is complicated and worth examining in terms of some of its unexpected and complicated effects.

Twelve years after the genesis of the movement, many undocumented women have been legalized as members of families (as spouses and mothers). Most of the individuals commonly left out of the process of regularization are single men not likely to obtain a change of status in the near future. The early focus on the humanitarian need to keep families together is now used by the state to deny legalization to many individuals who cannot claim familial linkages in France, including undocumented gays and lesbians.

Nongovernmental organizations and *sans-papiers* allies have also been quite successful at presenting immigrant and undocumented women as victims in need of protection (from sex traffickers, abusive husbands, exploitative bosses, and so on).[41] One of the pernicious, and often unintended, effects of this strategy is to reinscribe problematic notions about women and the Third World.[42] However, immigrant women are hardly simply victims, and their active participation in struggles such as that of the *sans-papiers*, even when orchestrated around family (mother-wife) issues, can inflect their strategies and transform their agendas.[43]

As immigrant organizations and the *sans-papiers* movement continue to challenge French immigration laws and create breaches for autonomous actions and development for immigrant women, French legislation still pronounces (and French popular and scholarly discourses still construct) these women as dependent on their husbands. This chapter has begun to address the problems generated by such legal and discursive contradictions and to invite feminist scholars and activists to understand the limits and the dangers (for all women) of representational practices that uncritically rely on tropes of women as dependants and victims.[44] As long as some immigrant women are imagined and constructed as wives and mothers in a meaning system that continues to ignore that wives and mothers are engaged in all kinds of productive and resistive activities in and outside of the wage-labor force and in and outside of the polity, we will fail to see them and engage them as the complex social actors they truly are.

4 FAMILY MATTERS: IMMIGRATION, DEMOGRAPHY, AND NATIONAL POLITICS

> *A piled-up family, with a father, with three or four wives and some*
> *twenty kids. He gets $8,000 from entitlements without, it goes*
> *without saying, working. If on top of that you add the smell and the*
> *noise, the French worker next door loses his mind.*
>
> **Jacques Chirac, Orleans, June 19, 1991**

IN THIS CHAPTER I look at the discursive framing of immigrant women from Africa in contemporary France. I begin with a rhetorical analysis of the quote that opens the chapter. I then move on to show how some immigrant women—especially from Africa—are constructed as mothers and wives and locked into "domestic" and "traditional" roles within French society. By analyzing French scholarly production, media constructions, legal texts, and social service practices, my aim is to shed light on the layered ways in which discourses on African motherhood constitute, in part, the material realities of African mothers in France. I close the chapter with the perspective of two undocumented African women who provide related but very different analyses of the impacts that hegemonic discourses and their attendant administrative practices have on the lives of immigrant women like them. By ending with these narratives, I want to underscore how African women themselves, especially in the *sans-papiers* movement, critique, resist, and transform the discursive and material processes analyzed in this chapter and in the previous one. Throughout I suggest the various ways in which the image of the "African mother" rearticulates old colonial understandings of African people and of Africa to racialize certain immigrant communities and the question of immigration in France.

Although this chapter focuses in some detail on the complex construction of the immigrant "mother," it also explores the broad processes that hail and lock immigrant women and their daughters into a narrow range of "tradi-

tional" and "domestic" roles.[1] Once firmly located in the realm of domesticity and tradition, immigrant women become the blatant sign and constant
reminder of certain immigrant communities' failure to integrate into French
society. Here I suggest that these roles are neither natural nor freely chosen
and yet provide normative and socially approved scripts for immigrant women
trying to carve out new spaces and new lives for themselves in the locales they
now inhabit.[2] I further argue that old notions of African women drawn from
France's colonial imaginary are rearticulated into the current context of postcolonial population movements. In particular, I contend that the image of an
overly fecund African mother haunts current discussions of the French "immigration problem."[3]

The discursive and material effects of such reformulations are many. First
and foremost, they conjure up and place the very concepts of the "domestic"
and the "traditional" (the discursive space occupied by the immigrant woman)
in contrast with the "public" and the "modern" (the space occupied by the
French woman). In the process, each term in these binary pairs (domestic/
public, tradition/modern, immigrant/French) is anchored as a commonsense
notion and naturalized in everyday parlance. Once these binary structures are
in place, it becomes almost impossible to think about social actors outside the
dichotomous understandings and frameworks they establish.

These rearticulations place immigrant women at the center of anti-
immigrant and racist developments in contemporary France and render them
particularly vulnerable to those developments. It is only through a gendered
analysis of the processes of racialization of certain immigrant communities
that we can begin to understand and unravel the complex gender and racial
technologies of power that inform current French politics of immigration
and in turn shape the lived realities of immigrant women.[4] I further argue
here that, where women are concerned, the recurring invitation to take up
domestic and familial roles is central to the mechanisms that turn them into
impossible subjects.

The presence of the woman (mother/wife/daughter) figure within popular discussions of immigration in France is of crucial importance. Indeed,
whether constructed as agent or as victim, whether understood as promoting or as resisting "integration," the immigrant woman emerges as a key element in the racialization of immigration and citizenship in France. In *Le sol
et le sang: Théories de l'invasion au XXe siècle* (Blood and soil: Theories of
invasion in the twentieth century), French demographer Hervé Le Bras ana-

lyzes the emergence of an ideology of (immigrant) invasion in France in the twentieth century. Le Bras points out that the immigrant in France presents a Janus face, "that of the worker and that of the dweller. One hides the other: we only see the worker during periods of economic growth and only see the dweller during economic crises."[5] However, Le Bras fails to notice that the face of the immigrant-dweller is more often than not the face of a woman. As already noted in Chapter 2, the wearing of Islamic scarves in French schools, polygamy, forced marriages, and female genital cutting are recurring themes within anti-immigrant discourses that present Africans as undesirable immigrants. Within each of these themes it is women who, though often robbed of any real agency, are conjured up to capture the cultural distance between the French and their postcolonial others.

Against the backdrop of international economic transformations, the construction of Europe, and increased national anxieties, "the immigrant mother" (imagined as poor and illiterate but skilled at draining the resources of the state) and her children have indeed emerged as threats to the nation. It is against this imaginary backdrop that French understandings of national inclusion and belonging as political and cultural become less central and make room for the reiteration of racist distinctions between "blood" French citizens (*Français de souche*) and "paper" French citizens. In this chapter, I contend that the recycling of existing forms of racism, xenophobia, and nationalism in France with deeply rooted patriarchal understandings of citizenship has created a context in which some immigrant women and their daughters find themselves particularly vulnerable to processes of exclusion.

"LE BRUIT ET L'ODEUR," OR CHERCHEZ LA MÈRE. . . .

The statement that opens this chapter, uttered by an elected official, did not lead to his resignation from public office.[6] Quite the contrary: in spite of the polemic the statement generated, Jacques Chirac not only retained his position but went on to pursue his political career and to become the president of the French Republic in 1995. Chirac's successful political fate in the aftermath of his infamous "noise and smell" comment is telling in itself and warrants further analysis.[7] It highlights the deep contradictions (and hypocrisy) embedded within French politics and evokes what some commentators describe as the lingering blemish of French republican racism.[8] In this chapter, however, I want to focus on something else. Rather than analyzing Chirac's fate in French politics, I want to focus on a key, if evanescent, character in the "noise and smell" story. Indeed, I want to bring to the fore a background but extremely potent figure—namely the African mother in the French-immigration-problem narrative evoked by Chirac in 1991.

Let me begin by pointing out that, at first sight, Chirac's story opposes two male characters. The African immigrant and the French citizen are locked in a close but conflicted relationship that gradually and dramatically ushers the French guy to the verge of madness. These two male characters, however, are cast in very different lights. The French citizen, who appears only at the end of the story, when he "loses his mind," is cast as a French worker (*travailleur Français*). So the French citizen evoked here is clearly established as a French national (he is French, *c'est un français*), but he is also portrayed as a productive member of French society (he is a worker, *c'est un travailleur*). The African immigrant, however, is never clearly named as such but rather evoked through a series of linguistic and imaginary linkages.

The scene opens with "the father" and his family. The kinship categories used to introduce the African immigrant serve at least two purposes. First, they locate him in the realm of family and settlement immigration. In contradistinction to the single male migrant worker who is emblematic of the 1960s and 1970s, the immigrant presented in the "noise and smell" story is someone who is not in France alone but has brought wife and children along.[9] No longer a temporary "guest," he is here to stay. Second, the "father" who opens the story is opposed to the "worker" who closes it. By contrasting a kinship category to an economic one, Chirac's scenario introduces a variation on the theme of immigration as economic threat.

The economic threat invoked here is not so much that the African immigrant will compete with the French worker in the labor market, even though that threat has not fully disappeared in the French imaginary. Far-right political parties and their leaders still bank, and score political points, on the spurious connections they make between rising French unemployment figures and unbridled immigration. Rather, it is the fact that the immigrant father is collecting welfare benefits "without working." So, Chirac's script in fact opposes the French worker to the non-French immigrant welfare recipient who drains the resources of the French state without contributing anything: "it goes without saying!"

Moreover, the unproductive welfare-recipient father lives in cramped quarters "with three or four wives and some twenty kids." The binary pair set up here is that of the "traditional" large unproductive African polygamous

family versus the "modern" productive French monogamous nuclear family. So, although the African wife and mother makes only a brief apparition
in the "noise and smell" script, she is of course fundamental to the logic of
the narrative. It is because she (and other African wives and mothers) are in
France that the face of immigration has fundamentally changed and become
so problematic! It is indeed these African mothers who give birth to five or
more children (compared to the 1.8 figure for French women) who enable
the immigrant father to collect so much in "family allowances" (*allocations
familliales*) and other welfare benefits.[10] It is because she does not come alone
but in duos and trios that France now has a "polygamy problem" on its hands.
It is also because she is not acquainted with the refinements of French culture
and cooking that unsavory "smells" emerge from her kitchen. Finally, it is
because she cannot control her children that raucous sounds disturb French
peace and public order.[11] Would it be too far-fetched here to suggest that on a
symbolic level it is precisely because she is here that the French social order is
perceived to be under threat and that madness emerges as the grim but ines-
capable denouement of Chirac's narrative?

LOCKING IMMIGRANT WOMEN INTO FAMILIAL ROLES

The "smell and odor" story is one among many that insidiously uses the figure of the African mother to ultimately present certain immigrants and their
families as unable or unwilling to embrace French culture. It must be noted,
however, that this notion is counterbalanced by a parallel focus on immigrant
women and daughters of immigrants as privileged agents of integration.[12]
This has been the case, as we saw in Chapter 2, of the media coverage of the
Beurettes. The idea that immigrant women are vectors of integration (because
of their privileged location within the family as mothers and daughters) cir-
culates widely in France and stands as the flip side of the imagined immigrant
woman evoked by Chirac in his speech. In both cases, women (and gender) are
conjured up to render problematic the presence of certain immigrants within
the French national space. Whether bearers or breakers of tradition, women
are called forth precisely to raise the specter of a "tradition" that stands in
the way of the successful integration of African and Muslim immigrants and
their children.

The French imaginary construction of immigrants and immigrant communities is replete with contradictory images of women, especially as mothers
and family members. This hypervisibility of immigrant women, especially

those from the African continent, in political discourse and media representations is interestingly accompanied by a real paucity of (scholarly) knowledge
about them. Indeed, in spite of such symbolic and media foregrounding, studies of immigration have only begun to pay serious attention to the presence
of women within a variety of immigrant communities and to the political
reactions such a presence has generated.

Sabah Chaïb, in a report commissioned by a French labor union, provides an
excellent review of the French scholarship on gender and immigration.[13] Among
other things, Chaïb highlights the many ways in which immigrant women are
discursively locked into the private sphere, occupying, by and large, domestic
and familial roles. Nouria Ouali, author of one of the studies reviewed by Chaïb
on the representation of immigrant women on francophone TV channels, notes
that subjects treating immigrant women directly figure in only a minority of
the programs. Images of women are omnipresent in the background, however.
Indeed, veiled women, wives, mothers, and daughters abound in these programs. Ouali's study also highlights that these women are rarely given a voice
and are almost never portrayed as active members of the labor force. Moreover, both documentaries and fictional accounts seem to privilege stories about
young women being victims of or revolting against their families.[14]

Figure 4.1 *Sans-papière* and son at demonstration. Photo by C. Raissiguier.

Daughters of immigrants made their entry onto the French political and media scenes in 1989 during an incident that created a national polemic and that has been widely referred to as the "headscarf case" (*l'affaire du foulard*). The case involved three young women of North African descent who were expelled from a public school because they refused to remove their headscarves on school grounds. The headscarf incident and the controversy surrounding it focused mainly on the inability of certain immigrants to "melt" into French society and on the waning integrative power of French republican institutions. These young women and others like them (constructed as either willing or manipulated agents) came to symbolize the notion that some immigrants were unable or unwilling to embrace French republican and secular principles. It also established Islam as one of the main roadblocks to the successful integration of postcolonial immigrants in France.[15]

The hypermediatization of issues such as the *hijab* (Islamic scarf), forced marriages, female genital cutting, and honor killings tend to construct these young women as prisoners of religion and the private-familial sphere. Through these representations, they emerge as supervictims of "tradition" or as rebels in rupture from their families and that tradition. In the process, I argue, the women not only come to symbolize the radical difference of certain immigrant communities but also are blamed (and therefore can be punished) for it.[16] I am not suggesting here that these painful realities are not present in the lives of immigrant women and should not alarm us. What I am pointing out, along with Ouali and Chaïb, is that the French media tend to focus on certain women and certain realities and not others and therefore offer dangerous and reductive constructions of immigrant women. First and foremost, they conflate immigrant women and African women and therefore fail to convey the incredible heterogeneity of backgrounds and lived experiences of immigrant women in France. They also frame certain immigrant women within narratives of victimhood and personal suffering.

Reductive constructions of immigrant women are also present in scholarly articles. This is particularly problematic because such articles ultimately inform media and popular understandings of the women under scrutiny. For instance, Chaïb notes that the crucial question of immigrant women's participation in the labor force has been underanalyzed in the vast majority of the studies she reviewed. "What are the reasons why the professional activity of immigrant women has not emerged as a 'phenomenological reality'?" Chaïb ponders at the beginning of her report.[17] She attributes this particular blind spot to the fact that many of these studies cast their analysis within a familial (women as family members) or cultural (women as agents of cultural reproduction or transformation) approach. Chaïb also points out that the overrepresentation of women from the Maghreb in these studies contributes to the general lack of attention to work-related issues. Maghrebian women tend to have one of the lowest rates of labor-force participation among immigrant women in France.

These patterns of knowledge production contribute to the formation and circulation of highly problematic "commonsense ideas" about immigrant women (which has almost become a code word for African women in France) and certain immigrant communities. One of the most pernicious ideas is that these women are only marginally involved in the work force. Although this might be true for some immigrant women, the fact of the matter is that immigrant women, regardless of their country of origin and regardless of their familial status, are entering the French labor force in greater and greater numbers.

Scholarly and media constructions cannot but help to shape the kinds of social services and programs that are delivered to immigrant women. Another study reviewed by Chaïb, for instance, describes how in the PACA (Provence-Alpes-Côte d'Azur) region, social programs focusing on economic insertion are few in number (20 out of the 186 programs listed); the majority of programs instead target immigrant women as immigrants in need of social integration and as mothers. The study's author ironically points out the sexist move that reduces women to their role as mothers: "[We] can hardly imagine associations offering [immigrant] men activities centered on their role as fathers."[18]

What I am arguing here is that (African) immigrant women are being constructed in ways that emphasize their domestic roles in the family and locate them primarily in the sphere of the private and the "traditional." In a complex and contradictory logic, immigrant women emerge as symbols of "tradition" and backwardness, and at the same time are locked into material realities that reinforce dominant perceptions of immigration in France. Old colonial and patriarchal beliefs about African women are rearticulated here to racialize certain immigrant communities and to politicize the very question of immigration. This pattern is particularly visible in the unique treatment of polygamy and polygamous families within the Republic.

THE PARTICULAR CASE OF POLYGAMOUS FAMILIES

In France, polygamy is a marginal phenomenon, yet it has received dispropor-
tionate media attention because it presents specific challenges to French law,
intensifies gender inequalities within the family, and has been exploited for
political reasons by anti-immigrant campaigns and their leaders. It is difficult
to quantify with accuracy the extent of polygamy in France. This is due in
part to the tightening of immigration policies since the mid-1970s, which has
led to the clandestinization of immigrant women in general and of women
within polygamous families more specifically. Various estimates suggest that
there are only a few thousand polygamous families in the French territory.
However, precisely because they can never be fully established, these numbers
are often inflated.[19] The trope of polygamy, then, has been shamelessly used to
politicize and racialize the question of immigration in France.

The polygamous family evoked by Jacques Chirac at the beginning of this
chapter, for instance, is a stock image in Jean-Marie Le Pen's discursive rep-
ertoire.[20] It is conjured up to symbolize the radical difference of postcolonial immigrants and to promote fear among French working-class families,
in particular blue-collar ones, who were especially hard hit by the economic
downturn of the 1970s and its accompanying waves of deindustrialization. It
is precisely "among blue collars that both the decline of The Left and the rise
of the extreme right, between 1978 and 2002, were the strongest."[21] Under late
capitalism, these families experience high levels of *précarité* and often have a
hard time securing decent and affordable housing.[22]

The increasing popularity and common usage of concepts and images once
found only in radical right political parlance does attest to the success of Le Pen
in defining the terms of the immigration debate in France. This movement from
the far right to the center of taboo topics and terminology has been described
as the *lepénisation des esprits*. The phrase evokes a process of normalization of
the themes and ideas that were once the province of Le Pen and his followers.
It also suggests that the French people, who used to know better, have progres-
sively been colonized (*lepénisation* linguistically and ironically echoes the term
colonization) and corrupted by extremists such as Le Pen and their ideas. So,
although the phrase does capture the normalization of extreme forms of racist
speech and acts in France, I would like to suggest that it might serve inadver-
tently also to obfuscate what it aims to uncover: French republican racism.[23]

Pierre Tevanian and Sophie Tissot, who offer useful analyses of this phenomenon, remind us that this discursive movement from right to center is

far from a linear one. They highlight two key moments in the progression of racialist thinking and language around the topic of immigration. They point to the politicization of the issue of immigration, which in the 1980s became a hot button for various regional and national elections in France. They also underscore the increased framing, in the mid-1990s, of immigration as a security issue.[24]

In the face of hegemonic discourses on polygamy in France, a few scholarly studies help us to dispel the myths surrounding this issue. Legal scholar Edwige Rude-Antoine, for instance, documents the marginal reality of polygamy in France and points out the pernicious effects of the media and political exploitation of the topic: "These polygamous situations, which in France principally affect families from West Africa (two ethnic groups, Soninké and Al pular [Peul], and three countries: Mali, Senegal, and Mauritania), Turkish families, and in a marginal way, Algerian and Moroccan families, are additional stones thrown on the terrain of immigration and symbols of the incompatibility of cultures."[25]

Foreigners who reside in France are allowed to follow, as far as their personal status is concerned, the legislation of their home country so long as it does not interfere with "public order." This legal compromise sometimes creates legal conflicts and oppressive situations that affect women in particular. This has certainly been the case for women who are part of polygamous families and reside in France. Polygamous marriages are *de jure* legal in France so long as they are contracted in the home country. The Pasqua law of August 24, 1993, however, prohibited the entry of polygamous families through the process of family reunification. It also forbade the renewal of residency permits for foreigners in polygamous situations, rendering polygamy de facto illegal in France. *Préfectures*, for instance, were asked not to renew sojourn papers for second or third wives present in the French territory.

At the time, the measure raised great criticism from the left and from pro-immigrant organizations. It was softened through a series of administrative memoranda. The first memorandum (February 8, 1994) stipulated that immigrant women who have French children or who have been living in France for fifteen years could not be deported. Women in polygamous families could then reside "illegally" in France while being protected from deportation.[26] The second (April 25, 2000) and third (June 10, 2001) memoranda allowed polygamous families who had entered the country before 1993 to have their sojourn papers renewed so long as they stopped cohabiting. This, according to the French press, placed many women in extremely precarious social loca-tions and untenable legal situations.

An article published in *Le Monde* in 2002, for instance, exposes the many difficulties (and contradictions) experienced by immigrant women living in France within polygamous families.[27] The article documents how, in the wake of the Pasqua laws, several *préfectures* simply removed residency papers from immigrants who could not be deported because they were parents of French children. Neither deportable nor legal residents, many women entered a zone of social and legal impossibility. In particular, without papers, they were no longer able to find legal work. It is precisely individuals like them who, having been relegated to impossible social locations, swelled the ranks of the *sans-papiers* in the early years of the movement. There is also ample evidence that when women become undocumented they become much more dependent on their husbands, which increases their vulnerability to abuse and domestic violence. In other cases, the French administration demanded that co-wives move out of the conjugal home and settle in their own apartment in order to maintain their legal status in France. Although this might have met the needs of some immigrant women caught in oppressive polygamous situations, many have been unable, because of the scarcity of affordable housing in the Paris region, to find decent housing. In fact, the *Le Monde* article documents the many women who opt to leave their husband and become homeless and squat in unoccupied buildings in Paris and its suburbs.[28]

Regardless of one's position on the gender dynamics involved in the prac-tice of polygamy, one can see that polygamous situations are extremely hard on the women and children concerned. Inadequate housing, the absence of women's solidarity networks, and the particular demands of French society make polygamous arrangements problematic and extremely volatile. In addi-tion, when women leave such situations, they encounter the inadequacy and limits of social services that are ill-equipped to deal with the impossible pres-ence of these women in France. As a result, these women are likely to find themselves with no resources and in total isolation. Indeed, many argue that immigrant women (and men) from Africa who oppose the practice in France are numerous.[29] When practiced "out of context," polygamy creates new, com-plex, and painful situations for the women concerned. These situations are partly shaped by the legal contexts out of which they arise.

Although immigrant women from Africa are still imagined and constructed primarily as mothers and wives, their actual lived realities in contemporary

France are far more complex and multifaceted. By focusing here on one *sans-papière*, I end this chapter by acknowledging the resistive consciousness that the women themselves develop in and through their involvement in a struggle for social change.

LOUISA

I met Louisa in Marseilles in the spring of 2002. She was twenty-five at the time of the interview. Louisa is a young Muslim woman from the Comoro Islands who arrived in 1993, when she was seventeen, to be with her older sister and to study in France. She entered the country with a three-month visa, hoping that she would obtain a change of status by having her sister become her legal guardian. Her applications took over a year to be processed and when she finally obtained an answer it was negative: by then she was too old, at eighteen, to be under the guardianship of her sister. Rather than going back to aging parents, a dislocated economy, and a bankrupt educational system, Louisa decided to stay and join the ranks of the thousands of undocumented immigrants who now live in France in the most precarious of conditions.

In 1995, Louisa enrolled in a French private school, learned French, and excelled in her studies. However, she was unable to take the national end-of-high-school exam (*baccalauréat*) because she did not have appropriate short-stay residency papers. In 1997 she applied for a change of status but her application was rejected. She became involved in the *sans-papiers* movement in 1998. Between her first application and the time she actually obtained a change of status in 2001, she appealed four times and was rejected four times.

In the interview, Louisa talked eloquently of the fact that her mother had insisted on her daughter's independence. Denied of real opportunities, the older woman wanted another set of life experiences for her young daughter:

> My mother was aware [of my activism in the *sans-papiers* movement]. She did not say anything. She used to say, "You can always protect your child but your child needs to learn how to protect himself because you cannot follow him wherever he goes."
>
> My mom always wanted us to be able to totally take care of ourselves because she was an orphan and got married at fifteen and started to have children immediately and so it has been hard for her to know the world around her so . . . she used to say that her children should not get married without understanding what marriage was about. . . .

Louisa thought that she had learned a lot from her mother and wanted to fight for both of them. Women, she thought, should stand on their own and fight to show their full worth to the world. Louisa's critique of the French authorities and how they handle undocumented immigrant women's applications for changes of status was quite telling. She recounted that Marseilles immigration officials recommended that she get married in order to obtain a change of status:

Literally, at the *préfecture*, they would say if you want . . . well you cannot obtain a change of status, but if you get married, then you will be able to—that's it and there won't be any problem . . . with a French national of course [laughter], but I did not want this situation! If you want papers you must have kids. . . . This is not a written policy but that is literally what the civil servants working the counter would tell us. Yes [they say that] to help us, perhaps they think they are helping us that way . . . but it is not my choice, it is not my choice! I wanted to build my life before . . . but that was the battle to win.

Louisa went on to discuss the dire effects of these administrative practices on women who follow the advice of various administrative agents. She referred in part to the perverse effects of the issuance of *récipicés* to women who are actually entitled to residency papers, and to the fact that women have to stay married for a minimum of two years before they can keep their papers:

I have seen women who listened to that, got married with guys they did not love, and then found themselves under their threat because even if you are married and you have your residency papers, you have to wait three years to be fully autonomous . . . you cannot divorce, you cannot argue with your husband because you are afraid that he will ask for a divorce. So these women found themselves in worse situations than mine—without papers. Some had kids with men who did not declare the children and therefore they were not able to get their papers in the end. . . . That's why [I am organizing,] to show to all these women that you can obtain what you want through struggle!

Louisa's testimony underscores the fact that immigrant women in France are literally being tied to the family through a variety of quasi-legal, political, and social practices. Later on in the interview she explained that single women are always suspect characters in the eyes of the French administration: "How can a single woman live in France for ten years without papers?" Because women are always thought of as depending on a man, it becomes impossible to imagine them independently migrating, getting an education, obtaining paid work, and supporting themselves, in spite of the fact that hundreds of them do just that. Louisa's testimony finally illustrates the arbitrary conditions of the review process and the importance of organized struggle for women like her:

> Today I obtained a change of status with the same case file I had in 1996. I was told you are not married, but I was not married when I obtained a change of status[. . . .] I was told that I did not have my family [in France]; now that's the same thing. So, I say that I obtained my change of status not by law, I say that I obtained my change of status through struggle, through the pressure put on by many activists!

CLAIRETTE

Here I contrast Louisa's interview with that of a much older woman whose middle-class background, religious beliefs, and educational attainment all contributed to making her a more reluctant participant in the *sans-papiers* struggle than Louisa and some of the other women I interviewed. Despite her lack of enthusiasm for organized struggle, Clairette was a member of a *sans-papiers* collective in one of the Paris *banlieues* (working-class outskirts of the city) when I met her. She attended most meetings and participated in demonstrations on a semi-regular basis. Although Clairette understood that her participation in the collective would probably help her situation, she felt strongly that, in part because of her education and her scientific expertise, she did not deserve stigma nor the material difficulties attached to her *sans-papiers* status. Often critical of other *sans-papiers'* uncouthness, Clairette (more than any other woman I met during my fieldwork) experienced her participation in the *sans-papiers* struggle as a form of social downward mobility.[30] Clairette's analysis of women's specific vulnerability, however, does echo that of many other women interviewed for this book, and of Louisa in particular.

A devout Christian and experienced scientist in her early fifties, Clairette is from the Republic of the Congo (RC).[31] Unlike Louisa, Clairette did not flee her homeland because of dire poverty and the destructuring of basic public services in her country. What set her on a trajectory of displacement and immigration were the brutal civil wars that have erupted in the RC since the early 1990s, and recurring health problems connected to the traumas she experienced during those civil wars. "If today I ask to stay in France, it is because I have nothing left. I have nothing left at home! If I retire, I do not have a house any longer. My house has been broken, destroyed. I have nothing left. . . . I know I can have a position there, but I would have to start again as if I were at the beginning of my career."

As for most of the other *sans-papiers*, Clairette's relationship to France preceded the troubles that made her leave the RC.[32] Connected with a Franco-African network of biomedical researchers (especially around the treatment and prevention of HIV/AIDS), she had already traveled to France many times before.[33] Clairette's only daughter and former husband lived in France with regular papers. In fact, Clairette made it quite clear in the interview that she could have invoked "family reunification" in the 1980s and early 1990s (when her daughter was still under eighteen) if her primary interest had been to stay in France for familial or economic reasons. Clairette was also clear about the class dislocation she had experienced as an undocumented immigrant in France. She knows that without papers her seniority as a scientist is meaningless.

Despite her downward mobility, Clairette needed to stay in France, she claimed, to protect her safety, to take care of her health, and to maintain a relationship with her daughter and her grandchildren. In fact, what Clairette saw as the ideal situation for her would be a legal status that would allow her to come and go between the two countries as she pleases:

> Yes, for me the ideal would be to be able to come and go. That would be perfect. That way, I could continue [to live] in my country because I am entitled to my retirement [benefits] back home. But when I need to come and visit my daughter and my grandchildren, to be able to do it without problems so that I can be the grandmother to my French grandchildren. Yes, to be able to come without difficulties so that I can get treatment [when I need it]. So for me the ideal situation is not necessarily to hold a position here—if they [the French authorities] are afraid of that—but to be able to work a little bit here, to draw a salary, to save some money, and then leave for my country.

The tightening of immigration laws throughout Europe in the 1980s and 1990s has made such legal standing and flexible arrangement next to impossible. Once in France, immigrants who have overstayed their legal sojourn (often after one month, or three months with a tourist visa) are likely to stay in the country without documents because they know that if they leave, their chances of coming back are slim to nil.

Clairette resented that she could not leverage her educational and class status to parlay her change of status or at least a job that would enable her to support herself while waiting for a legal decision to be made on her case:

> I personally think that if a person has difficulties getting a change of status, then they [the French authorities] should at least take into account the competency level of the person . . . to let that person support herself while she is waiting for her papers. Yes, at least check the skills of the person as far as work is concerned. It is not that, because you are an immigrant, you have nothing to offer. I personally think that it is the immigrants who build the country, so you should be more considerate [toward them]. Not only you don't give them papers, but you don't want them to work either. And then, later, people are surprised by the fact that [in France] we have an insecurity problem. . . . People become aggressive when they do not have . . . and the woman, if she is not grounded, it can even lead to prostitution! That's it! It pushes [some] women who are alone, who have no help, to turn to prostitution. Then we are surprised that HIV/AIDS rates [of infection] are on the rise . . . and those who have to beg because they are destitute. It is not a good thing for a country to have people begging on the street. Wouldn't it be better to give these people a job instead [of] to have them begging or turning to prostitution?

Clairette made a lot of interesting, and sometimes problematic, points. She was concerned with the fact that the *sans-papiers* have been rendered incapable of supporting themselves legally. This crucial economic point she saw as creating the larger social and epidemiological problems that are plaguing France and fueling the "immigration panic" in the country. She saw women as particularly vulnerable and, like Louisa, was highly critical of the social and political practices that push women to consider motherhood and marriage means to attain a change of status and leave behind their *sans-papiers* status:

> I want territorial asylum . . . because I am not safe [at home]. People are pushed. . . . I have seen other people who are forced to give birth or to marry in order to get their papers; that is something I disagree with. Often folks find themselves with a child that they do not want because that child for sure [was begotten] to have papers. . . . That is a terrible thing . . . or you get married . . . that is not, that is not, I think that it is belittling, I mean degrading, because I have seen some people who were married at home and here they are forced to remarry in order to obtain their papers . . . or to abandon their family back home.[34]

CONCLUSION

As Clairette and Louisa remind us, the French administration continues to treat (and therefore, I would add, participates in the construction of) immigrant women as perpetual minors. By inviting undocumented women to take up marriage or motherhood as a way to obtain a change of status, French immigration policies and their attendant administrative practices weaken women's autonomy and increase their vulnerability. Louisa pointed out the pernicious effects of such hailing. She countered strategies that rely on individual responses and, in turn, anchor women's domesticity by inviting immigrant women to embrace collective tactics such as the ones deployed by the *sans-papiers* since the mid-nineties. Most important, Louisa sees the fight for immigrant women's legal and personal autonomy at the core of the *sans-papiers* movement. I conclude this chapter by underscoring yet another danger for Louisa and other women like her. In particular, I highlight three ways in which the figure of the immigrant woman as "mother" is articulated with recurring themes within an overarching discourse on immigration as threat to the French nation. These three themes are interrelated and reinforce one another.

First, and most crassly, immigrant mothers from Africa are portrayed as prolific "breeders." This is the case in visual representations of African women surrounded by large numbers of children, as seen in the Plantu cartoon discussed in Chapter 2. This theme is also noticeable in the politicization of immigration figures in France. In particular, the number of immigrant children, especially undocumented ones, is constantly overstated. The "mother" and the numerous children who are attached to her emerge here to evoke an immigrant invasion and the failure of the French state to contain it.[35] As we saw in Chapter 3, in the context of postwar depopulation and mass immigration, France forged a policy matrix that favored European immigrants, who were expected to work and eventually populate France without threatening its ethnoracial composition. Against this legal and administrative backdrop, certain mothers, needless to say, have been more welcome than others. However, because this theme is unspeakable within the republican order, it emerges primarily sideways, through the related themes of immigration as economic and security threat to the nation.

I opened this chapter by discussing the economic threat present in the "noise and smell" story. In fact, the numbers of children that allegedly drain the coffers of the Republic are much smaller than what the French radical (and republican) right would have us believe. The case of polygamous families is worth revisiting here. Indeed, the 2006 *Commission nationale consultative des droits de l'homme* study discussed earlier (see note 18) found that only half of the polygamous families residing in France had the proper documentation to access certain social benefits and, more specifically, the *allocations familliales* evoked by Jacques Chirac in his Orleans speech. In other words, only nine thousand to ten thousand of these families have what it takes to access the financial support the French state affords families who are legally residing in its territory. In addition, because familial reunification for polygamous families has been forbidden since 1993, families that reside legally in the territory are aging and the numbers of individuals entitled to *allocations familiales* are in fact dwindling. Discourses that inflate the numbers of immigrants and their children instill economic fears. They also fuel anxieties about the much touted growing insecurity that plagues France in general and its urban regions more specifically.

Directly following the social unrest and violent outbursts of fall 2005, Nicolas Sarkozy (then minister of the interior) and other voices on the right blamed polygamous families for the violent behavior of African male youths from the *banlieues*. Sarkozy himself declared to the French weekly *L'Express* that the youths responsible for the urban violence were "French by law" but "polygamy and the [lack of] acculturation of a certain number of families [made] it more difficult to integrate a French youth of African descent than a French youth of another descent." Bernard Accoyer (who also distinguished himself for his homophobic comments during the PaCS [*Pacte Civil de Solidarité*—French civil union] debates), then president of the *Union pour un mouvement populaire* (Union for a Popular Movement, or UMP) group at the National Assembly, declared on the French radio station RTL that polygamy "was certainly one of the causes" of the social trouble. Polygamy, he added, "is the incapacity to provide the education necessary to an organized society—a society with norms." Finally, making the connection between the 2005 urban riots and family reunification gone wild, he stated, "For us to be able to integrate them [the male youths], we need to keep their numbers below our integration threshold."[36] Here the specter of polygamy and of different family structures is conjured up to racialize a particular group of immigrants and to demonize a group of French youths. African mothers (and fathers) are set apart in their incapacity to acculturate and, as a result, to rein in their violent sons. The particular and dangerous violence of these young men is also constructed through the discourse of the abused woman and the overcontrolled sister within Muslim and North African immigrant communities, discussed in Chapter 2.[37] It also paves the way for the connection of this population with another security threat: international crime and terrorism.

The progressive and *de facto* (if not *de jure*) closing of family reunification provisions within French immigration law since the 1970s tells many stories. The one I have chosen to underscore in this book places gender at the center. It emphasizes the fact that the figure of woman has been central in the processes of racialization and politicization of immigration that mark the same period. It is also a story that points out the material effects of such processes on women, children, and whole immigrant communities. It reminds us that blood and reproduction metaphors, which buttress all racialist thinking, are not marginal but central to the French republican tradition. Louisa, like many other *sans-papières* in France, lives at the crossroads of the processes discussed in both this chapter and the previous one. Her narrative imagines and hails immigrant women in ways that contrast sharply with those discussed in this chapter:

> It's a message. I did not know it was a message, but now I realize it is. It is a message to pass onto other African women, to other women who are here: you can live without being dependent . . . without being colonized by something, whether it is a country, a husband, or something else. You've got to find your life first. That's it.

5 OF POLISH PLUMBERS
AND SENEGALESE CLEANING LADIES

THE "POLISH PLUMBER" entered the French political scene in 2005 in the debate that preceded the referendum on the European Union's constitutional treaty. The expression had first appeared in 2004 in the French satirical political weekly *Charlie Hebdo*. Philippe Val, then editor and director of the newspaper, had conjured up the Polish plumber in his critique of a proposed European Commission directive aimed at deregulating internal European markets.[1]

The Polish plumber emerged again in March 2005, but this time in a declaration made by right-wing French politician Philippe de Villiers.[2] Resurrecting the imaginary character used by Val in *Charlie Hebdo*, de Villiers alarmingly declared that the European Commission's proposal would allow a "Polish plumber" or an "Estonian architect" to propose their services in France but with salaries and under the social regulations of their country of origin. This, he added, would threaten national labor and would ultimately lead to the dismantling of the French economic and social system. De Villiers also shared his worries about French workers losing jobs to "Latvian masons" and "Estonian gardeners."[3]

Frits Bolkestein, a Dutch senior member of the European Commission, also borrowed the image of an Eastern European worker when he told reporters he would have been happy to find a "Polish plumber" for hire when he found a leak in his secondary residence in Northern France and could not find a single plumber available in the area.[4] In response to Villiers' worries, Bolkestein added that he would also be happy to see "Czech nannies" and "Slovenian accountants" find work in France. Commentators on the right and left of the French political spectrum reacted to Bolkestein's tongue-in-cheek anecdote, and the media developed myriad stories that helped anchor the idea of an Eastern European worker ready to enter the French labor market and compete (unfairly) with honest, competent, and willing French workers.[5]

Bolkestein does not simply own property in France and have strong opinions about the scarcity of plumbers in the country where he likes to vacation. He is also the author of the directive that would allow employers offering long-distance or punctual services in France to pay workers hired from Poland and other European countries, where wages are lower than in France, the going rate in their home countries.[6] During the campaign leading to the referendum, Jacques Chirac tried to no avail to convince French voters that the European Union (EU) would not implement the Bolkestein directive.[7] At the same time, however, French news media were providing evidence that such a race to the bottom of the labor market was already taking place. One article in the daily *Libération*, for instance, documented in May 2005 that a subcontractor to France Télécom (the state-owned phone company) had hired one hundred Portuguese laborers who worked longer hours and were paid less than their French counterparts.[8]

In a country where one out of ten workers is unemployed, media stories about these economic shifts within the construction of Europe resonated with working-class actors, who might have good reason to fear the threat of Bolkestein-type EU economic directives.[9] The French rejected the EU constitution in May 2005 with 55 percent of the electorate voting no. The vote on the EU constitution highlighted deep class divisions within France. Blue-collar workers overwhelmingly rejected the Constitution, with 81 percent voting no, whereas 62 percent of those employed in upper-managerial positions and intellectual professions (*Cadre, profession intellectuelle*) endorsed it.[10] Among those who voted no, the primary reason invoked was a deep fear that the European constitutional treaty would negatively impact employment in France. This reason was selected as the primary one by 46 percent of all those who turned down the European constitution. The fear of losing one's job was especially strong among blue-collar workers and women. In each group, 51 percent of those who voted against the treaty chose "worsened employment prospects" as the primary reason for their decision.[11] Both right- and left-wing detractors of the European constitution, who played on French workers' fears of cheap foreign labor and increasing job insecurity in the new European economic landscape, helped make the Polish plumber a staple of French and European political and economic parlance.

In June 2005 the Polish office of tourism also used the Polish plumber and his infamous appeal in a publicity campaign, but this time to entice French travelers to venture all the way to Poland. Blond, white, muscular, and well-appointed with the tools of his trade, the young man was aimed at deflecting the economic fears of the French working class: "I am staying in Poland," he says on one of the posters. He is also inviting middle-class French tourists to come and spend their euros in Poland.

The image is funny and sexualized—campy, one might say. Interviewed for the *New York Times*, a "real" Polish plumber noted, "He is too lacquered, too handsome and too clean to be on a work site[....] He looks like something out of an x-rated fantasy film about women who are waiting for the plumber

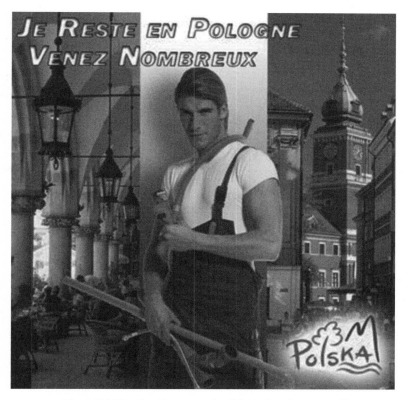

Figure 5.1 *The Polish Plumber.* Courtesy of Polish National Tourist Office.

to come."[12] The sexual fantasy invoked by the *New York Times* Polish plumber intersects with another fantasy that has currency in France and elsewhere. This is a gendered fantasy in which the woman plays a domestic role that locates her in the home and within heteronormative familial relations: she is at home "waiting." This stereotypical imagery is commonplace, as we saw in Chapters Three and Four, when the woman in question is an immigrant, especially when she is from Africa or from a Muslim community. The disco, "village people" aesthetics of the image, however, trouble the heteronorma-tive and sexist readings of the Polish tourism bureau posters and points to the multiple discursive threads that intersect to construct the publicity campaign and its visual narrative.[13]

I open this chapter with a brief discussion of the Polish plumber and con-trast his figure with that of the "Senegalese cleaning lady." The women who are involved in the *sans-papiers* movement, such as those I interviewed for this study, are often from sub-Saharan Africa and are likely to find their first job in the underground economy—cleaning French people's homes and taking care of their children and their elderly parents.[14] Here I bring these two characters into relation to make three simple but related points. First, I want to show that in order to understand the work realities of undocumented immigrant women in France, we have to place their experiences in a web of discursive and material relations that have given shape to these realities. In particular, I want to reemphasize the differential treatment of immigrants from Europe and those from outside the boundaries of the EU. Second, I argue that for these women "work" is at one and the same time a site of exploitation (and therefore disenfranchisement) and of active citizenship.[15] Finally, I want to bring light to the common processes through which "gender" and "race" and their troubling intersections are often made to disappear within immigration discourses in France.

For instance, it is important to note that, in addition to his recent role in the creation of the Polish plumber, in the 1990s Bolkestein was one of the first politicians in the Netherlands to argue that the "cultural" values of Muslim immigrants were incompatible with Dutch values. More recently, Bolkestein opposed Turkey's proposed membership in the EU on cultural grounds and argued that the entry of Turkey's large population and Islamic culture could bring an end to Europe as we know it. Invoking age-old notions of "barbarians at the gate" and quoting from historian Bernard Lewis, Bolkestein warned, "Europe will be Islamic by the end of the century."[16]

The Polish plumber, then, must be read as a multilayered narrative that can tell us who is welcome at the gates of the Republic. Indeed, whereas Polish plumbers, Latvian masons, and Czech nannies might be invited by Bolkestein and others like him to seek legal employment in France, Turkish electricians and Senegalese cleaning ladies need not apply. Indeed, as we saw in Chapter 3, most venues for legal entry and work have been closed off for non-European immigrants for the past three decades. What this chapter demonstrates is that—contrary to popular imaginings—immigrant women are more often than not working women. Often bringing home ridiculous wages and laboring under terribly precarious and difficult conditions, most of them sell their services as domestic, care, and sex workers. Although many of them provide lucid and complex criticisms of the transnational relations of production and exploitation that are shaping their work experiences, none of them express the desire to give up wage labor and its attendant but varying levels of economic independence and personal freedom.

This chapter links the emergence of the personal identities of the *sans-papières* to the larger phenomena of economic restructuring, national and transnational politics, and international population movements. For both men and women, the quest for residence papers is clearly linked to the ability to legitimately occupy a job in the "legal" economy. Without such a right, both men and women remain the vulnerable peons of a system of offshore production on the home front.[17] Because of a variety of international and local forces, women are more vulnerable than men to the excesses of globalization and advanced capitalism. As discussed in the previous two chapters, undocumented immigrant women have been locked, through discursive and material processes, within the realm of domesticity and familial relations. Their alleged lack of participation in productive labor is used against them and their communities. First, these women and their families are imagined as weakening the French economy as well as the core identity of the French nation. Second, their lack of modernity is used to racialize African and Muslim immigrant communities, who are thought unable to assimilate into the French cauldron. Here I argue that, in part because of this unique location within the French national imaginary, undocumented women actively involved in the *sans-papiers* movement forge identities in which wage labor, citizenship, and personal autonomy lie at the core of their hopes for the future. In doing so, ironically, they embody the very qualities that France is claiming they lack as a way of denying them entry into the Republic.

THE CHANGING FACE OF (LABOR) IMMIGRATION
AND IMMIGRANT LABOR IN FRANCE

Most studies of migration in France state that one of the characteristics of French immigration has been its rapid and steady feminization since the 1970s. Although it is true that the sheer augmentation of the immigrant population in France is due, by and large, to the arrival of new immigrant women, the statement needs some refining. The feminization of immigration in France is hardly a new phenomenon. Indeed, women already represented 46.9 percent of the total immigrant population in 1911 and this percentage hovered around 45 percent until the 1970s. Their proportion increased slightly but steadily to reach 48 percent in 1990.[18] In parallel with this increase, however, was the steady decline of European immigrants within the total immigrant population in France during the same period. Indeed, European immigrants representation shrank from 78.7 percent in 1962 to 50.4 percent in 1990 (45 percent in 1999). This decline was accompanied by the increased representation of immigrants from non-European countries. The proportion of immigrants from Africa increased from 14.9 percent in 1962 to 35.9 percent in 1990. In a similar manner, the proportion of immigrants from Asia increased from 2.4 percent to 11.4 percent between 1962 and 1990. In other words, what we see in the total immigrant population in France after the mid-1970s is the dual increased representation and feminization of immigrant communities from Asia and Africa and the related declining percentage of immigrants from Europe.[19]

When France formally closed its borders to work immigration in 1974, immigrants from Africa (outside the Maghreb) began to file for family reunifications in significant numbers. As a result, women from Africa began to arrive in sizeable numbers in the second half of the 1970s. In 1968 only 4,712 women from sub-Saharan Africa were present in France, and by 1975 their numbers had reached 16,470. In 1982 these numbers had more than doubled, with 42,400 women from sub-Saharan Africa present in the French territory, and in 1990 there were 73,000 of them (a 70 percent increase from the 1982 figure).[20] This exponential growth of women from sub-Saharan Africa in the 1980s contributed to the rapid feminization of this immigrant population. Indeed, whereas women represented less than 30 percent of all immigrants from sub-Saharan Africa in 1975 and 35 percent in 1982, by 1990 they represented 40 percent of that population.[21] Family reunification, along with the noted increase in single female work migration, launched the large-scale feminization and settlement of African immigrant communities in France.[22]

In other words, the feminization and settlement of immigrant communities did not start after France closed its borders to work immigration. They started much earlier, but at a slower pace for immigrants from southern and eastern Europe, as well as for those from the Maghreb. What I suggest here is that the peculiar phenomenological emphasis on the feminization of recent immigrant groups might be explained by the sheer fact that the women who entered France in the 1980s and the 1990s were simply more noticed because they had been rendered more "noticeable" through various processes of racialization and "othering" that I discussed in the previous chapter. In contradistinction to popular opinion, they also began to enter the workforce in large numbers, rendering their presence even more visible. As noted in an early study of migrant women in France, what we do see, since the mid-1970s, is "the sharp rise in the proportion of women in nationalities that are themselves on the rise, and the increasing tendency of foreign women to abandon traditional roles in the home and enter the labor force."[23]

In the context of an international economic downturn and rising rates of unemployment among nationals, French state representatives in the 1970s perceived and constructed family immigration as more acceptable than work immigration because it did not present, in the mind of these officials, a direct threat to male French workers. Notwithstanding the racist and sexist underpinnings of such assumptions, recent studies suggest that they also proved to be naive and unrealistic. Since the formal halt of work immigration, immigrant women have been entering the labor force in ever increasing numbers. This trend is true even within the national groups, such as Algerians and Moroccans, that have had traditionally low female labor force participation. In 1995, for instance, the labor-force participation of immigrant women (ages to fifty-nine) from the European Union was 66.2 percent; it was 40 percent for Algerian women, 37.8 percent for Moroccan women, 44.8 percent for Tunisian women, and 67.4 percent for women from Africa (outside of the Maghreb).[24]

What is particularly interesting about these numbers is that the labor force participation of women from sub-Saharan Africa is higher than that of their European counterparts (with the exception of women from Portugal, whose labor participation rate is 74.5 percent) and only slightly inferior to that of the total female labor force participation in France.[25] Because we lack disaggregated numbers by nationality and information about educational levels, language fluency, and geographical location in country of origin, it is difficult to interpret these figures. However, what is clear is that they debunk the racist and sexist notion that African women are simply consumers of a French welfare state and do not contribute to the national economy.

Immigrant women are working and, as the rest of this chapter shows, so are undocumented immigrant women. Yet they also suffer from high rates of unemployment, are often employed part-time or are underemployed, and draw lower salaries than their male and nonimmigrant counterparts. For instance, in 1990, almost 40 percent of all women of immigrant origin from outside the EU were unemployed.[26] Underemployment (*sous-emploi*) is a term used by French economist Margaret Maruani to describe all forms of flexible work arrangements, such as short-term contracts, internships, and temporary work, that have rendered employment precarious for larger and larger segments of the EU working population since the mid-1970s. Maruani further argues that underemployment, in part through part-time work, affects women in massive numbers. For instance, 81 percent of all part-time workers in the EU are women.[27] The jobs for which part-time employment is common are by and large female-dominated jobs: domestic work, child care, and elder care. They are also the jobs that undocumented immigrant women find until they are able to change their immigration status. What we see here is a structural continuity of women's work and underemployment patterns within the European community. So although women do occupy different positions within the economy depending on their class and national background as well as their legal status as immigrants, they all face "similar patriarchal constraints."[28]

WITHOUT PAPERS, BUT NOT WITHOUT WORK

Although I did not set out to find out what *sans-papières* did for a living, many of my interviews provide interesting information about the employment trajectories, the work realities, and the economic struggles of the women involved in the *sans-papiers* movement. All of the women I interviewed found positions in the black market [*travail au noir*] when they were undocumented and most saw the ability to secure legal work as one of the key benefits of their legal change of status. Many addressed the difficulty of making a living while sustaining their involvement in the struggle. Most of the interviews show that, regardless of their country of origin and regardless of their marital and familial status, *sans-papières* take wage labor for granted and are engaged in some form of income-generating activity. Some of the leaders of the movement are now legally employed within militant structures loosely connected to the *sans-papiers* struggle (labor unions, NGOs, and so on). However, the women I interviewed often downplayed this outcome of their involvement in the struggle, in part to avoid criticism of petty entrepreneurship and personal gains attained through their role in the movement.

Aminata, one of the few women still involved in the national leadership of the *sans-papiers* movement, is from Senegal and once worked as a cleaning lady. She explained to me that she already had a job before becoming active in the movement but she eventually lost it because of the disruption caused by her militant activities.[29]

> *Aminata*: Before I became involved with the [*sans-papiers*] struggle, I had everything. I was working when I became involved in the struggle. But then I lost my job. . . . I was often late because of the meetings, so at the end I had problems.
>
> *CR*: What were you doing?
>
> *Aminata*: I worked as a domestic help. They [my employers] pushed me aside without laying me off completely. They would give me two hours [of work] per day, one hour per day. . . . I would go and help the elderly. I would shop for them—two hours here, one hour and a half there!

Aminata evoked here the lack of regulation in these informal service-sector jobs. Employers recruit by word of mouth, pay in cash (or don't pay at all), and demand that workers work as little or as much as they need them to. They also extend work days and work weeks beyond what is normally acceptable. Aminata addressed the impossibility of supporting her family on the very low wages secured through this kind of labor. She also hinted at the fact that it might be difficult for women to maintain their involvement in the struggle for long periods. This is particularly true when they are single parents and solely responsible for the care and well-being of their children. In this case, Aminata's militant activity also got in the way of her making a living wage: "At the end I would work Saturday and Sunday. At the end they would give me two hours, an hour and a half [of work] per day. So at the end of the month I would be making roughly $300. With four children, all alone! No governmental help, nothing!"[30]

Aminata was now working in the cafeteria of a French labor union, where she had a regular salary and benefits. She tended to downplay that aspect of her accomplishments and regularly mentioned that people criticize the movement's leadership for its self-interest. She kept emphasizing throughout the interview that she became involved in the movement simply to help her daughters (to acquire a change of status through familial reunification) and that she now continues to help other *sans-papiers*. Although it is clear that Aminata, and others, have made some professional gains from their militant involvement in the struggle (if only through the personal contacts they have made within French activist circles), there seems to be a form of self-censorship about these connections and the personal gains made through them. Ironically, these are precisely the kinds of connections and successes that are often seen as indicators of integration into the host society.

Lisa had also been involved in the leadership of a collective, in the Paris region, for a couple of years and was about to obtain a change of status when I met her. Like most of the women interviewed for this project, she entered the country with a tourist visa—in this case a thirty-day visa—and stayed in France after it expired. After waiting for years to leave Algeria through the legal process of family reunification, Lisa joined her husband in 2000. In 2002, when I talked to her, Lisa was no longer a *sans-papiers* delegate but was present almost every day in the small locale that the collective used as a reception area and where undocumented immigrants came to seek information and, in some cases, to join the collective.[31] When I interviewed her, she stressed the physical drain caused by her involvement in the struggle and by the emotional labor she had often performed as a delegate and now as a regular volunteer for the collective:

> I thought [after I obtained my papers] that I would stay put at home, but when I obtained my change of status, I could not stay at home [laughter]. I am always here, I am still working at the front desk, I give folks appointments, I help people who do not know what they need to do, I try to lift their spirit. . . . I am here to do that, I help them, I can't let them down—even when I am tired.

Lisa went on to explain how the emotional labor she performed at the *coordination* was done on top of her wage labor and her domestic work at home. Like many of the women involved in the *sans-papiers* movement, Lisa was then doing a triple shift, which left her exhausted at the end of the day:

> *Lisa*: Yes, sometimes there are too many people [in the office]. I am here at the front desk and each one comes in to tell me about their life . . . so me, I have to talk nonstop, I [inaudible], now that I have started to work, as soon as I get off work, I come here directly, yes. And in the evening I still have to go home,

prepare dinner, clean the house. . . . I have so much to do during the day, at night I am exhausted.

CR: And now you are working in St. Denis?

Lisa: I take care of . . . no, no, I work at Boulogne-Billancourt [another town on the outskirts of Paris]. It's far.

CR: And you have to commute. . . .

Lisa: I have two hours of commute every day. I work in the black market.

CR: You are taking care of children, right?

Lisa: No, I am taking care of an elderly lady. I feed her and everything. I work simply to make a little money to go on vacation, but soon I will look for a real job.

CR: When you actually get your papers. . . .

Lisa: Yes, I don't have my papers yet, but I will soon. I have received the date of my interview. I went for my medical and soon I will get my ten-year residency card.

Lisa's interview also reveals that for the *sans-papières*, the reality of wage labor is closely linked to their immigration status. Women who are undocumented have no difficulty finding work in France, but they do so in an underground economic sector organized primarily around undocumented immigrant labor.[32] For women, this informal sector lands them jobs as domestic workers, child care workers, elder care workers, and sex workers.[33] Aminata D., another Senegalese leader of the movement who is currently located in Marseilles (and who also worked at some point as a cleaning lady), clearly points to this particular reality of the *sans-papières'* economic standing in France:

CR: And what were you doing then?

Aminata D.: Babysitting [in English during the interview]. What else? When you are undocumented in France all you can do is to become a cleaning lady or do babysitting: you take care of babies and the elderly.

Feminist scholarship has amply demonstrated that women's lives are shaped by a gendered division of labor that demands that they perform the bulk of domestic and care work in a household even when they are full-time wage earners.[34] Scholars of race relations and immigration have also demonstrated that domestic labor is a terrain where women are often divided across class, racial and ethnic, and national lines. Globalization and the increased movement of people across national borders have added a layer to the new economic world order wherein middle-class women from old and newly industrialized countries purchase the help of immigrant women who perform for them the tasks that are almost universally still considered "women's work." Indeed, wherever middle-class women have entered the waged work force in large numbers, the demand for foreign domestic workers has soared. Freed from some of this labor, middle-class women find themselves better able to compete in the economic sphere, enjoy the rewards of motherhood, and exert their citizenship rights. In France, undocumented immigrant women provide domestic and care work in an informal economy that thrives in part thanks to their precarious social location.[35]

Not surprisingly, women are also called to provide care work in the context of the *sans-papiers* movement. During my fieldwork I observed Lisa, Aminata, and other women in leadership positions do typically gendered emotional and care labor around the collectives and in the actions they organized. I have also seen many others, however, resist such calling. Nouria, a young woman from Algeria, remembered the leadership role played by Lisa but also cast her as doing "mother" work throughout the movement's occupation of a *gendarmerie*:[36]

> Yes, Lisa was there. She was a delegate. She was taking care of everything. She would do rounds at night. She would keep an eye on us, especially the girls, because she was afraid. When you occupy public buildings there are always people who you don't know. . . . She would keep an eye on us. Sometimes she would order us to go to sleep. She did not want us to linger in the courtyard. Then she would make sure that everyone had a bed that was comfortable[. . . .] She would take care of all the *sans-papiers*. Yes, Lisa, she'd keep her eye on everything, everything. She played a big, big role [in the occupation]; she was the mommy, she would make everyone feel better (she and Sam were staffing the reception desk). Yes she would work at the reception desk, she worked at the reception.

Other women addressed the gendered division of labor in the *sans-papiers* collectives, but many more were concerned about their working conditions and their overall *précarité* as undocumented workers in the informal economy. Most of the interviews I collected, in fact, are peopled by two staple characters: the unethical lawyer and the slimy exploitative employer. Indeed, the *sans-papières* I interviewed recounted stories involving themselves, their husbands, or people they know who had been exploited or literally robbed by an employer. Their vulnerability as workers was shaped by their particular location within French society and within a global economic order that relies on flexibility and lack of regulation. Aminata D.'s interview, for instance, sheds light on the informal networks that connect undocumented immigrants to their employers. She also described the recruitment and management techniques employed by her own employers. "I was working for a couple. They were teachers—they were young. They had a child who had just been born. I did not know them personally, but I knew their mother, who knew one of my cousins, who had worked for her in the past. They took me on trial for a month and then they trusted me. . . . I worked for them for four years."

Louisa, from the Comoro Islands, recalled her initial fear of illegal employment and the kind of extreme exploitation connected with this kind of work: "I was not working. I was afraid. I had seen people work for $8 a day! I could not do it." A sense of class dislocation and downward mobility is also a common experience for undocumented women. Clairette, whom we met in Chapter 4, is a good example of this phenomenon. She found herself somewhat "out of place" among the *sans-papiers*. Many of the women I interviewed left behind middle-class jobs and were now laboring in positions at the very bottom of the French labor structure. Of particular interest here is the recurring theme of women experiencing their downward mobility directly through their introduction to the *sans-papiers* movement and its collective infrastructure. The sense of shame and shock that comes with the loss of one's papers is particularly strong among young middle-class women, whose families often disapprove of the risks taken by becoming involved in the *sans-papiers* movement. Several of them used the language of "falling down" to describe their new déclassé status. In the process, the same women often become radicalized and more fully aware of their class location. Nouria, for instance, recalled her naiveté and her shock when she finally encountered the *sans-papiers* and their collective condition in France:

> I did not know it was going to be like that! Even I, who had the luck [of being protected by my family]—how could I imagine I was going to fall so low. When you live without papers, you live. . . . I mean [people live . . .], I did not experience *précarité* myself. I was nicely protected by my sisters. But I did not know that people could actually fall this far down! Human beings! Some people end up sleeping on the street. Some people go hungry. Some people never see doctors. I did not know *sans-papiers*; I did not even know they existed!

Sylvie, a young woman from Cameroon who entered France on a student visa, talked about her family's class and gender expectations. By becoming undocumented, but especially by joining an organized movement of undocumented immigrants, she felt she was failing them on both grounds:

> In a very short period of time I matured a lot. It has been very painful[. . . .] In some ways I had arrived in France with a certain idea of what it would be like. I was born in Cameroon, I thought I was coming to France to pursue my studies. I thought I would study, then get married and have a family. Certainly that's what was expected of me.
>
> For a young woman from Cameroon in Paris [being a *sans-papiers*] is not what was expected of me.
>
> It was like a big downward slide—"but what is she doing there?" I did not even try to explain.
>
> I felt like I had reached rock bottom, that I had fallen down very low by becoming a *sans-papiers*.
>
> The *sans-papiers* movement is like a crossroads. You find all kinds of people involved in it, but in the eyes of my community I did not belong there. As a *sans-papiers* you feel you are considered as an inferior; it's almost like having a venereal disease (*maladie honteuse*). It's a very negative image.

Laria, a resourceful student from Algeria who is now very active in a *sans-papiers* collective in Paris, does not mince her words about the shock of her arrival in the world of the *sans-papiers*. Her first encounter with the class and racial and ethnic diversity of the *sans-papiers* collective made her realize her own class dislocation:

> *Laria:* No, really, no, I did not think I would end up like this. In my head I thought I would quickly sort [out] my situation without any problems. I was telling myself, they will take into consideration . . . I am an intellectual, I am articulate . . . so I did not think it would be super difficult to obtain a visa.[37]
>
> I cannot hide the fact that the first time, the very first time [I attended a meeting] I was not very enthusiastic.
>
> *CR:* Why?
>
> *Laria:* Well, because of all the mixing. I am not racist when I say this, not racist at all. Well, when I saw the blacks, the Indians, the folks from different social classes, I told myself, "it can't be true, I cannot be mixed with all these people."

Despite her disclaimer, Laria's sense of class location and dislocation is also linked to a racial and ethnic pecking order that is being reinforced by global economic restructuring. Sub-Saharan Africans and South Asians (apart from a few students and civil servants) are relative newcomers in France. As such, they find themselves located at the very bottom of a class order that is being inflected by racialist thinking both within and outside the *sans-papiers* movement. Regardless of their class background, the women I interviewed in 2002 hoped to obtain a change of status through their active participation in the *sans-papiers* struggle. Some were successful. In the process, many became aware of a shared condition of lack that binds them to other undocumented immigrants in France. Some also learned lessons about the messy intersections that shape the complex reality of the *sans-papières* in France. Through her involvement with the *sans-papiers* struggle, Louisa finally obtained a change of status. She was now working for the CGT (*Confédération générale du travail*). She clearly connected the *sans-papiers*' economic vulnerability to global economic forces:[38]

> Helping other *sans-papiers* opened my eyes. Even if you have your papers, even if you are French, you can still be unemployed. . . .
>
> Why do you think we are here? *Sans-papiers* work for the bare minimum. People who work for a regular salary are threatened when they are told that some people work for less. . . . We must obtain papers, we must be employed. All of this is linked.

Louisa further pointed out that undocumented immigrants and French workers are linked in the global logic of late capitalism. Quite astute about the dangers that accompany the call of domesticity and natural caring for all women, Louisa saw undocumented immigrant women's access to wage labor as key to their overall independence and personal freedom: "I have an important message for other African women, for other women who are here: you can live without being dependant . . . or colonized by something, whether it is a country, a husband, or something else. You must find yourself (your life) first."

I end this section with the story of Malika—another cleaning lady from Morocco—because her story illustrates the contradictory nature of wage labor for many undocumented women. On the one hand, Malika's story highlights the vulnerability, isolation, and exploitation she experienced as a *sans-papière* at work. On the other hand, she recounted a trajectory in which employment was key to self-discovery and self-realization. One of the few women I interviewed who had entered the country illegally, Malika found work almost immediately after she crossed the border. Working as a live-in maid for three years, she managed to save money, learn French, and little by little reconstruct herself as a whole person.[39] She recounted with delight her first months at her employer's home:

> It was the first time in my life that I had a small room of my own. I knew, I totally knew my place—I was a maid, but it was something that I will never forget. For the first time in my life, a small room of my own: a bed, a small TV. I had never had a TV in my whole life, I mean until I was twenty-five. I was twenty-five when I arrived in France. See, that was amazing. They were good people. . . . I like to read, because I did not go to school for very long—five years: you can hardly accomplish anything. But I always loved to read. So I bought a little book. It is written in Arabic and translated in French. [I used it] to understand what the parents were saying to their children. I asked, what are you saying? What does this mean? Then I used the book to locate the words and memorize them. It is thanks to them that I learned how to speak little by little—they helped me improve my French.

Malika learned much more than language skills through her work experience. What the small "room of her own" provided her with was a personal space to look at her life, heal some of the wounds of gender oppression, and make crucial connections between different forms of oppressive and exploitative relations:

> See, I did not want to stay at my sister's. I wanted to work. I wanted to be independent. Because when you live like this, like an object, after, you revolt. I wanted to know what the freedom of a woman to decide all alone, to have a paycheck, to not depend on someone else, was. So for me it was great that I was able to work immediately. [. . .] But why was it great for me? Because at that time I did not know what it meant to work [for a wage]—I did not know about working hours. I did not know. All I could see was that I was in a castle. It was only a villa but for me it was a castle that I could not dream of; it was my little room that I never had until then; it was people who respected me. I did not care about the work, for me it was normal. I did not negotiate my salary, I did not . . . I did not know! Even if they had told me you have to work Saturdays and Sundays, I would have probably said yes, because I did not know.

Malika's desires to live on her own (free from, among other things, familial supervision), to be economically self-sufficient, and to experience freedom are all dependent on her ability to work. So work in itself, regardless of the working conditions, was what enabled Malika to "revolt" and to move from an object to a subject position. Malika's paycheck and her "little room" and the privilege they represent, however, can also be read as screens that initially mystified the exploitation she was experiencing and prevented her from "knowing." As time went by, however, Malika began to resist the exploitative working conditions that often come with the territory of live-in domestic work. Little by little, she recounted, her employers asked her to perform tasks that Malika saw as outside the boundaries of her live-in maid contract: working in the garden, washing her employers' car, and baking "specialty" cakes for the whole family. Malika also clearly resented that neither her family nor the family who employed her ever—in the three years she worked for them—took the time to take her to Paris (both families lived in the suburbs): "I never went to Paris, never! Each time I asked my sister, she'd reply: 'cops are everywhere.' So I thought the cops were circling the subway. I did not know!"

Again, the possibility of traveling from the suburbs to the center of Paris represents Malika's ability to move freely and to decide on her own what constitutes a dangerous activity. In this case, knowing that the cops are not "everywhere" and that many undocumented immigrant women do occupy and move within French space is a piece of information she had to acquire through a slow process of discovery and self-discovery. When she asked her employers to give her a formal work contract so that she could seek a change of status, her employers demanded that she sign a ten-year work contract. Malika refused the terms of their offer and walked out: "I said no. *No*, I said, ten years: that's a whole life! I don't know what is going to happen. I do not want to sign a contract. If you want to [employ me legally], then you do it; if you don't, you don't. What can I tell you?"

Malika found illegal work again, fast and easily. She was working as a maid in a third-class hotel run by a Kabyle.[40] She asked him to pay her at the end of each day of work ($25 when she started working for him and $50 before she moved on to another job) in order to avoid being robbed of a salary should the hotel close or her boss suddenly decide to disappear. Malika must have gleaned this wisdom through conversations with other *sans-papiers*.[41]

Malika's story also illustrates the common fate of the *sans-papiers* in France, where "black market employment also militates against the possibility of women of immigrant origin having access to legal residence cards in the future."[42] After almost nine years of life and full-time employment in France, Malika could not "prove" that she had been there for that long. She had no lease to show, no stamp dating her entry on her passport, and no other records that are asked for by the French authorities. Neither could she "prove" that she had been gainfully employed for all those years. She had no working contract, pay stubs, or even proof of a bank account in France.

SANS-PAPIÈRES AND THE GLOBAL ECONOMY

Migrant women play a specific, critical role in the global economy, as revealed by current economic transformations. Technological changes, the directions of capital flows and the increasing presence of transnational corporations all rely heavily on cheap female migrant labor to maintain their profit bases. For example, there has been a large shift from full-time jobs with benefits to contingent and temporary jobs. Exploitative working conditions with little or no benefits abound and migrant women provide the linchpin in the maintenance of these new structures.[43]

It is safe to say that the feminization of the non-European immigrant labor force in France is due in part to women's desire to find and secure paid employment, and to "the spreading urbanization and greater access to education [for women] in the countries of origin."[44] But it is also due to structural necessities in the French economy that favored the entry of these immigrant women into the labor force while relegating them to specific sectors of the economy. As a result, immigrant women generally and undocumented immigrant women in particular occupy the bottom rungs of the French occupational ladder. What must be noted, however, is that there have been clear differences among various immigrant communities in terms of employment opportunities and labor-market locations:

> Migrant women occupy the lowest levels of the manufacturing industries, and within these levels, hierarchies by nationality which correspond to the sequence of migration and length of residence in France have emerged. Thus, Italian women tend to be at the top, followed by Spanish, Portuguese, and Yugoslav women, who are in turn followed by North Africans and Turks.[45]

The hierarchies discussed by Caspari and Giles in the preceding quote must also be understood in light of the differential treatment of immigrant women by French immigration authorities. As we saw in Chapter 3, the late seventies saw a set of short-term measures restricting employment of foreign workers' wives and children. Women's access to the labor market was tolerated, until 1981, but connected to their husband's legal social position in France and in sectors that were not protected for French workers.[46] This enabled French authorities to select preferred national groups and allow them into particular sectors of the labor force. Catherine Wihtol de Wenden and Margo Corona DeLey argue that these measures in the context of a global economic recession worked to increase certain immigrant women's dependence on men, further weaken their precarious economic position, and boost illegal work for immigrant women:

> Married women who wished to separate from their husbands, or young women wanting to leave their parents, had no choice but to enter the underground labor market. Women who sought occupational mobility found themselves trapped in low-status, low-paying jobs due to government policy and/or their spouse's attachment to a particular locality. This double discrimination, as migrants and as women, was intensified by local administrative policy, which often took the form of refusing them entry into the French labor market.[47]

The effects of transnational economic forces and national immigration policies are multiple and complex. They create hierarchies among immigrant women. They also implement a dual process of inclusion/exclusion whereby some women *are* integrated into the French economy but occupy (to varying degrees) the lowest and most precarious positions within the occupational structure. Immigrant women are often found in domestic work, and in the garment and food industries, where a lot of illegal work is being done, in part, through home-based work. Fragmentary evidence and my own interviews suggest the significant participation of undocumented immigrant women in these illegal and informal forms of employment. This marked tendency, although impossible to measure exactly, does characterize the location of most undocumented immigrant women in the French economy.[48]

By successfully combining repressive immigration policies that render immigrants (especially undocumented ones) legally vulnerable with a soft (and differentiated) application of these policies, France has produced the conditions for the maintenance of a very flexible and somewhat compliant pool of workers within its national borders. Emmanuel Terray clearly documents how the existence of such a pool of illegal workers in France has driven wages down and created the conditions of an offshore economy on the home front.[49]

I am suggesting in this chapter that immigrant women, and undocumented immigrant women in particular, are central actors within this home-based offshore economy.

It is important to note, however, that these patterns echo and intersect with processes that have contributed to the overall feminization of the labor force within European markets, to the increased deregulation of these markets, and to the occupational segregation that still characterizes them. Gendered processes of economic restructuring have resulted in shifts in the European employment structure from full-time jobs with benefits to contingent temporary jobs and jobs with highly exploitative working conditions and few or no benefits. Jill Rubery and Colette Fagan demonstrate that women play a key role in the maintenance of these new employment structures. Their study shows how women within European markets are "providing the flexible labor force to be deployed in low paid casual or part time work."[50]

Most French people (whether in politics, academia, or on the streets) still ignore the gendered nature of immigration, work, and citizenship in the Republic. French commentaries about the Polish plumber polemic and the riots that set Paris on fire in November 2005, for instance, demonstrate an entrenched and enduring inability to see gender and race and the way they often intersect. Part of the racialization of certain immigrant communities in France operates through discourses and discursive practices that construct young "immigrant" men (*immigrés*) as shiftless, dangerous, and out of control.[51] It also operates through discursive practices that render some immigrant women invisible or at best located in the realm of domesticity and tradition. It is important to note here that, for instance, the outrageous rates of unemployment (in the formal economy) that were much discussed in the wake of the riots are even higher for women.[52]

The narrative about the Polish plumber builds on, feeds, and sometimes obfuscates the dual discursive threads of racialization of immigrants and erasure of women. The Polish plumber displaces the material workings of globalization and late capitalism onto a straw man: the foreigner. We cannot forget, however, that since the 1970s, discourses of foreign (labor) invasions and their related acts of racial hatred and violence have primarily targeted immigrant communities from France's former colonies. The Polish plumber narrative sanitizes (and distorts) this history.[53] It also renders invisible the central and necessary labor performed by women within these broad economic changes.

Senegalese cleaning ladies are indeed at work in France. They are at work in French women's homes. They are at work in run-down hotels run by men and women who migrated to France before them. They are at work in *sans-papiers* collectives organizing for their change of status and that of others. They are at work using the language of the Republic to construct new lives and new identities for themselves. They are at work prying open the fissures of that language and fighting its power and that of the Republic.

6 NANAS, PÉDÉS, IMMIGRÉS: SOLIDARITÉ?

IN THE FALL OF 1999—three years after the *sans-papiers* occupied the Saint-Bernard Church—France passed a law that established civil unions (*Pacte Civil de Solidarité*, or PaCS) for gay and heterosexual couples.[1] Supporters of the new law hailed the victory of the plural left and suggested that the PaCS was indeed a law born out of a strong French republican tradition. They further argued that the republican model of national integration had once again proved to be uniquely successful. Gay and straight couples alike—regardless of their sexual orientation and their group affiliation—were granted similar rights under the new law: "The PaCS refuses to consider citizens as parts of something else, as categories, as 'communities,' whose boundaries are rather vague, anyway. Rather, it proposes a new way of organizing one's life within a couple without taking account of the sex of each partner or prejudging the nature of the bonds that link them together."[2]

In this chapter, I propose an analysis of the PaCS law and the parliamentary debates that led to its passage in order to shed light on little-studied links between racism, homophobia, and sexism in France. In doing so, my aim is twofold. By analyzing the connections between anti-immigrant and anti-gay rhetoric, I illustrate some of the ways in which hegemonic discourses that construct certain people as impossible subjects borrow from and articulate with one another. I also ponder the kinds of transformational politics that might develop in the light of such analysis.

Little has been done in France, at least until recently, at the theoretical level or on the activist ground to better understand and fight these intersections.[3] In fact, observers—especially outside of France—have pointed to and

112

deplored the missed opportunities created by the single-term analyses that have dominated migration and feminist research in France. Jane Freedman, using Cathy Lloyd's phrase, summarizes the situation as a *rendez-vous manqué* between feminisms and anti-racisms in France, with both sides tending to prioritize one axis of domination (either sexist or racist) and failing to take full account of the multiple nature of women of immigrant origin's identities, experiences and situations."[4]

In the first part of this chapter I focus on the graffito *Islam = SIDA* (Islam = AIDS) to examine the ways in which racism and homophobia intersect at a specific historical moment in French political culture. I show how, in this slogan, *Islam* works to represent postcolonial immigrants as "barbarians at the gate." In a similar manner, I underscore how *AIDS* functions to represent "queers" as deviant and dangerous. In *Islam = AIDS*, both groups connote threat, criminality, and pollution. Both groups are discursively located outside the boundaries of the French Republic. As we saw in previous chapters, notions of threat, crime, and pollution are also built, in part, through gendered metaphors.

I then turn to the parliamentary debates on the PaCS reform in the fall of 1999 to demonstrate how the two terms of the equation *Islam = AIDS* are not simply linked in a catchy slogan tagged on Parisian walls by hateful right-wing extremists, but are in fact part of a discursive whole articulated and disseminated by a large and respectable fraction of the French polity. Indeed, *Islam = AIDS* not only functions as a key subtext to the PaCS debates in France, but also helps us understand how racism and homophobia are central to and intricately linked within contemporary postcolonial Western societies in general and within postcolonial France more specifically. By delineating continuities between street graffiti and mainstream debates over national legislation, I hope to show that racism and homophobia are linked in France to central themes within French republican discourse. Rather than seeing racism, homophobia, and sexism as anomalies that occasionally come to disturb the inclusive and egalitarian republican agenda, in this chapter I argue that they are in fact a troubling part of that agenda.

In *New Right Discourse on Race and Sexuality*, Anna Marie Smith offers a powerful analysis of the ways in which racism and homophobia function as nodal points within contemporary British politics.[5] By focusing on Thatcherism and Powellism, and on their position on immigration and homosexuality, Smith explores how a discourse emerged in Britain in the mid-1980s that successfully blended the prohibition of the "promotion of homosexuality" and the "regulation of black immigration."[6]

> The demonization of homosexuality was framed not only in terms of AIDS-panic discourse, but also in terms of Powellian and Thatcherite racism. The Section 28 supporters explicitly linked the promotion of homosexuality with the promotion of multiculturalism. They drew extensively upon already normalized racist metaphors around disease, foreign invasions, unassimilable 'other' cultures, dangerous criminals, subversive intellectuals, excessive permissiveness and so on.[7]

Smith's point here is that the demonization of homosexuality in 1980s Britain was possible and successful precisely because it built on already existing and normalized racist structures within the British state. Although Smith recognizes that queer and anti-racist activists are becoming more and more aware of these linkages and articulations, she calls for more scholarly studies that can help us locate them in specific political contexts. "It is only when," she writes, "we do the work of showing the actual connections between particular forms of racism and homophobia in specific contexts that our recognition of these linkages will become a strategically effective resource."[8]

In this chapter, I take on Smith's challenge seriously by showing that current homophobic and racist discourses in France borrow from each other and use similar metaphors. Through this analysis I hope to uncover how the deployment of anti-immigrant and anti-gay politics in the late 1990s contributed to the production of political and popular discourses that represent postcolonial immigrants and queers as threats to the French nation. I also suggest that a virulent anti-feminist agenda underlies both discourses and their dangerous intersection. I end the chapter by pointing out possibilities for coalitional politics that have yet to flourish in the French context.

The continuities between racism and homophobia in 1990s France can certainly be analyzed as traces of the nation's colonial project. Indeed, this dual and linked focus on queer and postcolonial subjects at this particular historical juncture echoes a colonial past when discourses of sexuality, racial thinking, and nationalist rhetoric intersected in the construction of the bourgeois national subject and its others.[9] Here, however, I choose to focus on something else. I analyze these discursive intersections and borrowings as part of an ongoing process of subjectification that articulates different hierarchies of power and locates individuals and collectivities in contradictory relations to the French state and its republican promise of universal inclusion and integration.

STREET TAGS

In the summer of 1997, Parisian walls were littered with the slogan "Islam = AIDS!" (*Islam = Sida!*).[10] The slogan, in its violent simplicity, captures the political climate of the moment. In the French collective imagination, Islam has been equated with a disease (a viral infection), which can spread and weaken—even destroy—the national body.[11]

By a series of metonymic shifts, we can see the larger implications of the slogan: *Islam* is used to represent a whole set of undesirable immigrants who will not or cannot be integrated into French society. These postcolonial immigrants are those from sub-Saharan Africa and the Maghreb. They—like their religion (assumed to be Islam and often equated with radical fundamentalism) and their culture (reduced to a monolithic backward and dangerous whole)—are invading and polluting our national space, constructed in contrast as white and Christian.

Figure 6.1 Street tag in Paris. Photo by C. Raissiguier.

AIDS, like Islam, is equated with a group of people: the homosexual community. And homosexuals, in particular white homosexual men, are persistently connected—and dangerously so—with the spread of AIDS within Europe and North America. AIDS, interestingly enough, has also been connected with Africans and people of the African Diaspora. Cindy Patton, for instance, writes, "[a] scientist of the stature of Luc Montaigne has persistently maintained, despite contrary epidemiologic data, that 'AIDS' started in 'Africa.' His claim is based on the genetic similarity of a simian immunodeficiency virus found in monkeys."[12] The racist implications of such a claim are obvious and noted by Patton. The rhetorical device in the slogan, which uses Islam to stand for the whole of Africa and African immigrants, rearticulates Montaigne's problematic claim. It suggests that immigrants from Africa are bringing the disease into France, where it is rapidly disseminated by (white) homosexuals. The final discursive link is made: immigrants and homosexuals and especially the subjects who embody both types of "deviance" are in collusion and together represent an acute danger to the stability and well-being of the French republic.[13]

Islam and AIDS can also be said to have generated a great deal of "(dis)ease" among French nationals in that they produced the kind of discomfort that both incites and legitimizes national sex panics. The (dis)ease here is both cause and effect of such panics, and it allows the body (individual, collective, national) imagined heretofore as "under threat" to think in terms of self-protection, border controls, and insularity. Needless to say, all these reactions pave the way for the emergence (or rather the rearticulation) of nationalist and racist narratives and practices that promise to contain and soothe such (dis)ease. The escalation of racist and homophobic violence in such contexts is one of the symptoms and releases of the (dis)ease.

Pointing out the multiple connections between the fears generated by postcolonial immigration and homosexuality, Barbara Browning, in *Infectious Rhythms*, argues, "HIV emerged as a pathogen simultaneously with new anxieties over the risks of these other [migrational, spiritual, cultural] 'contagions.' And while it may seem clear that one pandemic is painfully literal, the others figurative, they were quickly associated with one another." Browning further reminds us that "in fact, economic exploitation, cultural exchange, and disease are interrelated—but Africanness is hardly the deadly pathogen."[14]

Islam = AIDS, then, is a condensed political narrative that ironically borrows from the ACT UP slogan *Silence = Death* to conjure up the notion of a national body "at risk" and penetrated by infected foreign populations and sexual minorities. So the logic goes: immigrants from sub-Saharan Africa and the Maghreb, like and with homosexuals, are a threat to our culture and our values; they represent a danger to the national body, which should not tolerate them within its boundaries. This, of course, is a matter of life and death for the French nation and the French people—who are imagined to be racially pure and strictly heterosexual. The nation, in Western political parlance, is often associated with an imagined ideal human body. This idealized body "has been cast implicitly in the image of the robust, European, heterosexual gentleman, an ideal defined by its contradistinction to a potpourri of 'deviant' types."[15] Nations are also imagined through the trope of the reproductive heterosexual family.[16] Indeed, as McClintock argues, "despite their myriad differences, nations are symbolically figured as domestic genealogies."[17]

Feminist scholars have long argued that the control of women's sexuality and their reproductive power is central to colonial and nationalist projects. In the process, women's bodies become the symbolic markers of the nation. It is also over their bodies (literally and discursively) that national boundaries are drawn and redrawn.[18] The construction of the nation around bodily and familial metaphors suggests its ongoing reliance on and reinforcement of a gender hierarchy, which itself depends on a "natural" (but, ironically, strictly enforced) division of labor between the sexes. Women's bodies, then, are not simply used to embody the nation; they also often figure at the heart (even when invisible) of many national debates and struggles. Indeed, questions about female sexuality, reproductive rights, and respectability have been central to the ongoing process of nation-building and the centering of the male body-citizen within that process. Women thus appear within the discourse of the nation as static symbols upholding and reproducing the active male body-citizen described by Terry and Urla (see note 14).

Within recent political debates in France, however, this virile body is imagined as being assailed by a series of threats from foreign forces that, if not controlled, can weaken and ultimately destroy it. Current dominant representations of the national body, therefore, depend on the othering of a number of human bodies, including, most prominently, postcolonial subjects, women, and homosexuals.

The opposition of the national body as healthy but open to infections, and of all deviant bodies as bearers of infections, creates a dichotomy between health and pathology that is linked with notions of national security and social danger. The displacement of social conflicts (immigration and sexual politics in this case) onto the body has been analyzed as part of a discursive tradition that can be traced to the nineteenth century and that focuses on the "somatic territorializing of deviance." "In this late-twentieth-century form," Terry and Urla argue,

> "the idea that deviance is a matter of somatic essence—having passed through a period of disrepute following the 'excesses' of the Third Reich—has arrived again, through the back door facilitated by moral discourses concerning addiction as well as techniques of genetic engineering, neuroanatomical imaging and virology. In an age of 'compulsive behavior,' killer viruses, and dangerous genes, methods for finding a host of socially and scientifically menacing pathogens inside certain bodies are contributing to the construction of new, biologically demonized under-classes."[19]

This reemergence of the body and biological determinism is somewhat obscured, however, by an ongoing and parallel effort to explain difference and deviancy in terms of culture and religion. The juxtaposition of these two explanatory models of "difference" sheds some light on the continued racist practice of *contrôles au faciés* (identity check based on appearance) and the recurring cultural explanations of the inability of certain immigrants to assimilate and melt into the French crucible.[20]

What you have here, in a nutshell, is the political platform and the imaginary lexicon of the National Front and its outspoken leader, Jean-Marie Le Pen. As we saw in Chapter 4, this extremist message has become normalized and part of a hegemonic discourse about France and the "problem" of immigration. Etienne Balibar links this phenomenon to the emergence of what he sees as a form of "neo-racism."[21] Against the backdrop of a globalizing economy, the formation of the European Community, and the continuing pressures of international migrations, France—like many other European countries—is undergoing a deep national identity crisis. Within such a context, social anxieties about race, class, gender, and sexuality intersect to feed and transform the formation of this neo-racism.

Speaking of the United Kingdom, Anna Marie Smith defines the contours of the neo-racism invoked by Balibar:

> New racist immigration discourse never took the simple form of the defense of geographically fixed borders that protected one biologically defined group from the invasion by another biologically defined group, for it constructed

white-Christian-Englishness as an imaginary cultural space. In addition to its simplistic invasion logic, it organized the immigration crisis around the highly mobile metaphors of leeching, contamination, and subversion. In this manner, the very logic of the new racism prepared the way for the redeployment of its immigration discourse to other sites of contestation around the boundaries of 'normal' white Britishness."[22]

One such site of contestation in France can be found around the public and political discussions of the PaCS. This national form of domestic partnership open to heterosexual as well as homosexual couples was voted into law on October 13, 1999.[23] The empirical focus of this chapter lies in my analysis of the national discussions that have surrounded the passage and promulgation of the PaCS law. In particular, I focus on the National Assembly debates and on the unique contribution of Representative Christine Boutin (a member of the Union for French Democracy—*Union pour la démocratie française*, or UDF), who challenged the PaCS on twelve counts of unconstitutionality.[24] Boutin's thorough and time-consuming efforts (her presentation to the National Assembly lasted more than five hours) failed, but they provide a summary of the conservative and religious anti-PaCS and anti-gay sentiment in France. It is important to note, however, that the opposition to the PaCS involved a wide range of political actors and political parties broadly located within the republican right. In what follows, therefore, I offer an analysis of the ways in which racist and homophobic rhetoric inform the right-wing mainstream opposition to the PaCS.

I identify here two themes around which this national debate can be organized: homosexuality and PaCS as a threat to the family (and by extension as contributing to the "fall" [*décadence*] of France) and homosexuality and PaCS as an open door to illegal immigration. Both themes deploy, albeit in different ways, basic tropes of French anti-immigrant feelings. I conclude the chapter by pointing out some of the limitations of the new PaCS law. I also highlight missed opportunities in France to build broad coalitions that would strategically focus on related discursive and material processes that produce women, queers, and racialized immigrants as impossible subjects of the Republic.

THE PACS DEBATE

The PaCS law was first proposed in the French National Assembly on October 13, 1998.[25] After two round trips between the Assembly and the Senate, several amendments, and tumultuous debates, the law was finally promulgated on

November 10, 1999. The discussion of the text generated a wave of homophobic statements and reactions within the conservative ranks of the French Parliament. Similar reactions emerged from within the French religious right and its grassroots organizations.[26]

The bulk of the right's criticism of the PaCS proposal resides in its opposition to the codification of homosexuality into French law. In particular, conservative deputies underscored the ways in which such codification would eventually destroy both heterosexual marriage and the procreative family. Such criticism must be understood against the backdrop of what some observers have described as a French national identity crisis. For the past forty years, France has experienced deep structural changes brought about by the overall processes of decolonization, globalization, and France's gradual inclusion in the supranational body of the European Community. These profound changes have generated deep anxieties about the meaning of all things French. The ability to maintain and protect a core identity has become a central theme within national debates. Reimagined around blood and filial metaphors, this national identity, needless to say, is dependent on the existence and maintenance of "the French family." The republican family invoked here is heterosexual, monogamous, and civil. It stands as the cornerstone of the French republican edifice.

HOMOSEXUALITY AND PACS: THREAT TO THE FAMILY

"Two mommies or two daddies: we're heading toward disaster!" (Deux mamans ou deux papas: bonjour les dégats!)

Anti-PaCS demonstration in Paris, January 31, 1999

As illustrated by this slogan from an anti-PaCS demonstration, a recurring criticism leveled against the PaCS is that the new law would destroy the heteronormative bourgeois family. Needless to say, this family depends on a strict division of labor between the sexes and on a "natural" order in which the head of the family is male and his "helpmate" is female. It is not surprising, then, to see that Christine Boutin—one of the leaders of the anti-PaCS movement and a conservative Catholic—is also president of the anti-abortion association Right to Life Alliance (*Alliance pour les droits de la vie*). The complex connections between respectable bourgeois sexuality, racism, homophobia, and patriarchal forms of domination that run through these debates are dangerously reminiscent of those underscored by George Mosse in his important study of the construction of German national identity in modern Europe.[27]

Throughout the PaCS parliamentary debates, conservative politicians argued that homosexual unions and parenting would destabilize the traditional family. As a result, first children and then the whole country would suffer. These politicians claimed that, in spite of its false universal appeal (the PaCS is open to both homosexual and heterosexual couples), the basic and hidden goal of the text is to grant homosexual couples rights and duties heretofore extended only to heterosexual couples within the boundaries of civil matrimony. Jacques Kossowski, a member of the National Assembly and of the *Rassemblement pour la République* (Rally for the Republic, or RPR) party, stated on November 7, 1998, "I formally oppose this vision, which negates the role of the biological principle of reproduction and of the natural male-female relation in the legal definition of the couple[. . . .] We must privilege the marital model and its corollary, the family."[28] Kossowski and his colleagues stressed the naturalness (equated here with procreative capacity) and therefore superiority of the heterosexual "marital model," which they then linked to the very foundations of society. Christine Boutin's comments on November 3, 1998, are enlightening:

> It is not within our power here to modify a reality that has existed since the beginning of time, namely the natural relation between man and woman that forms the basis of society and sustains it. With this evidence in mind, societies have always tried to protect this natural and vital relation from what could distort or weaken it. Hence we can explain the rejection of homosexual proselytism and its condemnation to varying degrees that we encounter in all civilizations [. . . .] [Homosexuality] is not written within the frame of non-written laws that establish life within societies[. . . .] Not fecund by nature, it cannot meet the demographic and educational criteria that would entitle it to state protection.[29]

Homosexuality, then, is not natural because it is nonprocreative and therefore unworthy of state recognition and protection. In this contractual vision of the state's duties toward its citizens, homosexual couples are left out. The state needs only to protect the couples who produce its children and provide them with basic educational and socialization skills. The perverse logic of the French (religious) right does not stop here. Not only are homosexual couples not able to "breed" and parent—and therefore not protected under the law—but it is crucial to ensure that they can never do either. It is therefore the very possibility of homosexual procreation and parenting inscribed in the PaCS that needs to be stamped out. Indeed, conservative deputies argued that the PaCS must be opposed because it would eventually open the door to homosexual marriages, homosexual adoptions, and homosexual parenting (whether via artificial in-semination, medically assisted procreation, or adoption).

Christine Boutin recalled the current legal barriers to homosexual adop-tion and artificial insemination and warned the National Assembly that the PaCS "would inevitably lead to [homosexual] parenting (*filiation*) and adop-tion."[30] Citing statements made by several gay and lesbian organizations in favor of homo-parenting, she warned again, "If we adopt today this '*infra-marriage*,' the republican institution of marriage will be profoundly upset or destroyed."[31] Commenting on the new law, Dominique Dord (of the Liberal Democracy—*Démocratie libérale*, or DL, party) suggested that doing away with civil marriage as the legal basis of the family and opening parenting to ho-mosexuals would endanger the well-being and lawful protection of children:

> We would sacrifice then the right of the child to the right to a child, as if
> we did not measure every day the damage generated among many pre- and
> post-adolescents, by the absence of a father's image or by the breakup of fami-
> lies. In a century where everything is possible, even the most unreasonable
> choices, let's not play the apprentice sorcerer; let's not destabilize the funda-
> mental principles of social development and the most powerful symbols of
> our civilization.[32]

Dord starts here with the fear of homosexual parenting and its potentially damaging effects on children, then moves to an apocalyptic level where legal-ized homosexual parenting would lead to the general and global destruction of French society. Such fears are shared by Eric Doligé: "Why would [the leg-islative body] weaken the relationship between man and woman, the origin of society and of its renewal? Can we imagine a society composed of male and female couples? Can someone explain to me how children will be conceived then! [laughter on the left]."[33] Doligé's commentary is interesting because it captures the fantastic quality of the fears generated by the lawful presence of homosexuals within the nation. The French deputy here imagines a French society in which homosexuals have taken over and deprived France of its good reproductive heterosexuals so that it is now unable to renew and sustain it-self.[34] Homosexuality, then, like immigration is presented as not dangerous by itself but rather by its capacity to infiltrate and invade and eventually undo the very fibers of our societal order: "Homosexuality is not a fact that we need to combat, but its propagation and its publicity are."[35] This fear, as shown at the beginning of the chapter, is similar to the fear of immigrants "invading" and

diluting the "French stock" of the nation. In a shocking moment of homophobic lack of restraint, Emmanuel Hamel (of the RPR, Rhône) clearly associated
the PaCS with the notion of AIDS contamination and (male) homosexual
promiscuity. He renamed the PaCS "The Practice of AIDS Contamination"
(*pratique de la contamination sidaïque*).[36] The metaphor of contamination
runs through these debates. It opens up a discursive space for the linkage of
homosexuality and immigration.

Moreover, whether addressing homosexuality or immigration, the question
of who can constitute an acceptable family and who is allowed to reproduce is
of course at the core of this discussion. Christine Boutin helps us see the connection between homophobic and anti-immigrant feelings in this particular
construction of the French family: "Who will prevent cultural communities on
the margins of the Republic from claiming a special contract that would make
licit in France habits and customs that are contrary to our tradition?[...] Is
M. Jospin ready to accept polygamy in France?"[37] Boutin's point here is that
once we open up the legal definition of "family" to include homosexual couples and other duos, we lose the ability to preserve and protect the ideal of a
French marital and heterosexual bourgeois family. The gate is open to even
more dangerous and alien forms of families, such as the polygamous families
that are connected in France with immigrant communities from sub-Saharan
Africa, whose numbers, as we saw in Chapter 4, are often blown out of proportion. The connection between the deviant homosexual family and the deviant
postcolonial immigrant family is reiterated when Boutin, and her allies, claim
that the PaCS, which can be annulled unilaterally by one member of a couple,
introduces the principle of repudiation within French law and practices.

The PaCS should be called indeed the Open Repudiation Union Contract.[38]

You are legalizing repudiation.[39]

As an *infra-marriage*, the PaCS will be undone via an *infra-divorce*. By autho-
rizing a unilateral rupture [of the contract], the PaCS consecrates the insti-
tutionalization of an *infra-marriage* that can be annulled by repudiation—an
idea that, however, *horrifies* us.[40]

Here the idea of "repudiation," which again is associated with Islamic family law, "horrifies us." (Who is this "us" that Boutin claims to be speaking for?)
In a clever (and perverse) appropriation of feminist critiques of unilateral
annulment of matrimonial bonds that traditionally favor men, Boutin inserts

a common theme used to discredit the ability of certain immigrant families to "assimilate" within the French melting pot.

By waving the red flags of polygyny, repudiation, and by extension Islam within France, Boutin clearly and cleverly creates a semantic link between homosexuality, the PaCS, and postcolonial immigrants and the basic threat they pose to the very structure of French society. Having created such a link, there is no need any longer to insert an obvious referent; the dual threat, we now know, is subtly and dangerously established and silently (but powerfully) haunts the discourse of our conservative politicians:

> The PaCS defends the interest of a minority and risks destabilizing society as a whole.[41]

> This text is dangerous for society.[42]

> The model you propose is based on consumerism and violence[. . . .] It is the sign of a will to destroy the bases of society[. . . .] Your new PaCS is simply a return to barbarism. You follow the steps of those who, in order to destroy society, began with the destruction of the family. You are about to do violence to the most established law of our old civilization! You are playing with the very foundations of society! [. . .] The opposition will do all it can to prevent you from demolishing society, the family, and France![43]

> The cycle is irreversible and it is one that leads to decadence.[44]

In these quotes, the ideas of "minority," "danger," "violence," and "decadence" function—without "homosexuality" or "immigration" ever mentioned—as a refrain that continues to imprint and reassert the connections more clearly delineated by Boutin. Renamed "Pact of Social Destruction" (*Pacte de Destructuration Sociale*) by Bernard Accoyer, the PaCS can now be imagined as an evil and dangerous pact between homosexuals, immigrants, and leftist intellectuals who together work toward the subversion of a traditional French society.[45] The republican family rhetoric functions in the PaCS debates as a discursive thread that firmly establishes semantic connections between homosexuality, AIDS, promiscuity, Islam, and postcolonial immigrants. By positing the republican family as a "natural" unit, imagined as heterosexual, monogamous, and civil, opponents of the PaCS build on normalized racist and sexist structures within the French republican state.

The linkage between homosexuality, PaCS, postcolonial immigrants, and the dangers they represent for France is even more clearly established when French deputies begin to discuss Article 6 of the law.[46] This article stipulates that the signing of a PaCS between two individuals "constitutes one of the elements in the appreciation of the personal links" used to establish eligibility for legal entry and sojourn into France. I now highlight the disturbing ways in which the PaCS was often opposed on the grounds that it would create an open gateway to all kinds of fraudulent immigration.

HOMOSEXUALITY AND PACS AS AN OPEN DOOR TO ILLEGAL IMMIGRATION

The PaCS will be considered as a "personal reason" to obtain the right to sojourn: this is equivalent to completely opening our borders to immigration.[47]

The PaCS represents a new blow to the containment of migratory fluxes.[48]

This text is dangerous; I will not come back to Article 6, which as far as foreigners are concerned will open up the possibility for all kinds of abuses.[49]

Boutin and her colleagues, after symbolically linking homosexuality and PaCS to immigration, are now establishing some real material connections between the two. Since the 1970s, French politicians have maintained—at least in theory—the principle that France needs to contain immigration fluxes. In the context of rising unemployment rates and overall economic stress (and with the nationalist right having successfully linked unemployment and immigration in the minds of French people), this has been a "commonsense" and widely popular principle.

By underscoring the threat of uncontrollable immigration, Boutin perversely uses commonplace anti-immigrant feelings to discredit a law that would in fact benefit only a very small number of immigrants: heterosexual and homosexual partners of French nationals. These people have been denied legal entry and residency rights because they do not meet the marital requirement that currently qualifies immigrants for legal entry and long-term residency papers. In Boutin's imagination, immigrants and queers would combine efforts and generate massive fraud: "There will be a black market of fake [*blanc*] PaCS."[50] Here Boutin is directly tapping into the common process of the criminalization of immigrants in France (and elsewhere). Immigrants from France's former colonies as well as those from Eastern Europe are commonly constructed as potential criminals—always prepared to "work the system," cheat their way into undue benefits, and engage in criminal activities. Within such imagined constructions, the existence of the PaCS opens a new legal space within which immigrants can develop their never-ending fraudulent activities:

> This text is dangerous for society. It will lead to multiple forms of fraud.[51]

> Our country cannot afford to make any mistake here. If [the PaCS] gives the impression that the gates are open, it will generate, beyond the Mediterranean, hopes that will be exploited by unscrupulous individuals, who know our laws very well, and usher foreigners into our territory under the conditions that you well know[. . . .] Instead of having fake marriages [*mariages blancs*], we'll have fake PaCS—and it will be so much easier![52]

Goasguen's main focus is somewhat hidden behind his concern for the potential exploitation of immigrants, but a closer reading of his comment clearly demonstrates that Goasguen is simply elaborating on Boutin's fears and persistent stereotypes. The danger is imminent and potentially destructive; "no mistake" is permissible here! Goasguen is also very clear about the geographic location of the danger. It simply lies "beyond the Mediterranean." By invoking the hopeful masses just waiting to flood the gates, the fear of foreign invasion is rearticulated. Moreover, criminality is again associated with immigration by conjuring up notions of traffickers, fraudulent bundles, and black markets. The porous and weak borders of the French nation are now even further weakened by the presence of a law that is presented as a proxy for the open legalization of all forms of immigration within France:

> [We] remain absolutely hostile to the legalization of illegal immigration through the [PaCS].[53]

> [N]othing will prevent a French national to contract three successive PaCS in a year and help legalize three illegal immigrants [*clandestins*].[54]

The number of amendments generated to suppress or weaken Article 6 of the PaCS law reveals the clear connection that is perceived between homosexuality and PaCS and immigration.[55] This imagined connection has produced deep anxieties in the minds of conservative French politicians. These anxieties include, as in Mariani's comment, the fear that activists and intellectuals on the left will engage in collective acts of disobedience (such as those seen around the *sans-papiers* struggle) and help undocumented immigrants by repeatedly forming PaCS with successive partners.

CONCLUSION: THEORETICAL AND POLITICAL IMPLICATIONS

I end this chapter by pointing out the theoretical and political implications of my analysis. First and foremost, it must be noted that the discourses analyzed in this chapter are not innocuous. They create impossible subjects by establishing hierarchies of bodies, sexual practices, cultures, and religions. Once discursively located on the margins of the French citizenry, postcolonial immigrants and queers are "entitled" to different treatments and opportunities, uneven access to rights and civil protections, and unequal claims to social benefits. The demonization of queer and postcolonial subjects lays the ideological foundation for the development of new forms of discrimination that can rob entire segments of French society of the basic civil rights protection to which they are entitled by the constitutional texts of the Republic. Needless to say, discursive practices that construct certain subjects and collectivities as outsiders and threats to the national order also have the potential of legitimating and spurring individual, collective, and state violence against these subjects and collectivities.

With the analysis presented here I also hope to disrupt the naive notion that homophobia, racism, and their complex intersections with other axes of domination generate one-dimensional or simply additive forms of exclusion. Rather, I argue that although they are based on imagined fears, these discourses create "real" but different threats for postcolonial immigrants and queers in France. Queers and postcolonial immigrants inhabit parallel and linked locations within the French republican imaginary. Although there is no denying that there are resistive forces within republican political circles that do not partake in the demonization of either group, it is equally important to underscore the problematic ways in which the processes of demonization and exclusion rearticulate basic tenets of French republican discourse. An uncritical reliance on the notion of the republican family, for instance, on both sides of the debates contributed to the denial to French gays and lesbians of access to adoption and medically assisted procreation.

By and large, lesbian and gay groups in France welcomed the passage of the PaCS law. They saw it as a definite victory in the overall struggle toward equality between homosexual and heterosexual couples in that the text does recognize the existence of nonheterosexual couples and grants them some basic social rights. However, and to varying degrees, they deplored the limitations of the new law and the symbolic message attached to it. The law still denies marriage and parenting to homosexual couples. Few were the PaCS supporters who challenged the racist and anti-immigrant rhetoric used by conservative politicians to fight the passage of the law. Quite rare also are critiques that point out the multiple types of discrimination written into the law. The PaCS Observatory (*Observatoire du PaCS*), which was created after the passage of the law and defines itself as a "collective of associations of future users of the PaCS," did offer such a multifaceted critique, denouncing the following limitations of the law:[56]

- The PaCS does not write into French law equality among all couples— civil marriage is still unavailable to homosexuals.
- The PaCS are registered in court and not at the city hall (like civil marriages).
- The PaCS, unlike marriage, does not grant immediate fiscal benefits. (A three-year waiting period is required before these rights are open. This suggests that certain couples are less legitimate and automatically under suspicion. They need to go through a "probation" period before acquiring certain rights that are automatically granted to married people.)
- When you sign a PaCS, you immediately lose certain social benefits. These social benefits are particularly important for the poor future users of the PaCS. The observatory demands the individualization of these minimal social benefits (*minima sociaux*).[57]
- The PaCS does not grant immediate access to legal residency and, in turn, access to French nationality. Under the current text, the immigration administration is free to determine the personal links and to take a PaCS into consideration or not (an administrative memorandum gives specific directives on how to handle this particular issue).[58]
- The PaCS does not create a family and therefore does not give homosexual couples access to adoption or medically assisted procreation.

What is interesting about the Observatory is its coalitional basis. It involves queer, feminist, and immigrant groups, as well as organizations working on basic social welfare issues. All of them are interested in broadening the definitions of *couple, marriage,* and *family.* All of them are interested in broadening social coverage and rethinking the bases on which these benefits are granted. All of them are interested in translating formal rights into concrete benefits for excluded individuals and groups.[59]

CONCLUSION

AS THE RIOTS that set Paris *banlieues* on fire in November 2005 graphically demonstrate, France is still in crisis. This book has analyzed the varied meanings of the crisis. In particular, it has looked at the ways in which immigration and immigrants themselves have emerged as privileged scapegoats for France's lingering trouble. My analysis builds from the commonly noted fact that for the past forty years immigration has been highly politicized and constructed as a "problem" for the French nation and its people. For those who believe in or propagate such scenarios, national cohesion, cultural identity, economic health, and more recently security are threatened by the very presence of certain immigrants.[1]

By focusing on the gender underpinnings of the *sans-papiers* movement and of immigration politics in France, *Reinventing the Republic* has taken this insight further. It insists that women (and gender) are central figures within the reductive and dangerous scenario that posits certain immigrants at the heart of the French trouble. It also demands that we look at the often missed linkages between processes that position individuals and whole communities outside the reach of democratic inclusion. In the process, the book makes three different but related points about the question of immigration in France. First, it demonstrates that certain immigrants have been rendered much more vulnerable through the tightening of French immigration (and nationality) laws and through new forms of racialization of immigration and certain immigrant communities. Throughout I have argued that gender is a key element within both processes. As a result, although all racialized immigrants have come to experience great levels of civil and economic *précarité*, women and the children who depend on them experience these new conditions in different (specifically gendered) ways. Second, by focusing on (trans)national economic forces that shape the current realities of immigrants—with or without papers—the book explores the ways in which class relations in France (as well as in the European Community), are remapped along racial and ethnic and gender lines. These economic forces, I have argued, tend to be obfuscated when the troubles that ail the Republic are simply reduced to those brought about by unwelcome others. Finally, the book documents how the *sans-papiers* are appropriating and transforming (reinventing) notions of democracy, citizenship, and republican belonging. Women involved in the struggle have been active participants—often leaders—in these transformative interventions. Whether we like it or not, immigrants and their children—even undocumented ones— are actively engaged in the construction of new republican traditions.

Moreover, *Reinventing the Republic* explores the ways in which France treats and constructs subjects whose identity and strategies for claiming rights offend its universalist sensibility. The book is part of my ongoing effort at understanding and theorizing the multiple ways in which material and discursive forces produce subjectivities, and how subjects in turn transform social relations, personal and collective identities, and politico-cultural practices. Against the backdrop of global economic transformations, the construction of Europe, and increased national anxieties, the book documents how hegemonic discursive and material practices in France construct immigrants and other social actors as outside the reach of the democratic process. The book highlights contradictions within and between three contemporary political struggles (*Sans-papiers*, *Parité*, and PaCS). Within these sites of contestation, various actors borrow central tropes of the Republic to speak back and create spaces for alternative and irreverent subjectivities and politics. The book cannot do justice to all three struggles, but it underscores noteworthy points of connection between them. Throughout I have suggested that missing such linkages unfortunately renders coalitional work difficult within the French context.

In this book I have asserted the possibility—even in France—of political agencies framed outside of binary thinking, which demands that rights claims be based either on the principle of universal equality or on the corrective treatment deserved by subjugated communities. As I have shown in Chapter 2, organizing around an identity of "lack" not only reveals such conundrums but also anchors rights claims in the discursive and material processes that locate individuals and groups within particular social and symbolic spaces of impossibility. Following the lead of the *sans-papières*, I argue that we can work with and against the Republic to reveal its shortcomings and embrace its radical potentials. At the very least, we can use its idiom to imagine ourselves differently and disrupt the mechanisms that distinguish us from others and, in the process, create social rankings and inequalities. Throughout I have suggested that it is only when we fully recognize the intersecting ways in which "impossible subjects" are created that we can begin to envision a politics of inclusion, hospitality, and universal humanity. Such politics, I argue, can rely not on old notions of abstract subjects but rather on concrete and socially located ones.

In 2005 Nicolas Sarkozy, then minister of the interior, described the young men involved in the unruly politics of street rioting as scum (*racaille*). He also proposed to rid the *banlieues* of these troubling elements with a Kärcher (the brand-name of a high-powered hose used to wash off resistant street filth and graffiti).[2] In 2007, after campaigning on a political platform that called for the tightening of immigration policy and the promotion of "chosen" migration (*immigration choisie*), which favors economic migration over family reunification, Nicolas Sarkozy won his election bid and became president of the Republic. In October of the same year, the French Parliament codified genetic testing for immigration purposes into law.[3] Under the Hortefeux Law, DNA tests may be used by immigration candidates to prove a blood relation with a French person or a legal resident when applying for a long-term visa (for more than three months) under the legal provision of family reunification.

Although the human rights weaknesses and the racist effects of the new law have been discussed at length in France, very little attention has been directed toward the gender and sexual implications of a law that focuses, after all, on blood, bloodlines, and descent. As I have shown in Chapter 6, the impulse to exclude certain families from the French nation can be traced to the debates surrounding French civil unions and, more specifically, to what the French call *homoparentalité* (the capacity for queers to become parents, in particular through artificial insemination and adoption). The parliamentary debates that preceded the passage of the PaCS clearly demonstrate a strong attachment to heteronormative family structures within republican France. It is also interesting to note here that directly after the 2005 riots, Sarkozy and other voices on the right blamed polygamous families for the violent behavior of African male youths from the *banlieues*. As Eric Fassin judiciously comments about the law in a 2007 article, when the right of blood (*le droit du sang*) takes over, not only do we anchor dangerous forms of racialization, but we also reaffirm the myth of a national (and I would add patriarchal and heteronormative) family bound by blood, descent, and DNA.[4] Against such assertions, *sans-papiers* and *sans-papières* continue to battle in France by reiterating their right to live and work in France in "broad daylight."

Reinventing the Republic contends that gender is constitutive of the processes of immigration, racial formation, national identity, economic restructuring, globalization, and political representation. In the French context, this theoretical insight helps us see the contradictions that lie at the core of the Republic. Overall, *Reinventing the Republic* takes seriously the haunting presence of gender in the rhetoric of immigration in France. In particular, it asks that we think about discourses of family, mothering, and reproduction as part and parcel of French postcolonial and racial projects. This is particularly important because in France an emphasis on republican universalism and historical amnesia about the colonial past have until recently prevented thorough scholarly interrogations of these fruitful intersections.

As France continues to struggle with its national identity and its position in a global economy, the figures of the veiled Muslim girl, the Eastern European

Figure C.1 *Sans-papières* drumming and chanting, Porte St. Denis, Paris. Photo by C. Raissiguier.

laborer, the lesbian mother, and the polygamous father trouble the French universalist imagination. The *sans-papiers'* refusal to go away and their bold challenge to the logic that allows their entry in order to exclude them turns the notion of French egalitarianism based on universal rights on its head and help us envision subversive reconfigurations of the French Republic.

REFERENCE MATTER

APPENDIX

The Legal Construction of the *Sans-papiers* in France
(Laws, Decrees, and Administrative Memoranda),
1970–2006

1972 The Marcellin-Fontanet circulars (January 23 and 24, 1972) end the possibility of becoming a legal immigrant through a change of status (partially annulled by the *Conseil d'État* in 1975).

1974 On July 3, 1974, the Council of Ministers (*Conseil des Ministres*) suspends work immigration (except for certain categories of immigrants as stipulated by myriad bilateral agreements). This marks an end to the free circulation for workers from sub-Saharan Africa.

1980 The Bonnet Law of January 10, 1980, makes illegal entry and illegal sojourn grounds for deportation. It also legalizes the practice of "retention" for foreigners in instances of deportation.

1981 Socialist François Mitterand is elected president of the Republic.

1981 The law of October 29, 1981, prohibits forced deportations via administrative channels (only correctional judges can issue a deportation sentence). It also protects—except when they present a threat to state security—certain categories of immigrants from deportation (youths and persons with familial links in France).

1984 The law of July 17, 1984, creates the single residency/work card, valid for ten years and automatically renewable. Establishes automatic right (*plein droit*) to the single card for protected categories of immigrants. "Protected" immigrants—including youths who entered France before the age of ten, spouses of French nationals, parents of French children, veterans of French wars, retired workers receiving French pension benefits, persons who have legally resided in France for ten years, and so on—cannot be deported. Georgina Dufoix, in charge of the immigration dossier (as Secretary of

State under the Mauroy government and as Minister under the Fabius government), implements the first restrictions to familial reunification (the procedure must be initiated in the country of origin and becomes contingent on financial, housing, and health requirements).

1985   A Franco-Algerian agreement ends the privileged immigration status of Algerian immigrants established by the Evian treaty.

1986   The first Pasqua law reestablishes "administrative" deportations, limits to a consultative role the power of the Deportation Commission, and limits the automatic acquisition and renewal of the single residency card. It also establishes visas for all entrants (does not apply to European Economic Community residents) and limits family reunification according to housing and financial resources. It establishes the practice of random identity checks (*contrôle au faciès*).

1991   The Rocard government formalizes the already existing practice of requesting "hosting certificates" for legal entry (visitors and immigrants have to prove that they have a place to stay in France) and suppresses work permits for asylum seekers.

1993   The second Pasqua law limits to a mere consultative role the power of the Sojourn Commission, which functioned as a legal buffer between immigrants and the French administration. It increases to two years (instead of one) the length of legal residency before a request for family reunification can be filed. It includes a minimum of personal financial resources, as well as housing requirements for familial reunification, and lets the *préfecture* evaluate these resources by requesting the recommendation of the mayors as to where the immigrant family will reside (the first time that mayors are given this role in the assessment of family reunification requests). It increases the difficulty for certain children of foreign parents, students, and spouses of French nationals to obtain residency cards. It introduces the invalidation or nonrenewal of the single residency/work card to immigrants when they practice polygamy, lack adequate resources, have introduced family members outside the boundaries of family reunification, or present a threat to public order. It makes legal entry and current legal status prerequisites for the acquisition of residency papers.

1996   The law of July 22, 1996, criminalizes the act of offering help or shelter to illegal aliens.

1997   The Debré law institutes the "temporary sojourn card" for those categories of immigrants who cannot have access to the single residency card. It facilitates procedures for and lengthens the retention of illegal immigrants. Strong popular opposition defeated part of the project that requested that the host of a recent immigrant notify French authorities when she or he has stayed beyond the visa expiration date.

June 1, 1997 President Jacques Chirac dissolves the national assembly. Parliamentary elections are held and the plural left (*gauche plurielle*) wins the election. A second period of cohabitation starts with socialist Lionel Jospin at the head of the government.

1997 The Chevènnement administrative memorandum calls for the regularization of the *sans-papiers* along twelve criteria. Each case file will be reviewed independently according to these criteria.

1998 The Chevènnement law of May 11, 1998, also referred to as Reseda (which regulates the entry and sojourn of foreigners in France and the right to asylum— *Relative à l'entrée et au séjour des étrangers en France et au droit d'asile*), formalizes the Chevènnement administrative memorandum into law. The law makes it easier for certain categories of immigrants to receive residence cards. Requires that the administration justify a negative answer to a visa request. It also codifies the notion of "familial and private life" into French immigration law. It decreases to one year (instead of two since 1993) the length of legal residency before a request for family reunification can be filed. Limits the arbitrary power of the *préfecture* in assessing financial resources necessary for familial reunification. It replaces "housing certificates" with a simple declaration from the hosts. It creates specific measures for retired immigrants. It institutes the regularization of long-term residents (ten-year residency requirement).

May 5, 2002 Presidential election, The "Le Pen effect" ensures the overwhelming victory of Jacques Chirac.

2003 The Sarkozy law of November 26, 2003, increases from three to five years the duration of legal and uninterrupted sojourn in France before a ten-year residency card may be requested. The delivery of the ten-year residency card is now subordinated to the requirement of "republican integration." The law eliminates the 1984 provision that granted rejoining family members the same card as the legal resident (often a ten-year residency card). Now joining family members are granted a one-year temporary sojourn card. They will be able to request the ten-year residency card only after two years of legal sojourn in France. Housing certificates are reinstated. Minimum wage is required for family reunification. Resources are evaluated at the communal level by the mayor (the *préfecture* still makes the final decision). Sojourn papers can be removed if the familial link is severed by separation or divorce for up to two years (instead of one year until then) after issuance of papers. The law allows for the removal of legal residency papers from those who introduced family members outside the boundary of family reunification (a throwback to the Pasqua law of 1993; long-term residents are, however, protected from this new sanction). It increases to two years the period of communal living required before the temporary sojourn card can be replaced by a ten-year residency card to the foreign spouse of a French national. (Sojourn papers can be renewed, in spite of separation, in the case of domestic violence.) The period of potential administrative retention is increased from twelve to thirty-two days.

2006   The Sarkozy law of July 24, 2006, requires long-term visas for all would-be immigrants (outside the European Union). It offers sojourn and work papers to highly qualified immigrants. It increases from twelve to eighteen months the period of legal sojourn before a legal resident can submit a family reunification request. Minimum resources for family reunification cannot include familial allocation. The law increases to three years the period of communal living before the foreign spouse of a French national can request a ten-year residency card. New immigrants must sign "integration contracts." It eliminates the automatic renewal of the ten-year residency card and scraps the ten-year residency regularization provision included in the Reseda (Chevènnement) law.

May 16, 2007   Nicolas Sarkozy is elected president of the French Republic.

NOTES

Preface

1. French *banlieues* are more similar to inner cities than to suburbs in the United States. They are geographically located on the outskirts of larger urban centers. Immigrant families are overrepresented in the *banlieues*, which stand as blatant signs of *fracture sociale*—the deep structural inequalities (economic, educational, cultural) that are now experienced by people living in France. Parisian *banlieues* were the site of social unrest and rioting in the fall of 2005 and again in November 2007.

2. I spent a month (January 1 to January 31, 2002) in Marseilles collecting ethnographic data on the *sans-papiers* who were active in the Marseilles-region collectives. I also spent two months (February 1 to March 31, 2002) in Paris gathering ethnographic data on the *sans-papiers* involved in the Paris region collectives. Finally, I spent three months (April 1 to June 30, 2002) alternately in Marseilles and Paris conducting follow-up interviews with the *sans-papiers*.

3. Drawing from the work of Mae M. Ngai, Lisa Lowe, Lisa Duggan, and Sabah Chaïb, among others, I examine narratives as political and cultural interventions embedded in concrete institutions such as the law, academia, social services, and the media. Mae M. Ngai, *Impossible Subjects: Illegal Aliens and the Making of Modern America*; Lisa Duggan, *Sapphic Slashers: Sex, Violence, and American Modernity*; Sabah Chaïb, *Facteurs d'insertion et d'exclusion des femmes immigrantes dans le marché du travail en France: Quel état des connaissances?*; and Lisa Lowe, *Immigrant Acts: On Asian American Cultural Politics*.

4. For two analytical reviews of this scholarship, see Anne Golub, Mirjana Morokvasik, and Catherine Quiminal, "Evolution de la production des connaissances sur les femmes immigrées en France et en Europe"; and Chaïb, *Facteurs d'insertion*.

5. A notable exception is the collected volume *Women, Immigration and Identities in France*, edited by Jane Freedman and Carrie Tarr, which looks at ideological

constructs and addresses the ways in which gender and race intersect both in dominant representations of immigrant women and in their self-representations. See also, in French, Nacira Guénif-Souilamas, *Des 'Beurettes' aux descendants d'immigrants Nord-Africains*; and Nacira Guénif-Souilamas and Eric Massé, *Les féministes et le garçon arabe*.

6. *Sans-papières*, the feminine form of *sans-papiers*, is a term that the women involved in the movement have used to describe themselves. By challenging proper French grammatical form, these undocumented women embrace feminist linguistic practices that are now common in France.

7. Madjiguène Cissé, *Parole de sans-papiers*; Jane Freedman, *Immigration and Insecurity in France*; and Claudie Lesselier, "Femmes migrantes en France: Le genre et la loi." For partisan analyses of the struggle, see IM'média/reflex, *Chroniques d'un movement: Sans-papiers*; and Etienne Balibar, et al., *Sans-papiers: L'archaïsme fatal*. For an excellent sociopolitical analysis of sans-papiers struggles in France, see Johanna Siméant, *La cause des sans-papiers*. For personal accounts of the struggle, see Mamadi Sané, *"Sorti de l'ombre": Journal d'un sans-papiers*; Ababacar Diop, *Dans la peau d'un sans-papiers*; and Cissé, *Parole*.

8. Joan Wallach Scott, *Parité! Sexual Equality and the Crisis of French Universalism*; Enda McCaffrey, *The Gay Republic: Sexuality, Citizenship, and Subversion in France*.

Introduction

1. Third-country nationals are would-be immigrants who do not belong to other European Union countries.

2. Scholarly writing in France has contributed to this hegemonic narrative. Comparative studies help shed light on the enduring role of national intellectual traditions in shaping explanatory models and policy decisions. See in particular Adrian Favell, *Philosophies of Integration*; and Sandra Lavenex, "National Frames in Migration Research." Lavenex, for instance, looks at the discursive frames of reference that guide immigration research in France and Germany. She argues that, ironically and in contradistinction to commonly held views, ethnocultural concerns are more common in French discussions of "assimilation" and "integration."

3. Adrian Favell, *Philosophies of Integration*, 43.

4. Ibid., xvi–xvii.

5. The concept of *précarité* (precarity) has been used mostly in Europe to describe a social condition that lacks predictability and security and endangers a person's well-being. The term has been used to describe new labor conditions under globalization and their attendant social precariousness.

6. Sophie Wahnich, *L'impossible citoyen*; Ngai, *Impossible Subjects*. By focusing on South Asian politics in the United States, Gayatri Gopinah analyzes the mechanisms

that elide the possibility of a South Asian queer female subjectivity within dominant nationalist and diasporic discourses. See *Impossible Desires: Queer Diasporas and South Asian Public Culture.*

7. Wahnich, *L'impossible citoyen.*

8. Ibid., 81. Throughout, translations from French to English are mine unless indicated otherwise.

9. Ibid., 123.

10. Ngai, *Impossible Subjects,* 4–5.

11. Gopinah, *Impossible Desires,* 16.

12. Monisha Das Gupta, *Unruly Immigrants: Rights, Activism, and Transnational South Asian Politics in the United States.*

13. Ibid., 2.

14. Ibid., 16. For a discussion of the ways in which *sans-papiers* in France have used European Union structures to stake their claims, see Stephen Castles and Alastair Davidson, *Citizenship and Migration: Globalization and the Politics of Belonging.*

15. Texts that promote these ideas in France and elsewhere are too numerous to list here. For prominent ones, see Gérard Noiriel, *Le creuset français: Histoire de l'immigration XIXe–XXe siècle*; Patrick Weil, *La France et ses étrangers: L'aventure d'une politique de l'immigration de 1938 à nos jours*; Dominique Schnapper, *La France de l'intégration: Sociologie de la nation en 1990*; and Rogers Brubaker, *Citizenship and Nationhood in France and Germany.* Adrian Favell offers an interesting critique of the French republican hegemonic frame in his *Philosophies of Integration.*

16. See Françoise Gaspard, Claude Servan-Schreiber, and Anne Le Gall, *Au pouvoir, citoyennes! Liberté, égalité, parité*; Élianne Viennot, "Les femmes d'Etat de l'Ancien Régime"; and Joan Wallach Scott, *Only Paradoxes to Offer: French Feminists and the Rights of Man.*

17. See Brubaker, *Citizenship and Nationhood in France and Germany*; Weil, *La France et ses étrangers*; and especially Gérard Noiriel, "La nationalité au miroir des mots." See also Michel Wieviorka, *Une société fragmentée? Le multiculturalisme en débat*; and Alec Hargreaves, *Immigration, 'Race' and Ethnicity in Contemporary France.*

18. Noiriel, "La nationalité au miroir des mots."

19. For a historical account of the ways in which gender, class, and racial inequalities constituted citizenship in the U.S. context, see Evelyn Nakano Glenn, *Unequal Freedom: How Race and Gender Shaped American Citizenship and Labor.*

20. For a thorough analysis of the parity movement in English, see Scott, *Parité!* For the founding text of the movement in France, see Gaspard, Servan-Schreiber, and Le Gall, *Au pouvoir, citoyennes!*

21. *Manifeste des "577" pour une démocratie paritaire.* This manifesto was produced by the *Réseau femmes pour la parité* (a network of women parity activists). It appeared in Supplément 1 of *Parité Info* (the publication of the parity movement)

in the spring of 1993 and achieved national visibility when it was published in *Le Monde* in November 1993. The manifesto bears the signatures of 289 *citoyennes* (female citizens) accompanied by 288 signatures of *citoyens* (male citizens) (a total of 577 signatures) who associated themselves with this initiative. The number of signatures is important here. The French national assembly holds 577 seats and stands as the symbolic heart of democratic representation in France. The number 577 then symbolically renders visible what parity democracy would look like if it truly existed in France. In a national assembly with equal representation for women and men, one would indeed find 289 representatives of one gender and 288 of the other. See http://multitudes.samizdat.net/spip.php?article736.

22. For a discussion of France's opposition to Anglo-Saxon multiculturalism and communitarianism and of the way this rejection often frames conversations about rights claims made by various sectors of French civil society, see Scott, *Parité!*

23. Ibid., 5.

24. For a review of parity critics within France, see Scott, *Parité!* 66–73.

25. For an overall review of these criticisms and a discussion of the backlash, see McCaffrey, *The Gay Republic*, 45–74. For a different take on the backlash and an important discussion of the particular role played by French philosopher Sylviane Agacinski in the essentialist turn in the parity movement, see also Scott, *Parité!* 100–123.

26. Scott, *Parité!* 119.

27. See McCaffrey, *The Gay Republic*. Interestingly, this is not unlike Scott's argument about the inscription of the principle of gender equality through the *Parité* legislation.

28. *Pour l'égalité sexuelle* was published in *Le Monde* on June 26, 1999. It received the support of an array of intellectuals and organizations, including ACT UP, Aides Fédération, Aides Ile-de-France, Sida Info Service, SOS Homophobie, and others.

29. Linda Bosniak, *The Citizen and the Alien*, 1.

30. Aihwa Ong, "Cultural Citizenship as Subject-Making," 737.

31. For a similar argument calling for citizenship on the grounds of residence (in the specific case of voting rights for foreign residents), see Saïd Bouamama, *J'y suis, J'y vote.*

32. See David Jacobson, *Rights Across Borders: Immigration and the Decline of Citizenship*; Saskia Sassen, "Immigration Policy in a Global Economy"; and Yasemin Soysal, *Limits of Citizenship.*

Chapter 1

1. Sans-Papiers, "Manifeste des sans-papiers," originally published in *Libération* on February 25, 1997. The full text of the manifesto is available online at http://bok.net/pajol/film.html#texte. It is important to note here that this site is not the

official *sans-papiers* Web site. Volunteers who maintain the site clearly stipulate that the *sans-papiers* are present on the Web in a variety of locations and sites. This attests to the plurality and autonomy of the movement. The *Pajol* site, however, has existed since July 1996 and offers recent updates on the movement in both France and Europe (http://pajol.eu.org) as well an archive of the French movement from 1996 to 2000 (http://bok.net/pajol). It is an excellent online resource on the movement.

2. For a critical engagement with the term *postcolonial*, see Ella Shohat, "Notes on the 'Post-Colonial'"; Anne McClintock, "The Angel of Progress: Pitfalls of the Term 'Post-Colonialism'"; Ruth Frankenberg and Lata Mani, "Crosscurrents, Crosstalk: Race, 'Postcoloniality' and the Politics of Location"; Karen Kaplan, Norma Alarcón, and Minoo Moallem, eds., *Between Woman and Nation: Nationalisms, Transnational Feminisms, and the State.* Here I use *postcolonial* to signify that France has now lost most of its former colonies but has maintained strong neocolonial links. The breakup of the French colonial world and the emergence of global capitalism have created the conditions for the massive immigration of people from France's former colonies. The term also signals that in France a host of postcolonial subjects has now come to occupy a very vulnerable position within the social order. The presence, settlement, and precarious status of these postcolonial subjects within French metropolitan borders are posing serious challenges to France's republican foundational promise of universal inclusion and equality.

In France, *immigrant* is defined as a person born non-French in a foreign country who now lives in France. Following this definition, immigrants can be either nationals or nonnationals. In 1990, two-thirds of immigrants had kept their nationality of origin and one-third had acquired the French nationality.

3. Collectives (*collectifs*) are autonomous groups of individuals who organize around a particular set of demands—in this case, the regularization of undocumented immigrants, the repeal of certain immigration laws, and so on.

4. In Paris, the Saint-Bernard and Saint-Hyppolyte collectives organized around the occupation of a public space and limited their membership to a closed list of case files (three hundred in the case of Saint-Bernard). The third collective, which bears that name (*Le troisième collectif*), followed the first two Parisian collectives but maintained an open membership. All *Sans-papiers* in need of representation were welcome to join. In the summer of 1996, the third collective represented more than thirty nationalities and had collected fourteen hundred case files. Chinese and other Asian immigrants appeared in the *sans-papiers'* struggle within the formation of the third collective. The movement also spread to the outskirts of Paris and eventually to the rest of the country. On July 20, 1996, the first national coordination of the *sans-papiers* collectives was created and met at the *Bourse du travail* in Paris.

5. Madjiguène Cissé, "The Sans-Papiers: A Woman Draws the First Lessons." The Democratic Republic of the Congo was called Zaïre between 1971 and 1997.

6. For a thumbnail summary of these texts, see the Appendix. For a regularly updated guide to French immigration laws, see Groupe d'information et de solidarité aux travailleurs immigrés, *Le guide de l'entrée et du séjour des étrangers en France*. For a brief overview of French immigration politics, see Philippe Bernard, *L'immigration: Les enjeux de l'intégration*. For more detailed discussions, see Weil, *La France et ses étrangers*; Danièle Lochak, *Étrangers: De quel droit?*; and the exhaustive Vincent Viet, *La France immigrée: Construction d'une politique 1914–1997*.

7. The Pasqua laws were passed in 1993 under the leadership of then Interior Minister Charles Pasqua and his minister of justice (*garde des sceaux*), Pierre Méhaignerie. They reformed the nationality code and modified the Order of November 2, 1945, which has provided the foundational structure of immigration laws in France since World War II. Charles Pasqua's tough stance on immigration and his impossible and therefore dangerous call for "zero immigration" set the tone for the toughening of immigration laws and the repressive stance against undocumented immigrants that led in part to the *sans-papiers* crisis of 1996. The Pasqua laws included the tightening of visa requirements and led to increasing police identity checks and a narrowing of protective measures for immigrants and refugees. For a critique of the Pasqua laws, see Sami Naïr, *Contre les lois Pasqua*. I discuss French immigration laws at greater length in Chapter 3.

8. Sans-Papiers, "Manifeste."

9. The *déboutés du droit d'asile*, a total of 117 from among the 300 Saint-Bernard case files, were the "weakest" of all the files presented to the Minister of the Interior. For the most part they were single men from Mali who had exhausted all legal channels in the effort to obtain a change of status, which could now be granted only through an exceptional measure of the French government. A case file is the narrative along with accompanying documents that a *sans-papiers* provides to the French administration in order to obtain a change of status. Immigrants themselves, French allies, NGOs, and sometimes lawyers participate in the construction of these narratives.

10. See Brun and Laacher, "De la régularisation à l'intégration"; Gérard Neyrand, "Le suivi social des étrangers régularisés au titre de la circulaire de 24 Juin 1997"; Roza Cealis et al, "Immigration clandestine: La régularisation des travailleurs 'sans-papiers' (1981–1982)."

11. In two volumes recently published by the Institut national de la statistique et des études économiques, *Les femmes* and *Les immigrés en France*, a total of four pages focus on immigrant women per se. In fact, the volume on immigrants does not have a segment specifically about women. Data on women must be gleaned from the volume's sections on family and couples.

12. The exact numbers of successful case files from the 1997 procedure are difficult to come by. One study published by the Institut national d'études démographiques claimed that the actual numbers could range between 87,000 and 100,000, and that the rate of successful change of status could be as high as 74 percent. See Xavier Thiery,

"Les entrées d'étrangers en France: Evolutions statistiques et bilan de l'opération de régularisation exceptionnelle de 1997." For obvious (but different) political reasons, both state representatives and activists tend to rely on more conservative figures. It is also important to note that the criteria used to evaluate each case file have changed over time and point in the direction of key transformations within the population of undocumented immigrants in France. In 1981 the main criteria used were stability of employment and length of stay in France, pointing out the clear focus on the immigrant as worker. In 1987 to 1988 the criteria for legalization were multiplied to respond to the changed nature of immigration in France. Notably, they also included "private and family life" to address the right of individuals to live with their families, and "territorial asylum" to address—as in the case of Algerian nationals suffering from a specific form of nonstate political persecution—dramatic situations not yet recognized by traditional asylum law.

13. It has been pointed out that *sans-papiers* have historically used hunger strikes to help focus national attention on their plight. See Siméant, *La cause des sans-papiers*; and Mogniss H. Abdallah, "Les sans-papiers, d'hier à aujourd'hui, pour une mémoire collective de l'immigration."

14. Siméant, *La cause des sans-papiers*, 92. This point was also made by Claudie Lesselier (interview on file with author).

15. Madjiguène Cissé, "Sans-Papiers: Un combat pour les droits de l'homme."

16. The priest of the Saint-Ambroise parish demanded that the French authorities remove the *sans-papiers* from his church. In the early stages of the movement, although each *sans-papiers* did have to constitute a case file, the call of the movement was a change of status for all undocumented immigrants.

17. For a detailed chronology of the movement, see Cissé, *Parole*, 245–249.

18. For an interesting discussion of French republicanism and racism, see Michèle Lamont, *The Dignity of Working Men: Morality and the Boundaries of Race, Class, and Immigration*, 186–194. For a feminist critique of the French republican tradition, see Catherine Raissiguier, "Gender, Race, and Exclusion: A New Look at the French Republican Tradition."

19. Sans-Papiers, "Manifeste."

20. Jean Marie LePen is the leader of the *Front national* (National Front party).

21. Sans-Papiers, "Manifeste."

22. Republican *marrainages* and *parrainages* appeared in 1998 and 1999. The *marrainage* organized by the RAJFIRE (*Réseau pour L'autonomie juridique des femmes réfugiées/ immigrées*, or Network for the Legal Autonomy of Immigrant and Refugee Women) was staged on June 6, 1999. Comments provided by Claudie Lesselier (interview on file with author).

23. The petition was signed by Pierre Bourdieu and Étienne Balibar, among many others. Cissé, *Parole*, 245.

24. Stéphane Hessel, French ambassador and spokesperson for the mediators, quoted in IM'média/reflex, *Chroniques d'un movement: Sans-papiers*, 17. The quote (which has been translated here) is from the documentary *La ballade des sans-papiers* (directed by Samir Abdallah and Raffaele Ventura), which chronicles the movement from the occupation of Saint-Ambroise to the forced removal from Saint-Bernard. The demand for the legalization of all undocumented immigrants and refugees did not, however, meet with the support of a segment of The Left and several antiracist associations.

25. The *collège des médiateurs* was composed of French intellectuals, jurists, human rights activists, and representatives of the clergy. According to these criteria, *sans-papiers* can rightfully claim a change of status if they are: (1) parents of French children; (2) spouses or established partners of French nationals; (3) spouses or children of a legal resident; (4) parents of children born in France; (5) asylum seekers (whose claims have been denied) who entered France before January 1, 1993; (6) closely linked to a legal resident (brother, sister, parent); (7) mentally or physically ill and their departure would interrupt a medical treatment; (8) in danger if they return to their home country; (9) students currently enrolled in a course of study; or (10) individuals successfully integrated into French society.

26. Besides receiving overwhelming support from progressive French intellectuals and artists, the *sans-papiers* also secured the support of French labor organizations, leftist parties and organizations, and wide segments of the French population. A CSA-*Le Parisien* poll indicated that 50 percent of the French population supported the *sans-papiers* and their cause. See Sylvain Salaün, "Régularisations: Retour sur un mouvement en devenir," 6.

27. Cissé, "The Sans-Papiers: First Lessons," 3.

28. Emphasis added. Jean-Pierre Allaux, *Groupe d'information et de solidarité aux travailleurs immigrés* (GISTI). Quoted in Commission immigration Scalp-Reflex, "Quand le sage montre la lune, l'imbécile regarde le doigt," 63.

29. Ibid.

30. See in particular "Les fluctuations d'une cause hérétiques," 157–221.

31. Ibid. In 1996, Jean-Louis Debré, then interior minister, proposed a text of law that removed basic human rights protection in the case of an immigrant's expulsion from the French territory. It also made it mandatory for people to inform their local authorities (*mairies*) when a foreign guest on a tourist visa left his or her home or overstayed his or her welcome. Charles Pasqua, Debré's predecessor, had earlier put into law an already existing practice (instituted during the socialist government of Pierre Mauroy in 1982), requesting that any visa required for a family visit be accompanied by a hosting certificate delivered from and approved by the city hall of the municipality in which the host family resided. Siméant remarks that both the temporal coincidence of Debré's proposed text and the National Front victory in the municipal

elections of the southern town of Vitrolles contributed to the success of the mobiliza-tion. A petition launched by a group of filmmakers garnered thousands of signatures and led to the massive demonstration of February 22, 1997, that rallied more than a hundred thousand persons in the streets of the French capital. According to Siméant, both events provided a venue for French progressive political actors to display publicly their opposition to the right and the far right. The *Conseil d'État*, France's highest administrative court, found the proposed text unconstitutional. The court criticized the text mainly for its attack on individual freedom and the right to privacy. Redrafted and toned down, the text was voted into law on April 24, 1997.

32. Cissé, "The Sans-Papiers: The First Lessons," 3.

33. Ibid.

34. Cissé, *Parole*, 140. Pajol is an unused railway site made available to the *sans-papiers* by the CFDT.

35. Ibid.

36. Cissé, "The Sans-Papiers: The First Lessons," 3.

37. Ibid., 4.

38. Ibid., 4.

39. Claudie Lesselier noted that they did use the space for meetings (interview on file with author).

40. Cissé, *Parole*, 141.

41. Cissé, "The Sans-Papiers: The First Lessons," 4.

42. Sharon Dubois and Martin Benoit, "The Sans Papiers Success."

43. Comments provided by Claudie Lesselier (interview on file with author).

44. Johanna Siméant lists more than ten hunger strikes between 1972 and 1996 that involved women. Among these, only one other strike was initiated, in 1981, by two immigrant women. They were then joined by three French allies (*La cause*, 464).

45. There have been reports of violence against women within some of the col-lectives and at least one report of sexual harassment in one of the retention centers. These centers, which "house" *sans-papiers* awaiting deportation, do not have separate women's facilities. One Moroccan woman was harassed by the French police in one of these centers. See Libération, "Une sans-papier harcelée de 'câlins' policiers."

46. Cissé, quoted in Abdallah and Ventura, *La ballade*, 17.

47. See Cissé, *Parole*, 11–38 and 185–206.

48. The *sans-papiers* have made strong and interesting connections with these other have-not groups that in the recent past have also emerged as political actors (such as *Droit devant!* [Right Ahead!], *Droit au logement* [Housing Rights, or DAL], and *Agir ensemble contre le chômage* [Acting Together Against Unemployment, or AC!]). Together they form coalitions to address the general question of social exclu-sion in France. For an interesting discussion of these connections, see Abdallah, "Les sans-papiers."

49. This focus on the family within some collectives (the Saint-Hyppolyte collective, for instance) is complicated and worth examining in terms of some of its unexpected effects. Three years after the genesis of the movement, many of these women had been legalized as members of families (as spouses and mothers). Most of the individuals left out of the process of regularization were single and not likely to obtain a change of status in the near future. Therefore, the early focus on the humanitarian need to keep families together has been used by the state to deny legalization to many individuals who cannot claim familial linkages in France—including gays and lesbians without papers.

Chapter 2

1. I use the terms *frame* and *framing* here not only to refer to the material and discursive construction of the subject, but also to suggest that this construction is indeed a setup. After being constructed in and as "a certain way," the subject is then blamed for being "that way." This aspect of "framing" will be more fully developed in Chapters Three and Four.

2. African women and Muslim women in general are the targets of the mechanisms I describe here. However, it is important to note that different narratives circulate about different groups of women.

3. For a brief discussion of the media construction of the case, see Catherine Raissiguier, *Becoming Women/Becoming Workers: Identity Formation in a French Vocational School*, 139–142. For a more detailed analysis see Françoise Gaspard and Farhad Khosrokhavar, *Le foulard et la République.*

4. See Catherine Raissiguier, "Scattered Markets, Localized Workers: Gender and Immigration in France."

5. I am not suggesting here that the unwillingness to assimilate is in itself a bad thing. To the contrary, it is the very possibility of certain immigrants' subversive interventions, such as nay-saying to hegemonic integration and assimilationist scripts, that a loud and relentless republican chorus renders inaudible.

6. For discussions of the difference between "women" as historical actors and "woman" as a discursive production, see Teresa de Lauretis, *Alice Doesn't: Feminism, Semiotics, Cinema*; and Chandra Talpade Mohanty, "Under Western Eyes: Feminist Scholarship and Colonial Discourses."

7. *Beur* and its feminine (and diminutive) form, *Beurette*, are expressions that came out of French *banlieues* culture, where youth used a speech form called *Verlan*, in which words are turned around. *Verlan* itself, for instance, is the youth equivalent of *envers* (inside out) and *Beur* is the "inside out" version of *Arabe* (Arab). For a discussion of the offensive quality of both terms, but especially of *Beurette*, see Jane Freedman and Carrie Tarr, *Women, Immigration and Identities in France*, vii. For a brilliant analysis of the discursive construction of the *Beurettes* in France, see Guénif-Souilamas, *Des 'Beurettes' aux descendants d'immigrants Nord-Africains*, which charts

the genealogy of the term and these young women's social location in France. Among her other useful insights, Guénif-Souilamas analyzes the contradictory injunctions that invite these young women either to emancipate (and lose sight of their culture) or to conform (and lose sight of their freedom). By focusing on discursive practices and the "impossible choice" they offer, Guénif-Souilamas reminds us that the *Beurettes* are as much a product of French modernity as they are of its colonial past.

8. Chapter 4 offers a more detailed discussion of this gap in the literature. On this topic, see also Françoise Gaspard, "De l'invisibilité des migrantes et de leurs filles à leur instrumentalisation"; and Catherine Raissiguier, "Is Gendering Immigration Enough? The Case of France."

9. These are articles in which the title makes it clear that the focus is on women. It is interesting to note that the term *sans-papières* appears for the first time in the title of a short piece on Madjiguène Cissé (*La Croix*, January 9, 1997).

10. This was particularly true at the beginning of the movement. See Siméant, *La cause des Sans-Papiers*.

11. It is clear that left-wing parties have been vying to represent the immigrants and the *sans-papiers* more specifically. On this topic, see Siméant, *La cause des Sans-Papiers*; and Jacobson, *Rights Across Borders*.

12. Scott, *Only Paradoxes to Offer: French Feminists and the Rights of Man.*

13. See Dominique Schnapper, "The Debate on Immigration and the Crisis on National Identity," quoted in Sandra Lavenex, "National Frames in Migration Research: The Tacit Political Agenda," 256.

14. It is only in the past decade that France has begun to engage its colonial history seriously. Both new research and political interventions invite us to look at the history of the French colonial project and its traces in French society today. The emergence of groups such as *Les indigènes de la République* (the natives of the Republic) as well as the passage of the February 23, 2005, law that requires history programs in French schools to address the positive impact of France in its colonies are the product, opposite and yet related, of these new developments. For an interesting discussion of French republican colonialism, see Philippe Bernard's interview of Emmanuelle Saada in *Le Monde* (January 21, 2006). For a critique of the February 23, 2005, law, see Claude Liauzu, "Une loi contre l'histoire."

15. *Le Monde*, August 14, 1996.

16. Some of the names in the RAJFIRE interviews have been changed by the RAJFIRE activists who compiled and published them to protect the anonymity of the speakers.

17. It must be noted that the role of Claudie Lesselier, one of the RAJFIRE activists, is instrumental here.

18. The RAJFIRE produced its first brochure on the movement, *Femmes sans papiers: En lutte!* in 1997. It also produced a documentary: *Sans-papières: Des papiers et*

tous nos droits! In VHS format, the documentary features interviews of *sans-papières* and their feminist allies. In addition, the RAJFIRE activists maintain a Web site that is an excellent source of information about immigrant women in France. Some of the interview transcripts are available, in French, on the RAJFIRE Web site: http://rajfire.free.fr

19. RAJFIRE Brochure No. 2.

20. Nicole Genoux in RAJFIRE Brochure No. 2.

21. Claire Rodier and Nathalie Ferré, "Visas: Le verrou de la honte." Gérard Noiriel, in *Le creuset français*, brilliantly discusses how papers, permits, and codes have in fact created the categories of nationals and foreigners. In a similar way, here visa requirements and the administration's reluctance to deliver them have become part of a process that creates documented and undocumented immigrants.

22. The *préfecture* is the governing body of the Interior Ministry at the level of the *département* (administrative unit). As such, it is in charge of delivering identity papers and immigration documents at the local level.

23. Nacira Guènif-Souilamas offers a pertinent analysis of the tradition/modernity binary in *Des 'Beurettes' aux descendants d'immigrants Nord-Africains.*

24. For a discussion of the health care challenges facing certain immigrant women in France, see Catherine Raissiguier, "Women from the Maghreb and Sub-Saharan Africa in France: Fighting for Health and Basic Human Rights."

25. Emphasis in the original. Nacira Guénif-Souilamas and Eric Massé, *Les féministes et le garçon arabe*, 21.

Chapter 3

An earlier version of this chapter titled "French Immigration Laws: The Sans-Papières' Perspectives" was presented at Gendered Borders: International Conference on Women Immigration Law in Europe, Amsterdam, The Netherlands (September 30–October 2, 2004) and appeared in Catherine Raissiguier, *Women and Immigration Law in Europe: New Variations of Feminist Themes.*

1. For the most part, names have been changed to protect the anonymity of the women I interviewed. I did not change the name when the woman has been interviewed elsewhere under her given name.

2. The Évian Accords, signed in 1962, allowed Algerians to continue circulating freely between their country and France for work. The free circulation of Algerians was somewhat curtailed in 1968 and ended in 1974 when France closed the country to work immigration. Other former French colonies have signed bilateral agreements with France to permit the free circulation of people. For instance, Mali and France signed such an agreement on March 8, 1963. Senegal and France did as well on March 4, 1964. For a detailed discussion of the special treatment of Algerians within French immigration policies, see Viet, *La France immigrée.*

3. Family reunification is codified by the Order of November 2, 1945 (articles

29 through 30 *bis*), which has been amended numerous times since its first implementation. At the same time, the National Immigration Office (*Office national d'immigration*, or ONI) was created to oversee and manage the introduction of migrant workers (*travailleurs immigrés*) and their families. Family reunification did not apply to Algerians, who could move freely between Algeria and France until 1969. Since 1975 it does not apply to members of the European Community, who can move freely inside the member countries. It must also be noted that residency requirements were lengthened (to two years) after 1993, reduced in 1998, and lengthened again in 2006. The meaning of "adequate" resources has also been modified over time.

4. For a detailed history of French immigration politics that charts the development of French immigration policy from the perspective of administrative structures see Viet, *La France immigrée*.

5. Within this broad framework, two patterns emerged as early as the first decades of the twentieth century: first, immigration practices have continuously contradicted state-controlled policies; and second, European immigration has been favored over immigration from outside of Europe. For a good introduction to this history see Bernard, *L'immigration*.

6. Georges Mauco, secretary of the Committee on Population and the Family from 1945–1970, had already advocated for such practices in the 1930s, paving the way for the ethnic politics of the Vichy government. Mauco remained an influential force in the French administration until the 1970s. For an analysis of the European preference in France during the interwar period, see Ralph Schor, *L'opinion française et les étrangers*. For an analysis of Mauco's influence on French immigration and nationality laws, see Patrick Weil, *Qu'est-ce qu'un français? Histoire de la nationalité française depuis la révolution*. For Mauco's own ethnic theories, see Georges Mauco, *Les étrangers en France, leur rôle dans l'activité économique*.

7. Although French law excluded discrimination based on the national and ethnic origin of immigrants, it did not provide sanctions for actual practices that did so.

8. Against the backdrop of national independence struggles and decolonization, European preference emerged to counter the growing number of immigrants coming from Algeria. Algerians had started to arrive in France in noticeable numbers after 1919, when they were allowed to enter metropolitan France without permits. Their numbers grew in the mid-1950s because of increased economic opportunities in cities such as Paris and Marseilles and in spite of the war France was staging against their country. See Bernard, *L'immigration*; and Viet, *La France immigrée*.

9. Between 1945 and 1974, France also aimed to integrate new immigrant populations while protecting French nationals from foreign competition in employment, housing, and an array of social benefits. See Viet, *La France immigrée*.

10. Viet, *La France immigrée*, 153. For a short synthesis, see also Catherine Kolher and Suzanne Thave, "Un demi-siècle de regroupement familial en France."

11. They stayed under ten thousand entries per year. Algerians and members of other French colonies are not counted in these figures.

12. During that time many immigrants, recruited directly by employers, were entering the country without documents. They would request and obtain a change of status later, when they processed immigration applications for their families. Between 1965 and 1968, for instance, the ONI records show that 80 percent of all immigrant workers follow this two-step pattern. In 1968, in an early effort to control immigration, only Portuguese workers were granted the privilege to regularize their situation after the fact. See Kolher and Thave, "Un demi-siècle de regroupement familial en France," 10.

13. Ibid.

14. It is important to note here that this is done at a time when the European Community is being constructed. See Weil, *La France et ses étrangers*.

15. Ibid.

16. Claudie Lesselier, "Pour une critique féministe des lois sur l'entrée et le séjour des personnes étrangères en France."

17. André Lebon, *Immigration et présence étrangère en France en 2002*.

18. Roxanne Silberman, "Regroupement familial: Ce que disent les statistiques."

19. Lesselier, "Femmes migrantes en France: Le genre et la loi."

20. On derivative rights, see Judy Scales-Trent, "African Women in France: Citizenship, Family, and Work"; Edwige Rude-Antoine, "Des épouses soumises à des régimes particuliers"; Françoise Gaspard, "Statut personnel et intégration sociale, culturelle et nationale"; and Saïda Rahal-Sidhoum, *Éléments d'analyse de statut socio-juridique des femmes immigrées en vue d'un statut pour l'autonomie des femmes immigrées en France*.

21. Before 1984, spouses and children introduced through the procedure of family reunification were granted a residency card that mentioned their status as "family member" and did not include the right to seek employment. Residency and work permits were separate documents. Those family members who wished to work for a wage needed to request a work permit once they could document they had secured a job. Stoléru also instituted financial "help" for those immigrants who agreed to go back to their home countries.

22. The *Conseil d'État* is France's highest administrative court.

23. Catherine Wihtol de Wenden and Margo Corona DeLey, "French Immigration Policy Reform and the Female Migrant," 201. It is important to note that French law has provisions that protect the employment of French nationals.

24. Andrea Caspari and Winona Giles, "Imigration Policy and the Employment of Portuguese Migrant Women in the UK and France: A Comparative Analysis."

25. Wihtol de Wenden and Corona DeLey, "French Immigration Policy Reform and the Female Migrant."

26. The immigration law of 2003, in fact, codified the practice by stipulating that

rejoining spouses would be granted only a temporary card for the first two years—a clear setback from the gains of 1984.

27. Already in 1983, Georgina Dufoix, then in charge of the immigration dossier, had declared that family reunification through introduction would have priority. The administration also doubled the cost of the application in cases of regularization.

28. The law of September 9, 1986, broadened the list of countries that necessitate a visa for entry into France. The generalization of visa requirements for entry is part of the larger politics of immigration control in France. See Viet, *La France immigrée*.

29. Not only did this government amend the Order of November 2, 1945, but it also introduced important changes to the civil code (on marriage) and to the code of health insurance (*code de la Sécurité Sociale*).

30. A second salary or welfare benefits cannot be counted to meet these requirements. The mayor of the city where the immigrant resides approves the housing and resources of those who request family reunification. The mayor appears as "the discretionary master of quotas." See Naïr, *Contre les lois Pasqua*, 24. An article in *Le Monde* (Paris, March 15, 1996) documents that 58 percent of the mayors in the Languedoc-Roussillon region, for instance, apply the law by systematically denying familial reunification. Cited in Naïr, *Contre les lois Pasqua*, 105.

31. Foreigners who reside in France are allowed to follow, as far as their personal status is concerned, the legislation of their home country as long as it does not interfere with "public order." This legal compromise sometimes creates legal conflicts and oppressive situations that affect women in particular. So, although polygamy is de facto legal in France, as long as polygamous unions are contracted in the home country, polygamous families and the wives within them are not granted the right to have their families reunited. The question of "personal status" is another area of French law that inscribes immigrant women into subservient roles within the private/personal sphere.

32. Naïr condemns and documents instances of *infra-droit* that were created under the Pasqua laws, and Lochack theorizes the legal contours of the concept. See Naïr, *Contre les lois Pasqua*; and Lochack, *Étrangers: De quel droit?*

33. The 1998 law reduced the legal residency requirement to one year before an immigrant can apply for family reunification. Under the Chevènement law, the person requesting the procedure must demonstrate housing considered "normal for a family living in France," a stable income (equivalent to the minimum wage), and a full-time job. Authorization to enter the territory can be granted only after the *Office des migrations internationales* has determined that housing and resource requirements have been met.

34. See Wihtol de Wenden and Corona DeLey, "French Immigration Policy Reform and the Female Migrant," 201. Withol de Wenden and Corona DeLey also point out that the main reason for the increase in undocumented women after 1974 was due to the entry of independent single women seeking employment in France.

35. See Michèle Tribalat, *De l'immigration à l'assimilation*, cited in Chaïb, *Facteurs d'insertion*, and in personal interview with Claudie Lesselier from the RAJFIRE (on file with author).

36. In the 1960s, economic forces superseded France's plans to use immigration to stave off its population decline. Employers actively recruited workers in Southern Europe and the Maghreb. A minister publicly stated that illegal immigration should be considered as a solution to the country's need for labor power. Indeed, the 1960s were laissez-faire years as far as immigration was concerned. See Bernard, *L'Immigration*, 80–81.

37. Children born in France to parents born in Algeria before 1962 are French at birth through the principle of double *jus soli*.

38. Edna de Oliviera a Silva and Martine El Mahalawi-Nouet, "L'aspiration à l'autonomie des femmes immigrées," 40.

39. Lesselier, "Femmes migrantes en France."

40. Mady Vetter, *Situation juridique et sociale des femmes âgées étrangères*, 12. The 2003 law of Nicolas Sarkozy includes a provision that protects immigrant women who sever a familial link, and hence might lose their legal status in France, because of domestic violence.

41. For a discussion of this phenomenon in France, see Lessellier, "Femmes migrantes en France." For a more general discussion, see also Jacqueline Bhabha, "Border Rights and Rites: Generalizations, Stereotypes and Gendered Migration."

42. Chandra Talpade Mohanty, *Feminism Without Borders: Decolonizing Theory, Practicing Solidarity*.

43. See Chapter 1 on this issue.

44. For a detailed analysis of this danger in relation to the French organization *Ni Putes Ni Soumises*, see Catherine Raissiguier, "Muslim Women in France: Impossible Subjects?"

Chapter 4

An earlier version of this chapter titled "Troubling Mothers: Immigrant Women from Africa in France" was presented at the African and Nordic Perspectives Conference in Dakar, Senegal, February 15–18, 2003, and appeared in *JENdA: A Journal of Culture and African Women Studies* in 2003.

1. The children of immigrants from Africa, who often are French themselves, are still considered immigrants (*les jeunes issus de l'immigration*). Needless to say, this idea constitutes a violent discursive denial of their legally and lawfully belonging to the French nation. For a layered analysis of these discursive practices, see Nacira Guénif-Souilamas, *Des "Beurettes" aux descendants d'immigrants Nord-Africains*.

2. The agency invoked here is not conceptualized as simply a willed or chosen position. Rather, borrowing from Judith Butler's work on iteration in *Bodies That Matter*,

NOTES TO CHAPTER 4   157

this analysis is attentive to the power relations and reiterative processes (both discursive and material) that produce "impossible" subjects and subversive political practices. Through repetition, commonsense and normative ideas about France, French nationals, and immigrants (assimilable and unassimilable) are produced. "And yet, it is also by virtue of this reiteration that gaps and fissures are opened up as the constitutive instabilities in such constructions, as that which escapes or exceeds the norm, as that which cannot be wholly defined or fixed by the repetitive labor of the norm" (10). It is in this inevitable instability that new forms of citizenship and new modalities of belonging are produced.

3. Here I build on the work of Catherine Quiminal, who has written about the necessity to study immigration politics in France through the lens of and in relation to its colonial history. See, in particular, "Le rapport colonial revisité: les luttes des africains et des africaines en France." Speaking specifically about the African context, Quiminal argues that the colonial relationship binds male actors through a hierarchical and unequal relationship by which cheap labor is extracted from the colonized. Colonized women, in this schema, are either simply neglected or relegated to the role of "fecund mothers" or oversexualized and evil temptresses.

4. Racialization is used the way Omi and Winant define it, "to signify the extension of racial meaning to a previously unclassified relationship, social practice or group." Michael Omi and Howard Winant, *Racial Formation in the United States from the 1960s to the 1980s*, 64.

5. Hervé Le Bras, *Le sol et le sang: Théories de l'invasion au XXe siècle*, 77.

6. Jacques Chirac was the mayor of Paris when he made this speech to some 1,500 party activists in the provincial town of Orleans. An audiovisual excerpt from the speech is available on the Web site of the Institut national de l'audiovisuel (http://www.ina.fr).

7. Chirac's political career is long-standing and of the highest order. His tenure in the French government spans three decades and can be briefly summarized as follows: agriculture and rural development minister, 1973–1974; interior minister, 1974; prime minister, 1974–1976, 1986–1988; mayor of Paris, 1977–1995; president, 1995–2007.

8. Pierre Tévanian, *Le racisme républicain: Réflexions sur le modèle français de discrimination*.

9. At that time, *l'immigré* was typically represented as a North African male worker in *bleu de chauffe* (the blue cotton suit worn by many manual workers in France) at work or on his way to work. This image, which conjures up a secular, unattached, with-a-home-elsewhere male laborer, has been replaced by images of North African women and girls in schools, supermarkets, or social service agencies, often wearing some variation of the *hijab*, or images of young mothers from sub-Saharan Africa in traditional attire with children in tow.

10. The French fertility rate in 2000 was 1.89 children per woman. See http://

www.info-france-usa.org. For a brief history of French family allowances and their relation to the French concept of citizenship, see Edwige Liliane Lefebvre, "Republicanism and Universalism: Factors of Inclusion or Exclusion in the French Concept of Citizenship."

11. It must be noted here that mothers of youths of immigrant parentage were blamed in the aftermath of the 2005 riots.

12. See Chaïb, *Facteurs d'insertion.*

13. Ibid.

14. Nouria Ouali, "Les télévisions francophones et l'image des femmes immigrées," cited in Chaïb, *Facteurs d'insertion.*

15. Fifteen years after the "headscarf case," the issue of the *hijab* was back on the front burner in France. On December 17, 2003, Jacques Chirac declared that he was in favor of a law that would prohibit ostentatious signs of religious belonging in schools. The Islamic scarf was undeniably the main target of the presidential address and rekindled the debate on France's *laïcité* (a political and philosophical concept that organizes French society and demands the strict separation of church and state, sometimes referred to in English as *laicity*) principle, its republican tradition, and its relationship with the French Muslim community. In February 2004, French legislators overwhelmingly approved the law, which went into effect in the fall of the same year. For a brief analysis of the French *hijab* polemic and what it tells us about the French republican model, see Judith Ezekiel, "French Dressing: Race, Gender, and the Hijab Story."

16. A good illustration of this point can be found in the decision of June 27, 2008, by the *Conseil d'État* to uphold a 2005 judgment to deny a Moroccan woman the French nationality because of lack of assimilation (*défaut d'assimilation*). Because she wears the *burqa* (a garment for women that covers the entire body), her request was denied on the ground that "she adopted, in the name of a radical practice of her religion, a social behavior incompatible with the essential values of the French community, notably the principle of gender equality." Stéphanie Le Bars, "Une marocaine en burqa se voit refuser la nationalité française."

17. Chaïb, *Facteurs d'insertion,* 16.

18. Chantal Deckmyn, *Les "actions femmes" dans la politique de la ville en région Provence-Alpes-Côte d'Azur.*

19. The well-respected *Commission nationale consultative des droits de l'homme* (CNCDH) recently commissioned a paper on the state of polygamy in France. The paper estimates that around 180,000 individuals, including adults and children, are part of polygamous families in France. This constitutes less than 0.3 percent of the national population. For a summative memorandum on the paper's basic findings and the CNCDH policy recommendations, see Commission nationale consultative des droits de l'homme, "Avis sur la situation de la polygamie en France. For the com-

plete study, see Françoise Hostalier, *Étude et propositions: La polygamie en France.* Some politicians have been known to multiply these figures by ten. On this issue, see, for instance, Octave Bonnaud, "De Villiers décuple le nombre de familles polygames en France."

20. Jean-Marie Le Pen founded the National Front party in October 1972. It occupied a marginal place within French political life until the early 1980s. In the 1974 presidential elections, for example, the National Front party won less than 1 percent of the total vote. It remained a marginal party until the beginning of the next decade. In 1981 it won only 0.3 percent of the vote in the legislative elections. Combining its populist and nationalist agenda with a strong anti-immigrant rhetoric, the National Front emerged in the 1980s as a key player within French politics. By the middle of the decade, it had reached 10 percent of the votes in European and parliamentary elections. In 1988 it scored 14.4 percent of the total vote in the presidential election. The steady ascendance of the National Front culminated in the presence of Jean-Marie Le Pen in the second round of the presidential election in 2002, after obtaining almost 17 percent of the votes in the first round. For a discussion of the role of the National Front in French politics, see Peter Morris, *French Politics Today.*

21. Nonna Mayer, "Radical Right Populism in France: How Much of the 2002 Le Pen Votes Does Populism Explain?"

22. It is important to note here that the idea of an increased popularity of Le Pen and his message within the working class must be somewhat tempered. Indeed, this notion has been challenged by recent scholarship that looks closely at French electoral numbers and reveals that other groups, such as farmers, small business owners, and self-employed workers (*professions indépendantes*), in fact form the political base of the French National Front. These scholars argue that explanations of Le Pen's spectacular electoral rise that rely on his populism are mistaken and dangerous. They overstate the appeal of the National Front on sheer populist grounds and they present working-class actors as the principal supporters of Le Pen and his racist agenda. This exaggerated focus on the working class also functions to exonerate other culprits, such as political, media, and intellectual elites in France. See Mayer, "Radical Right Populism in France." See also Annie Collovald, *Le "populisme du FN," un dangereux contresens,* 18, cited in Pierre Tevanian and Sylvie Tissot, "La lepénisation des esprits: Éléments pour une grille d'analyse du racisme en France."

23. Pierre Tévanian, *Le racisme républicain.*

24. Tevanian and Tissot, "La lepénisation des esprits."

25. Edwige Rude-Antoine, "La polygamie face au droit positif français," 64. For additional discussions of polygamy by Edwige Rude-Antoine, see "Des épouses soumises à des régimes particuliers"; "Le statut personnel: Liberté ou sujétion?"; "Le statut personnel en France"; and "La polygamie et le droit Français." See also Brigitte Thomas, "La gestion quotidienne des problèmes générés par des questions de statut

personnel"; Gaspard, "Statut personnel"; and Saïda Rahal-Sidhoum, "Du statut des femmes."

26. It is important to note here that an immigrant with appropriate sojourn and residency papers is allowed, under the Pasqua law, to bring in a second or third wife through the process of family reunification as long as she is the mother of a French child. Whether or not the family will succeed in securing the necessary documents to obtain an entry visa is another matter.

27. Bissuel, "Divorcer ou vivre sans papiers."

28. It is worth noting here that for undocumented women, who often cannot generate the revenues necessary to apply for low-income housing, the difficulty of secure housing increases their overall *précarité*. French allies involved with *Femmes urgence droit au logement* (Women Emergency Housing Rights) noted, for instance, that shelters, which are not allowed to turn down undocumented women because they lack papers, often release them after a few days of emergency housing. They further note that these shelters are already full of women who do have papers but whose insufficient resources prevent them from accessing low-income housing. Lacking shelter, these women find it impossible to fight for their change of status. Housing emerges here as a fundamental social condition for the development of civil rights. See Eliane, "Logement: Femmes sans papiers, doublement opprimées."

29. Quoted in Claudette Bodin and Catherine Quiminal, "Le long voyage des femmes du Fleuve Sénégal," 26.

30. Indeed, several women from middle-class backgrounds recounted how "shocked" they were to find themselves in a *sans-papiers* collective. I develop this point further in the next chapter.

31. The Republic of the Congo became independent in 1960.

32. Civil wars erupted in the RC in 1993, 1997, and 1998. In 1992 the people of RC approved a new constitution that established multiparty rule. Pascal Lissouba was elected president in the first democratic presidential election in the country. A dispute over parliamentary elections in 1993 led to violent clashes between progovernment forces and opposing factions. Although some of the militias disarmed in 1994, civil unrest continued until 1997, when a full-scale civil war erupted. The fighting in Brazzaville caused material damage, large-scale population displacements, and thousands of casualties. Clairette herself recounts that she fled Brazaville in 1997 and walked 600 kilometers (400 miles) to reach Pointe Noire and Dolizi, which were protected because of the oil industry located in the area. She vividly recounted the atrocities she witnessed during the journey, which still haunt her today.

33. In 1990 she even did a three–month internship at the Pitié-Salpêtrière Hospital in Paris.

34. Territorial asylum may be obtained when political asylum has been denied. It was introduced under Jean-Pierre Chevènnement to protect Algerians, in particular,

whose life or liberty might be threatened in their home country but not necessarily by state authorities.

35. The theme of immigrant invasion is present in the language of numbers that speaks of a tolerance threshold (*seuil de tolérance*) beyond which the social order is in danger and France cannot possibly "integrate" its foreign population. For a discussion of the myth of an "immigrant invasion" that is attentive to gender, see Freedman, *Immigration and Insecurity in France*, 17–19.

36. Polygamy has also been evoked at times to explain employment discrimination and the housing crisis in France. See Ligue des droits de l'homme (LDH), "C'est pas la faute aux polygames."

37. Fadela Amara (who is now part of the Sarkozy government) and her organization *Ni Putes Ni Soumises* (Neither Whore nor Submissive) have unfortunately also contributed to this very problematic construction. For a fuller discussion of Ni Putes Ni Soumises, see Raissiguier, "Muslim Women in France."

Chapter 5

1. Interestingly, Val made the news when *Charlie Hebdo* was brought to trial under French antiracism laws for publishing cartoons depicting the prophet Muhammad. In February 2006 the newspaper had put out a special issue on the controversial Danish cartoons. It featured twelve drawings first published in the daily *Jyllands-Posten*. Val and *Charlie Hebdo* argued that they had made the choice to reprint the cartoons in the interests of freedom of speech in France. The Paris court agreed with them. It acquitted Val in 2007 when it ruled that in the context of the special issue and of the satirical and defiant tradition of the paper there had been "no deliberate intention of directly and gratuitously offending the Muslim community." See Bernard Schmidt, "Verdict in 'Charlie Hebdo' Satirical Newspaper Case."

2. De Villiers is the president of the far-right Movement for France (*Mouvement pour la France*) party. A social conservative with strong ties to the pro-life movement in France, he was one of the leaders of the "no" vote for the European constitution referendum in 2005. Running on an anti-immigration platform, and competing for Le Pen's votes, de Villiers made an unsuccessful bid for the French presidency in 2007.

3. Elaine Sciolino, "Unlikely Hero in Europe's Spat."

4. Bolkestein was commissioner for the Internal Market in the European Commission.

5. See *Libération*, "Des pages jaunes pour Frits Bolkstein."

6. On January 13, 2004, the European Commission presented a proposal for a directive on services in the internal European market, also known as the Bolkestein directive. The Bolkestein directive eases the processes through which European companies can offer cross-border services. When services are not offered in France or are offered in France for a period inferior to eight days, the work regulations

(minimum wage, work hours, vacation time, hygiene, and security regulations) will be that of the country of origin. When services are offered in France on a long-term basis, French work regulations are to be followed except for social benefits, which will be determined by the regulations of the country of origin. This, critics have pointed out, would still make the Polish worker much cheaper to hire than the French one.

7. In March 2005, Chirac won the support of several member states—including Germany, Belgium, and Sweden—in his effort to introduce changes in the Bolkestein directive and to protect the "European social model." A softer version of the directive was approved by the European parliament in 2006 without the "country of origin" principle. The first draft of the directive included such a principle, which meant that workers were subject to the laws of their country of origin. Instead, the directive now stipulates "that companies from all member states will be free to provide services in any EU country but must respect the labour and collective bargaining laws and health and safety and environmental standards of the host country." Catharina Gnath, "The Services Directive Has Passed the European Parliament," 4–5.

8. Cited in Thomas Fuller, "The Workplace: For French, Cheap Labor Is the Specter." It must be noted that in 1997 *France Télécom* went through a partial privatization.

9. Discourses that link immigration to the loss of jobs for French nationals have been in circulation for years and are commonly redeployed in times of economic crisis.. For an in-depth analysis of such discourses during the interwar period, see Schor, *L'opinion française*. Today such linkages help deflect the global forces that have produced the economic dislocation of many working people in France. The National Front and its leader, Jean-Marie Le Pen, have aptly triangulated unemployment, insecurity, and immigration and drawn, in the process, increased support from the French working class. For a brief essay developing this thesis, see Alain Bihr, "L'extrême droite à la conquête du prolétariat," 4–5. Although this is an important phenomenon, it can also obfuscate the fact that the political stronghold of the National Front remains the traditional middle classes. On this caveat, see Chapter 4, especially endnote 24.

10. For a detailed analysis of the referendum in France, see Dominique Reynié, "29 Mai 2005, un paysage dynamité." See also European Commission, *The European Constitution: Post-Referendum in France*. It must be noted here that the overwhelming majority of the voters supporting far-right parties (*Front national* and *Mouvement national républicain*) as well as those supporting the French communist party voted against the treaty (94 percent and 95 percent, respectively). Also noteworthy is the urban/rural discrepancy, with 61 percent of those living in rural areas voting no compared with 47 percent in urban areas voting no. Interestingly, 55 percent of people living in the Paris region voted yes for the constitution.

11. Philippe Le Coeur, "La crainte pour l'emploi." Overall, French women voted against the constitution in higher numbers (72 percent) than their male counterparts (69 percent).

12. Elaine Sciolino, "Unlikely Hero in Europe's Spat."

13. The meanings produced by the Polish plumber are indeed multiple and contradictory. They draw from, rearticulate, and transform imaginary scenarios about the nation and its "others." One might read him, for instance, as a sexualized threat to hegemonic working-class French masculinities. The Polish plumber evokes the weakening of traditional working-class male roles brought about by large-scale economic forces. Immigrant men in France are cast not only as those who take "our jobs" but also as those who take "our women." This displacement of an economic threat onto the realm of sexuality is a common feature of these scenarios. In addition, the uniquely and undeniably "queer" sensibility of the image undermines the macho heteronormative subtext.

14. The *sans-papiers* have diversified since 1996. Today *sans-papiers* are from China, Eastern Europe, and other parts of the globe. Because of the specific composition of the *sans-papiers* collectives I observed during my fieldwork, however, the women I interviewed for this project are mostly from Africa.

15. Active citizenship can be simply defined as active and direct participation in the polity. On the *sans-papiers* and active citizenship, see Balibar Étienne, "Le droit de cité ou l'apartheid?" 89–116.

16. Quoted in Alain Gresh, "Malevolent Fantasy of Islam," *Le Monde Diplomatique*. Lewis later became a valued advisor to the Bush administration.

17. Terray convincingly writes about the global processes that create local forms of labor delocalizations. By employing undocumented immigrants in various sectors of the French economy, employers accrue the benefits of labor delocalization (low wages, low social cost, and soft labor laws) without having to deal with the problems generally linked with off-shore production. See Emmanuel Terray, "Le travail des étrangers en situation irrégulière ou la délocalisation sur place," 9–34.

18. Institut national de la statistique et des études économiques (INSEE), *Les Immigrés en France*, 21.

19. As we saw in Chapter 3, women have traditionally entered France by joining their husbands and fiancés and have been active participants in processes of family and community settlement. It is important to note that autonomous feminine immigration did occur, to a small degree, among immigrants from Spain and Yugoslavia prior to 1974, and instances of independent female immigration into France have been on the increase in the recent past. Brun and Laacher, for instance, document the emerging phenomenon, in the *régularisation* procedure of 1997, of single and isolated women—notably from Mauritius, Cape Verde, Haiti, and the Philippines—working as maids and nannies. Brun and Laacher, "De la régularisation," 2.

20. Catherine Quiminal et al, "Mobilisation associative et dynamiques d'inté-gration des femmes d'Afrique subsaharienne en France," 4.

21. INSEE, *Les immigrés*. Catherine Quiminal and her colleagues note that the bulk of these new immigrants are also young women: 52 percent under twenty-five and 33 percent between twenty-five and thirty-four. Quiminal et al, "Mobilisation associative et dynamiques d'intégration," 4.

22. It is worth noting here that immigrants from Asia entered France in large number only in the 1980s. In the case of immigrants from South East Asia, they did so as refugees and families.

23. Wihtol de Wenden and Corona DeLey, "French Immigration Policy Reform and the Female Migrant," 198.

24. INSEE, *Les immigrés*, 73.

25. The labor-force participation of all women in France in 1992 for ages 25 to 49 was 78.3 percent. INSEE, *Les immigrés*, 73. For 1994, labor-force participation rates for all women in France were the following: 77.0 percent (ages 30 to 34), 77.0 percent (35 to 39), 79.0 percent (40 to 44), 76.9 percent (45 to 49), 68.3 percent (50 to 54), and 46.3 percent (55 to 59). INSEE, *Les femmes*, 117. These figures, of course, do not account for the involvement of many immigrant women in underground economies, which cannot be measured by national statistics.

26. Freedman and Tarr, *Women, Immigration and Identities*, 24.

27. This feminization of part-time work is more visible in the northern than in the southern members of the EU. France is located somewhere between these two poles, with 29.5 percent of women's work part-time as opposed to 5.2 percent for men's work in 1996. In contrast, part-time work represented 68.5 percent of all women's work in the Netherlands and only 9 percent of all women's work in Greece. Part-time work emerged in France in the 1990s in the context of a weak economy and a national labor crisis. Margaret Maruani, *Travail et emploi des femmes*, 81.

28. Pei-Chia Lan, *Global Cinderellas*, 13–14. Pei-Chia uses the term *structural continuity* to highlight two related processes. First, it underscores the similar ways in which women of various social backgrounds find themselves primarily responsible for domestic labor. Structural continuity also refers to the different ways in which womanhood itself is constructed at the intersection of several social forces. So, although all women are hailed as "natural" domestic and care workers, they are invited to take up this type of work in a broad range of ways and locations.

29. Aminata arrived in France in 1990 to reconnect with her estranged husband, who had left for France six years earlier and left Aminata and their three children behind without support and information about his whereabouts. Determined to find him and ask that he take care of his family, Aminata left for France and had no dif-ficulty finding him with the help of the Senegalese immigrant community. The couple reunited and Aminata's husband asked her to go and fetch their daughters in Senegal.

However, when she arrived with them and pregnant with her fourth child, the couple began to unravel and they separated.

30. Aminata's story echoes the analysis developed by Margaret Maruani on women's work in the EU. Women who are employed part-time often work the least favorable hours and are forced to accept these shifts for fear of losing their job. See Maruani, *Travail et emploi des femmes*, 102–103.

31. The space had been made available by the local communist municipality. This particular collective regularly added names to its list that it presented to the *préfecture* for review.

32. An International Monetary Fund study interestingly titled "Hiding in the Shadow: The Growth of the Underground Economy" claims that in France the percentage of the total labor force involved in the underground economy doubled between 1975 and 1998. Indeed, the share of workers involved in this "shadow" economy was "3–6 percent in 1975–82 but doubled to 6–12 percent in 1997–98." Friedrich Schneider and Dominik Enste, "Hiding in the Shadows: The Growth of the Underground Economy." Although undocumented immigrants are overrepresented in the underground economy, legal immigrants and French citizens are also engaged in it. Indeed, workers look for employment in this informal sector because they need second jobs, because they find it more lucrative to do so, or because they are not allowed to secure jobs in the regular economy.

33. Although none of the women I interviewed revealed that they had themselves worked as sex workers, there are enough references in these interviews (and in interviews with French allies) to such labor to indicate that this is indeed a real option for many of the women who find themselves undocumented in France.

34. In France, recent studies show that almost 80 percent of domestic tasks are still performed by women. See Sophie Ponthieux and Amandine Schreiber, "Dans les couples de salariés, la répartition du travail domestique reste inégale." Women are also overrepresented in waged work that provides direct services (domestic and care work). In 1997, for instance, women represented 86 percent of all workers in these positions. Maruani, *Travail et emploi des femmes*, 38.

35. For an early study of domestic work, gender, and race relations in the United States, see Judith Rollins, *Between Women: Domestics and Their Employers*. See also Evelyn Nakano Glenn, *Issei, Nissei, War Bride: Three Generations of Japanese American Women in Domestic Service*; and May Romero, *Maid in the U.S.A.* For a groundbreaking study of domestic workers in newly industrialized countries, see Nicole Constable, *Maid to Order in Hong Kong: Stories of Filipina Workers*. For more recent scholarship that focuses on immigrant women in a global context, see Anderson Bridget Anderson, *Doing the Dirty Work? The Global Politics of Domestic Labor*; Rhacel Salazar Parreñas, *Servants of Globalization: Women, Migration and Domestic Work*; Barbara Ehrenreich and Arlie Russel Hochschild, *Global Woman: Nannies, Maids and Sex Workers in the New Economy*; and Pei-Chia, *Global Cinderellas*.

36. The *gendarmes* in France are a military police force. The *gendarmerie* is their police station.

37. Laria came to France with a tourist visa and thought she would be able to obtain a student visa easily once people saw her pedigree. When her visa expired, she enrolled in a French university, where she is now pursuing a postsecondary degree.

38. The CGT is a labor union closely connected to the French communist party. The Marseilles *sans-papiers* collective is housed in the CGT locale and receives generous support from the union.

39. Malika had left Morocco to escape domestic violence and sexual objectification at the hands of her husband.

40. *Kabyles* are African Berber people located primarily in Morocco, Tunisia, western Libya, and the coastal mountain regions of northern Algeria.

41. As indicated earlier, in the course of this study I heard several stories of *sans-papiers* being robbed of their salary by unsavory employers who take advantage of their illegal status. Like many other *sans-papiers*, Malika described a situation in which the unethical employer was an immigrant who exploited other immigrants. Claudie Lesselier, in the interview I conducted with her, clearly pointed to this pattern and indicated that sometimes patterns of extreme exploitation develop through and within familial and gendered networks. This is particularly true for labor in small independent businesses and domestic work.

42. Freedman, *Immigration and Insecurity in France*, 24–25.

43. Malika Dutt, Leni Marin, and Helen Zia, *Migrant Women's Human Rights in G-7 Countries: Organizing Strategies*, 1.

44. Wihtol de Wenden and Corona DeLey, "French Immigration Policy Reform and the Female Migrant," 200–201

45. Caspari and Giles, "Immigration Policy and the Employment of Portuguese Migrant Women in the UK and France," 169.

46. Wihtol de Wenden and Corona DeLey, "French Immigration Policy Reform and the Female Migrant," 201.

47. Ibid.

48. See Emmanuel Terray, "Le travail des étrangers"; Yeza Boulahbel-Villac, "The Integration of Algerian Women in France: A Compromise Between Tradition and Modernity"; and Georges Tapinos, "Female Migration and the Status of Foreign Women in France."

49. Terray, "Le travail des étrangers."

50. Jill Rubery and Colette Fagan, "Does Feminization Mean a Flexible Labour Force?" 140.

51. The term *immigré* in France is very interesting and somewhat confusing. The census definition of "immigrant" refers to those who were born not-French outside of France and have actually migrated into France (and this includes naturalized French

citizens). In popular parlance, however, *immigré* refers to anyone who has migrated into France or who is of immigrant descent, especially those from France's former colonies. As a result, a recent immigrant from Argentina—especially if she or he "looks" white, appears educated, and is of the middle-class—is less likely to be called *immigré* than the son of an Algerian who was born in France and carries a French identity card. In other word, the term *immigré* itself connotes "race" in a country that until very recently did not dare speak its name.

52. FASILD, *Femmes d'origine étrangère: Travail, accés à l'emploi, discriminations de genre.*

53. Ralph Schor, in *l'opinion française*, documents that during the interwar years the new immigrants from Poland were both appreciated for their good work habits and criticized on human and cultural grounds. See, in particular, 143–145.

Chapter 6

This chapter appeared in slightly different forms as "The Sexual and Racial Politics of Civil Unions in France," in the *Radical History Review*, and as "Bodily Metaphors, Material Exclusions: The Sexual and Racial Politics of Domestic Partnership in France," in Arturo Aldama's *Violence and the Body.*

1. This law is introduced in the Preface and mentioned in my discussion of polygamy in Chapter 4.

2. Jean-Paul Pouliquen and Denis Quinqueton, "Le PaCS est-il républicain?"

3. It must be noted that activists in France are more and more aware of these connections. It is also interesting to note that theoretical explorations of such intersections began to emerge in France in the mid-1990s. Complex struggles like that of the *sans-papiers and sans-papières* and outside scholarly influences might have contributed to this recent shift. A recent special Issue of *Cahiers du Genre*, for instance, directly engages the theoretical concept of *intersectionality*. See Fougeyrollas-Schwebel, Dominique Éléonore Lépinard, and Eleni Varikas, *Féminisme(s): penser la pluralité.*

4. Cathy Lloyd, *"Rendez-vous manqués:* Feminisms and Anti-racisms in France," cited in Freedman, *Immigration and Insecurity in France*, 107.

5. Anna Marie Smith, *New Rights Discourse on Race and Sexuality: Britain 1968–1990.* See also Anna Marie Smith, "The Centering of Right-Wing Extremism Through the Construction of an 'Inclusionary' Homophobia and Racism."

6. Under Thatcher's government, Section 28 of the Local Government Act specifically prohibited the promotion of homosexuality by local governments.

7. Smith, *New Rights Discourse*, 22.

8. Ibid., 23.

9. Recent historical, feminist, and postcolonial scholarship has mounted ample evidence of the deep and ongoing connections between racial, sexual, and national thinking within the context of Europe's colonial project. See Homi Bhabha, "The

Other Question"; Sander Gilman, "Black Bodies, White Bodies: Toward and Iconography of Female Sexuality in Late Nineteenth-Century Art, Medicine, and Literature"; Anne McClintock, *Imperial Leather: Race, Gender and Sexuality in the Colonial Context*; and Ann Laura Stoler, *Race and the Education of Desire: Foucault's History of Sexuality and the Colonial Order of Things.*

10. This analysis of the *Islam = Sida!* slogan was first developed in my article "Women from the Maghreb and Sub-Saharan Africa in France: Fighting for Health and Basic Human Rights." In this chapter, I use a slightly different and expanded version of the analysis. I introduce the importance of bodily metaphors in the parliamentary discussions of the PaCS and I locate these discussions within a larger discursive context where layered and complex constructions of race and sexuality articulate and deploy specific forms of differences and exclusions.

11. George Mosse has documented how, especially in the German context, the racist imaginary often revolves around tropes of disease, infection, and contagion: "Racism branded the outsider, making him inevitably a member of the inferior race, whenever this was possible, readily recognized as a carrier of infection, threatening the health of society and the nation." See *Nationalism and Sexuality: Respectability and Abnormal Sexuality in Modern Europe*, 134.

12. Cindy Patton, "From Nation to Family: Containing African AIDS," n6.

13. Mosse argues that from its inception the concept of racism was associated with (deviant) sexuality. In the context of German nationalism and anti-Semitism, Mosse shows that both Jews and homosexuals were seen as "decadents" who weakened the nation and deprived it of "healthy sons and daughters." See *Nationalism and Sexuality*, 109.

14. Barbara Browning, *Infectious Rhythms: Metaphors of Contagion and the Spread of African Culture*, 7.

15. Jennifer Terry and Jacqueline Urla, *Deviant Bodies: Critical Perspectives on Difference in Science and Popular Culture*, 4.

16. On the concept of the nation as "imagined community," see Benedict Anderson, *Imagined Communities.*

17. McClintock, *Imperial Leather*, 357.

18. See, in particular, Nira Yuval-Davis and Floya Anthias, *Women-Nation-State*; Floya Anhias and Nira Yuval-Davis, *Racialized Boundaries: Race, Nation, Gender, Colour, and Class and the Anti-Racist Struggle*; and Nira Yuval-Davis, *Gender and Nation*. See also Radhika Mohanram, *Women, Colonialism and Space.*

19. Terry and Urla, *Deviant Bodies*, 1–2.

20. The focus on looks and visible characteristics of these *contrôle au faciés* (you can actually tell an "illegal immigrant" when you see her or him) clearly inscribes current anti-immigrant politics in France within the logic of a long racist tradition that relies on visual clues to infer the character and status of individuals and entire communities.

21. Etienne Balibar, "Is There a `Neo-Racism'?"

22. Smith, "The Centering of Right Wing Extremism," 120.

23. The PaCS law is a contract that two adults of the same sex or of different sexes sign in order to organize their communal life. The PaCS cannot be signed by parents and children or by siblings. It needs to be recorded in court (*Tribunal d'instance*) and consists of a mutual declaration stipulating the nature of the contract. The PaCS grants basic social benefits such as the ability to file a joint tax form (after three years) and health coverage, and is considered one of the elements attesting to a "personal link" with a French national in relation to the acquisition of entry and residency permits for foreigners. The duties of the partners who have signed a PaCS are a "mutual material aid" that is codified more specifically in each contract, and they are jointly responsible and accountable for common living debts. The PaCS is ended when one partner dies or marries. It can be annulled by simple declaration by both or one of the partners. If the rupture is a unilateral one, one party needs to "signify" the rupture to the other, after which the PaCS is annulled within three months. It must be noted, however, that individuals joined in a PaCS are not considered a "family" and are not given rights to adoption or medically assisted procreation.

24. Christine Boutin, representative from the Yvelines, was one of the strongest opponents to the PaCS in the National Assembly debates. She was asked to intervene on the PaCS by the UDF on November 3, 1998; she was then criticized within the party for the extremity of her homophobic comments. Her speech generated a wide range of protest across the political spectrum. Boutin is now part of the Sarkozy government.

25. An earlier text, introduced on October 9, 1998, had been rejected by the National Assembly because several Socialist deputies were absent.

26. *Générations famille* and *Jeunesse action chrétienté* are two representatives of this movement. Organized in a collective "for marriage and against PaCS," these groups organized educational campaigns, demonstrations, and lobbied then President Jacques Chirac to call for further discussion of the text when it had already been voted into law and approved by the *Conseil constitutionnel*—a constitutional right of the president. See *Décision du Conseil Constitutionel* at http://www.conseil-constitutionnel .fr/conseil-constitutionnel/francais/les-decisions/acces-par-date/decisions-depuis -1959/1999/99-419-dc/decision-n-99-419-dc-du-09-novembre-1999.11849.html

27. Mosse suggested, for instance, a clear connection between "the persecution of homosexuals and the effort to maintain the sexual division of labor" in his study of nationalism in Nazi Germany. See *Nationalism and Sexuality*, 164.

28. Particularly homophobic statements from sessions on November 3, 7, and 8, 1998, have been compiled by gay and lesbian activists. These excerpts are available at http://altern.org.ardhis/etrangers.htm. Jacques Kossowski, RPR, November 7, 1998. Official Analytical Summary (*Compte rendu analytique officiel des comptes rendus*) of November 7, 1998. http://www.assembleenationale.fr/2/dossiers/pacs/981107.htm

29. Christine Boutin, November 3, 1998. Integral Report (*Compte rendu intégral*) of session held on November 3, 1998. http://www.assemblee-nat.fr/2/cri/19990057 .htm

30. Ibid. Although adoption by a single adult has been allowed by French law since 1966, on October 9, 1996, the *Conseil d'État* stipulated that the right to adoption is not extended to homosexuals. Similarly, artificial insemination and other forms of medical assistance for procreation (*Procréation médicalement assistée*) are exclusively granted to married couples and common-law heterosexual couples who have lived together for a period of at least two years.

31. Ibid.

32. Dominique Dord, "PaCS, un mauvais projet."

33. Eric Doligé, RPR, November 7, 1998. Official Analytical Summary of November 7, 1998. http://www.assembleenationale.fr/2/dossiers/pacs/981107.htm

34. This hallucinatory scenario taps into an old French anxiety about the country's demographic weakness: "While our society is undergoing a demographic crisis without precedent, you choose to grant official status to couples who cannot procreate." Jacques Kossowski, RPR, November 8, 1998. Official Analytical Summary of November 8, 1998. http://www.assemblee-nationale.fr/2/dossiers/pacs/981108.htm

35. Eric Doligé, November 7, 1998. Official Analytical Summary of November 7, 1998. http://www.assembleenationale.fr/2/dossiers/pacs/981107.htm

36. Statement made during last reading of the bill in the Senate, June 30, 1999. http://altern.org.ardhis/etrangers.htm

37. Christine Boutin, November 3, 1998. Integral Report of session held on November 3, 1998. http://www.assemblee-nat.fr/2/cri/19990057.htm

38. Thierry Mariani, RPR, December 8, 1998. Summative Report (*Sommaire des comptes rendus*) of December 8, 1998. http://www.assemblee-nationale.fr/2/dossiers / pacs/9812o8.htm

39. Christian Estrossi, RPR, November 7, 1998. Official Analytical Summary of November 7, 1998. http://www.assembleenationale.fr/2/dossiers/pacs/981107.htm

40. Christine Boutin, November 3, 1998. Emphasis added. Integral Report of session held on November 3, 1998. http://www.assemblee-nat.fr/2/cri/19990057.htm

41. Jacques Masdeu-Arus, RPR, November 7, 1998. Official Analytical Summary of November 7, 1998. http://www.assembleenationale.fr/2/dossiers/pacs/981107.htm

42. Thierry Mariani, RPR, November 7, 1998. Official Analytical Summary of November 7, 1998. http://www.assembleenationale.fr/2/dossiers/pacs/981107.htm

43. Philippe Le Jolis de Villiers de Saintignon, Movement for France (*Mouvement pour la France*) or MPF, November 7, 1998. Official Analytical Summary of November 7, 1998. http://www.assembleenationale.fr/2/dossiers/pacs/981107.htm

44. Philippe Houillon, DL, November 7, 1998. Official Analytical Summary of November 7, 1998. http://www.assembleenationale.fr/2/dossiers/pacs/981107.htm

45. Bernard Accoyer, RRR, December 8, 1998. Summative Report (*Sommaire des comptes rendus*) of December 8, 1998. http://www.assemblee-nationale.fr/2/dossiers/pacs/9812o8.htm

46. Article 12 in the final version of the PaCS. The one-year period that was included in the initial text has also disappeared from the final text. See *PaCS Bill 1118* (*Proposition de Loi no 1118 relative au pacte civil de solidarité*). http://www.assemblee -nationale.fr/2/dossiers/pacs1118.htm

47. Christine Boutin, November 3, 1998. Integral Report of session held on November 3, 1998. http://www.assemblee-nat.fr/2/cri/19990057.htm

48. Jacques Masdeu-Arus, RPR, November 7, 1998. Official Analytical Summary of November 7, 1998. http://www.assembleenationale.fr/2/dossiers/pacs/981107.htm

49. Thierry Mariani, December 8, 1998. Summative Report (*Sommaire des comptes rendus*) of December 8, 1998. http://www.assemblee-nationale.fr/2/dossiers /pacs/9812o8.htm

50. Chrisine Boutin, December 1–2, 1998.

51. Thierry Mariani, November 7, 1998. Official Analytical Summary of November 7, 1998. http://www.assembleenationale.fr/2/dossiers/pacs/981107.htm

52. Claude Goasguen, DL, December 1–2, 1998.

53. Dominique Dord, UDF, November 7, 1998. Official Analytical Summary of November 7, 1998. http://www.assembleenationale.fr/2/dossiers/pacs/981107.htm

54. Thierry Mariani, RPR, November 7, 1998. Official Analytical Summary of November 7, 1998. http://www.assembleenationale.fr/2/dossiers/pacs/981107.htm

55. Accoyer introduced amendment 434, which would forbid aliens illegally residing in France from contracting a PaCS. Boutin introduced an amendment that would make the PaCS available to French citizens only (it was rejected). Mariani introduced several amendments (200 and 300) aimed at the exclusion of the *sans-papiers* (both were rejected), and Amendment 301, which would forbid a foreigner who had entered France illegally from being able to contract a PaCS. Goasguen's Amendment 220 demanded the removal of Article 6 (it was rejected). Mariani introduced Amendment 322, which would forbid the contracting of a PaCS outside of France (it was rejected); Amendment 329, which demanded that one of the persons signing a PaCS must be a French citizen (the same as Amendment 717—both were rejected); Amendment 323, which demanded a five-year limit before it would opened rights to legal sojourn; Amendment 324, which demanded a three- year limit; Amendment 325, which demanded a two-year limit; Amendment 908, which also demanded a two-year limit; and Amendment 907, which demanded a one-year limit. All were rejected.

56. *L'observatoire du PaCS* includes the following organizations: *Agir ensemble contre le chômage* (*AC!*), ACT UP-Paris, *Aides fédération nationale* (National Federation HIV/AIDS Help), *Aides* (HIV/AIDS Help) Paris-Ile de France, *Association des parents et futurs parents gais et lesbiens* (Association of Parents and Future Parents of

Gays and Lesbians), *Association pour la reconnaissance des droits des personnes homosexuelles et transexulles à l'immigration et au séjour* (Association for the Recognition of the Right to Immigration and Sojourn of Transsexual and Homosexual Persons), *Centre gai & lesbien* (Gay and Lesbian Center), *ProChoix-Paris* (Pro-Choice-Paris), and *SOS homophobie* (SOS Homophobia).

57. These benefits are the Allocation for Isolated Parents (API), the Specific Solidarity Allocation (ASS), the Minimum Insertion Revenue (RMI), and the Handicapped Adult Allocation (AAH).

58. The administrative memorandum of December 10, 1999, specifies that the person seeking legal sojourn and residency papers must prove—regardless of the date of the PaCS—three years of common life with a French citizen.

59. More than three hundred thousand PaCS have been contracted since the passage of the law.

Conclusion

1. See Lochak, *Étrangers: De quel droit?*; Étienne Balibar, *Les frontières de la démocratie*; Naïr, *Contre les lois Pasqua*; Didier Fassin, Alain Morice, and Catherine Quiminal, *Les lois de l'inhospitalité: Les politiques de l'immigration à l'épreuve des sans-papiers*; Monique Chemillier-Gendreau, *L'injustifiable: Les politiques françaises de l'immigration*; and Freedman, *Immigration and Insecurity in France*.

2. Elaine Sciolino, "Sarkozy Pledges Crackdown on Rioters."

3. The law was promulgated on November 20, 2007, and is often referred to as the Hortefeux Law. Brice Hortefeux is the minister of immigration, integration, and national identity in the Sarkozy government. The Senate vote was 185 yes, 136 no, and the National Assembly vote was 282 yes, 235 no. Socialists voted unanimously against the bill.

4. See Eric Fassin, "Statistiques de la discorde."

BIBLIOGRAPHY

Abdallah, Mogniss H. "Les sans-papiers, d'hier à aujourd'hui, pour une mémoire collective de l'immigration." In IM'média/REFLEX, *Chroniques d'un movement: Sans-papiers.* Paris: Editions REFLEX, 1997.

Abdallah, Samir, and Raffaele Ventura, dirs. *La ballade des sans-papiers.* Paris: Agence Im'média, 1997.

Aldama, Arturo, ed. *Violence and the Body.* Bloomington: Indiana University Press, 2003.

Anderson, Benedict. *Imagined Communities.* London: Verso, 1983.

Anderson, Bridget. *Doing the Dirty Work? The Global Politics of Domestic Labor.* London: Zed Books, 2000.

Anthias, Floya, and Nira Yuval-Davis. *Racialized Boundaries: Race, Nation, Gender, Colour, and Class and the Anti-Racist Struggle.* London: Routledge, 1992.

Balibar, Étienne. *Les frontières de la démocratie.* Paris: La Découverte, 1992.

———. "Is There a 'Neo-Racism'?" In *Race, Nation, Class: Ambiguous Identities*, edited by Étienne Balibar and Immanuel Wallerstein. 17–28. New York: Verso, 1991.

———. "Le droit de cité ou l'apartheid? " In *Sans-papiers: L'archaïsme fatal*, edited by Etienne Balibar, Monique Chemillier-Gendreau, Jacqueline Costa-Lascoux, and Emmanuel Terray. Paris: La Découverte, 1999.

Balibar, Étienne, Monique Chemillier-Gendreau, Jacqueline Costa-Lascoux, and Emmanuel Terray. *Sans-papiers: L'archaïsme fatal.* Paris: La Découverte, 1999.

Bernard, Philippe. *L'immigration: Les enjeux de l'intégration.* Paris: Éditions Le Monde, 1998.

Bhabha, Homi. "The Other Question." *Screen* 24, no. 6 (1983): 18–36.

Bhabha, Jacqueline. "Border Rights and Rites: Generalizations, Stereotypes and Gendered Migration." In *Women and Immigration Law: New Variations on Classical Feminist Themes*, edited by Sarah Van Walsum and Thomas Spijkerboer. 15–34. New York: Routledge, 2007.

173

Bihr, Alain. "L'extrême droite à la conquête du prolétariat: En France, désespérance populaire et démagogie politique." *Le Monde Diplomatique* (December 1995): 4–5.

Bissuel, Bertrand. "Divorcer ou vivre sans papiers." *Le Monde* (February 10, 2002).

Bodin, Claudette, and Catherine Quiminal. "Le long voyage des femmes du Fleuve Sénégal." *Hommes et Migrations* 1141 (March 1991): 23–26.

Body-Gendrot, Sophie. "Models of Immigrant Integration in France and the United States." In *The Bubling Cauldron: Race, Ethnicity, and the Urban Crisis*, edited by Michael Peter Smith and Joe Feagin. Minneapolis: University of Minnesota Press, 1995.

Bonnaud, Octave. "De Villiers décuple le nombre de familles polygames en France." *Marianne* 2 (April 12, 2007), http://www.marianne2.fr/index.php?action=article&numero=1121

Bosniak, Linda. *The Citizen and the Alien: Dilemmas of Contemporary Membership*. Princeton, NJ: Princeton University Press, 2006.

Bouamama, Saïd. *J'y suis, J'y vote: La lutte pour les droits politiques aux résidents étrangers*. Paris: L'Esprit Frappeur, 2000.

Boulahbel-Villac, Yeza. "The Integration of Algerian Women in France: A Compromise Between Tradition and Modernity." In *International Migration Policies and the Status of Female Migrants*. Proceedings of the United Nations Expert Group Meeting on International Migration Polices and the Status of Female Migrants, San Miniato, Italy, March 28–31, 1990. New York: United Nations, 1995.

Browning, Barbara. *Infectious Rhythms: Metaphors of Contagion and the Spread of African Culture*. New York: Routledge, 1998.

Brubaker, Rogers. *Citizenship and Nationhood in France and Germany*. Cambridge, MA: Harvard University Press, 1992.

Brun, François, and Smaïn Laacher. "De la régularisation à l'intégration: Stratégies, atouts, obstacles . . . ." *Migrations Études* 97 (January–February 2001): 1–12.

Butler, Judith. *Bodies That Matter: On the Discursive Limits of "Sex."* New York: Routledge, 1993.

Caspari, Andrea, and Winona Giles. "Immigration Policy and the Employment of Portuguese Migrant Women in the UK and France: A Comparative Analysis." In *International Immigration and the Female Experience*, edited by Rita James Simon and Caroline B. Brettell. 152–177. Totowa, NJ: Rowman and Littlefield, 1986.

Castles, Stephen, and Alastair Davidson. *Citizenship and Migration: Globalization and the Politics of Belonging*. New York: Routledge, 2000.

Cealis, Roza, Delalande François, Jansolin Xavier, Marie Claude-Valentin, and Lebon André. "Immigration clandestine: La régularisation des travailleurs 'sans-papiers' (1981–1982)." Numéro Spécial Supplément 106. Paris: Ministère des Affaires Sociales et de la Solidarité Nationale, 1983.

————. *Facteurs d'insertion et d'exclusion des femmes immigrantes dans le marché du travail en France: Quel état des connaissances?* Paris: Confédération Française Démocratique du Travail, 2001.

Chemillier-Gendreau, Monique. *L'injustifiable: Les politiques françaises de l'immigration.* Paris: Éditions Bayard, 1998.

Cissé, Madjiguène. *Parole de sans-papiers.* Paris: La Dispute, 1999.

————. "Sans-Papiers: Un combat pour les droits de l'homme." 1998. http://www.bok.net/pajol/international/allemagne/liga/madjicombat.html

————. "The Sans-Papiers: A Woman Draws the First Lessons." *Politique, La Revue* 2 (October 1996): 1–6.

Collovald, Annie. *Le "populisme du FN," un dangereux contresens.* Broissieux: Le Croquant, 2004.

Commission immigration Scalp-Reflex. "Quand le sage montre la lune, l'imbécile regarde le doigt." In IM'média/REFLEX, *Chroniques d'un movement: Sans-papiers.* Paris: Editions REFLEX, 1997: 62–65.

Commission nationale consultative des droits de l'homme. "Avis sur la situation de la polygamie en France," March 9, 2006. http://www.cncdh.fr/article.php3?id_ article=100.

Constable, Nicole. *Maid to Order in Hong Kong: Stories of Filipina Workers.* Ithaca, NY: Cornell University Press, 1997.

Das Gupta, Monisha. *Unruly Immigrants: Rights, Activism, and Transnational South Asian Politics in the United States.* Durham, SC: Duke University Press, 2006.

Deckmyn, Chantal. *Les "actions femmes" dans la politique de la ville en region Provence-Alpes-Côte d'Azur.* Rapport pour la délégation régionale des droits de femmes PACA. Marseille: Délégation Régionale des Droits de Femmes PACA, Préfecture de Région PACA, March 1999.

de Lauretis, Teresa. *Alice Doesn't: Feminism, Semiotics, Cinema.* Bloomington: Indiana University Press, 1984.

de Oliviera a Silva, Edna, and Martine El Mahalawi-Nouet. "L'aspiration à l'autonomie des femmes immigrées." *Hommes et Libertés* 33 (1984): 39–41.

Diop, Ababacar. *Dans la peau d'un sans-papiers.* Paris: Editions du Seuil, 1997.

Dord, Dominique. "Pacs: un mauvais projet." *Le Figaro* (October 9, 1998).

Dubois, Sharon, and Martin Benoit, "The Sans Papiers Success." 1997. http://www.llb.labournet.org.uk/1997/february/news1.html

Duggan, Lisa. *Sapphic Slashers: Sex, Violence, and American Modernity.* Durham, NC: Duke University Press, 2000.

Dutt, Malika, Leni Marin, and Helen Zia. *Migrant Women's Human Rights in G-7 Countries: Organizing Strategies.* San Francisco: Family Violence Prevention Fund; New Brunswick, NJ: Center for Women's Global Leadership, 1997.

Ehrenreich, Barbara, and Arlie Russel Hochschild, eds. *Global Woman: Nannies, Maids and Sex Workers in the New Economy.* New York: Macmillan, 2003.

Eliane. "Logement: Femmes sans papiers, doublement opprimées." *Alternative Libertaire* 112 (2003): 14.

European Commission. *The European Constitution: Post-Referendum in France.* Wavre, Belgium: European Commission, 2005.

Ezekiel, Judith. "French Dressing: Race, Gender, and the Hijab Story." *Feminist Studies* 32, no. 2 (Summer 2006): 256–281.

Fassin, Éric. "Statistiques de la discorde." *Le Monde* (October 6, 2007).

Fassin, Eric, Alain Morice, and Catherine Quiminal (dirs.) *Les lois de l'inhospitalité: Les politiques de l'immigration à l'épreuve des sans-papiers.* Paris: La Découverte, 1997.

Favell, Adrian. *Philosophies of Integration: Immigration and the Idea of Citizenship in France and Britain.* New York: Palgrave, 2001.

Fonds d'aide et de soutien pour l'intégration et la lutte contre les discriminations (FASILD). *Femmes d'origine étrangère: Travail, accés à l'emploi, discriminations de genre.* Paris: La Documentation Française, 2004.

Fougeyrollas-Schwebel, Dominique, Éléonore Lépinard, and Eleni Varikas, eds. "Féminisme(s): Penser la pluralité." *Cahiers du Genre* 39 (2005): 13–26.

Frankenberg, Ruth, and Lata Mani. "Crosscurrents, Crosstalk: Race, 'Postcoloniality' and the Politics of Location," *Cultural Studies* 7, no. 2 (1993): 292–310.

Freedman, Jane. *Immigration and Insecurity in France.* Aldershot, UK: Ashgate, 2004.

Freedman, Jane, and Carrie Tarr. *Women, Immigration and Identities in France.* New York: Berg, 2000.

Fuller, Thomas. "The Workplace: For French, Cheap Labor Is the Specter," *International Herald Tribune* (May 25, 2005).

Gaspard, Françoise. "Statut personnel et intégration sociale, culturelle et nationale." *Hommes et Libertés* 84 (June–July–August 1995): 3–15.

———. "De l'invisibilité des migrantes et de leurs filles à leur instrumentalisation." *Migrants Formation* 105 (June 1996): 15–30.

Gaspard, Françoise, and Farhad Khosrokhavar. *Le foulard et la République.* Paris: La Découverte, 1995.

Gaspard, Françoise, Claude Servan-Schreiber, and Anne Le Gall. *Au pouvoir, citoyennes! Liberté, égalité, parité.* Paris: Éditions du Seuil, 1992.

Gilman, Sander. "Black Bodies, White Bodies: Toward an Iconography of Female Sexuality in Late Nineteenth-Century Art, Medicine, and Literature." In *Race, Writing and Difference*, edited by Henry Louis Gates Jr. 223–261. Chicago: University of Chicago Press, 1985.

Glenn, Evelyn Nakano. *Unequal Freedom: How Race and Gender Shaped American Citizenship and Labor.* Cambridge, MA: Harvard University Press, 2002.

———. *Issei, Nissei, War Bride: Three Generations of Japanese American Women in Domestic Service.* Philadelphia: Temple University Press, 1986.

Gnath, Catharina. "The Services Directive Has Passed the European Parliament: Business as Usual?" *European Newsletter* (March–April 2006).

Golub, Anne, Mirjana Morokvasik, and Catherine Quiminal. "Evolution de la production des connaissances sur les femmes immigrées en France et en Europe," *Migrations Société* 9, no. 52 (July–August 1997): 19–37.

Gopinah, Gayatri. *Impossible Desires: Queer Diasporas and South Asian Public Cultures.* Durham, SC: Duke University Press, 2005.

Gresh, Alain. "Malevolent Fantasy of Islam." *Le Monde Diplomatique* (August 2005). Available in English at http://www.mondediplo.com/2005/08/16lewis

Guénif-Souilamas, Nacira. *Des 'Beurettes' aux descendants d'immigrants Nord-Africains.* Paris: Bernard Grasset, 2000.

Guénif-Souilamas, Nacira, and Eric Massé. *Les féministes et le garçon arabe.* Paris: Editions de L'aube, 2004.

Hargreaves, Alec. *Immigration, 'Race' and Ethnicity in Contemporary France.* New York: Routledge, 1995.

Hollifield, James. "Ideas, Institutions, and Civil Society: On the Limits of Immigration Control in France." Paper prepared for a workshop on Immigration Control in Europe, University of Bologna, Italy, April 1997.

Hostalier, Françoise. *Étude et propositions: La polygamie en France.* L'Annuaire au féminin, March 9, 2006. http://www.annuaire-au-feminin.net/06–polygamieFH.html

IM'média/reflex. *Chroniques d'un movement: Sans-papiers.* Paris: Reflex, 1997.

———. "La ballade des sans-papiers." IM'média/REFLEX, *Chroniques d'un movement: Sans-papiers.* 15–22. Paris: Éditions REFLEX, 1997.

Institut national de la statistique et des études économiques. *Les femmes: Portrait social.* Paris: INSEE, 1995.

———. *Les immigrés en France: Portrait social.* Paris: INSEE, 1997.

Jacobson, David. *Rights Across Borders: Immigration and the Decline of Citizenship.* Baltimore, MD: John Hopkins University Press, 1996.

Karen Kaplan, Norma Alarcón, and Minoo Moallem, eds. *Between Woman and Nation: Nationalisms, Transnational Feminisms, and the State.* Durham, SC: Duke University Press, 1999.

Kolher, Catherine, and Suzanne Thave. "Un demi-siècle de regroupement familial en France." *Synthèses* 3 (October 1999): 7–19.

Krulic, Joseph. "L'immigration et l'identité de la France, mythes et réalités." *Pouvoirs* 47 (1988): 31–43.

Krook, Mona Lena. "Competing Claims: Quotas for Women and Minorities in India and France." Paper presented at the General Conference of the European Consortium for Political Research, Budapest, Hungary, September 8–10, 2005.

http://krook.wustl.edu/doc/krook-competing%20claims.doc

Lamont, Michèle. *The Dignity of Working Men: Morality and the Boundaries of Race, Class, and Immigration.* Cambridge, MA: Harvard University Press, 2000.

Landes, Joan. "The Performance of Citizenship: Democracy, Gender, and Difference in the French Revolution." In *Democracy and Difference: Contesting the Boundaries of the Political*, edited by Seyla Benhabib. 295–313. Princeton, NJ: Princeton University Press, 1996.

Lavenex, Sandra. "National Frames in Migration Research: The Tacit Political Agenda." In *International Migration Research: Constructions, Omissions, and the Promises of Interdisciplinarity*, edited by Michael Bommes and Ewa T. Morawska. 243–264. Aldershot, UK: Ashgate, 2005.

Le Bars, Stéphanie. "Une marocaine en burqa se voit refuser la nationalité française." *Le Monde* (July 12, 2008).

Le Bras, Hervé. *Le sol et le sang: Théories de l'invasion au XXe siècle.* Paris: Editions de l'aube, 1994.

Le Coeur, Philippe. "La crainte pour l'emploi est la raison principale du rejet de la Constitution par les Français." *Le Monde* (May 31, 2005).

Le guide de l'entrée et du séjour des étrangers en France. GISTI. 8ème edition. Paris: Syros/Guides GISTI, 2008.

Lebon, André. *Immigration et présence étrangère en France en 2002.* Paris: La Documentation Française, 2003.

Lefebvre, Edwige Liliane. "Republicanism and Universalism: Factors of Inclusion or Exclusion in the French Concept of Citizenship." *Citizenship Studies* 7, no. 1 (2003): 15–36.

Lesselier, Claudie. "Femmes migrantes en France: Le genre et la loi." In *Genre, travail et migrations en Europe*, edited by Madeleine Hersent and Claude Zaidman. 45–59. Paris: Publications Paris 7, 2003.

———. "Pour une critique féministe des lois sur l'entrée et le séjour des personnes étrangères en France." *Brochure du RAJFIRE* 2 (March 2000).

Liauzu, Claude. "Une loi contre l'histoire." *Le Monde Diplomatique* (April 2005). http://www.mondediplomatique.fr/2005/04/LIAUZU/12080

Libération. "Une sans-papier harcelée de 'câlins' policiers," *Libération* (September 28, 1998).

———. "Des pages jaunes pour Frits Bolkstein," *Libération* (April 11, 2005).

Ligue des droits de l'homme (LDH). "C'est pas la faute aux polygames. . . ." Ligue des droits de l'homme. November 16, 2005. http://www.ldh-toulon.net/spip.php?article1004

Lloyd, Cathy. "*Rendez-vous manqués*: Feminisms and Anti-racisms in France." *Modern and Contemporary France* 6, no. 1 (1998): 61–73.

Lochak, Danièle. *Étrangers: De quel droit?* Paris: Presses Universitaires de France, 1985.

Lowe, Lisa. *Immigrant Acts: On Asian American Cultural Politics.* Durham, SC: Duke University Press, 1996.

Maruani, Margaret. *Travail et emploi des femmes.* Paris: La Découverte, 2000.

Mauco, Georges. *Les étrangers en France: Leur rôle dans l'activité économique.* Paris: Librairie Armand Colin. 1932.

Mayer, Nonna. "Radical Right Populism in France: How Much of the 2002 Le Pen Votes Does Populism Explain?" Symposium on Globalization and the Radical Right Populism, Centre for the Study of European Politics and Society, Ben Gurion University of the Neguev, Beer Sheva, Israel, April 11–13, 2005: 5–6. http://hsf.bgu.ac.il/europe/uploadDocs/csepspnm.pdf

McCaffrey, Enda. *The Gay Republic: Sexuality, Citizenship, and Subversion in France.* Aldershot, UK: Ashgate, 2005.

McClintock, Anne. *Imperial Leather: Race, Gender and Sexuality in the Colonial Context.* New York: Routledge, 1995.

———. "The Angel of Progress: Pitfalls of the Term `Post-Colonialism.'" *Social Text* 31/32 (1992): 1–15.

Mohanram, Radhika. *Women, Colonialism and Space.* Minneapolis: University of Minnesota Press, 1999.

Mohanty, Chandra Talpade. *Feminism Without Borders: Decolonizing Theory, Practicing Solidarity.* Durham, NC: Duke University Press, 2003.

———. "Under Western Eyes: Feminist Scholarship and Colonial Discourses." *Feminist Review* 30 (Autumn 1988): 61–88.

Morris, Peter. *French Politics Today.* Manchester, UK: Manchester University Press, 1994.

Mosse, George. *Nationalism and Sexuality: Respectability and Abnormal Sexuality in Modern Europe.* New York: Howard Fertig, 1985.

Naïr, Sami. *Contre les lois Pasqua.* Paris: Arléa, 1997.

Neyrand, Gérard. "Le suivi social des étrangers régularisés au titre de la circulaire de 24 Juin 1997." *Migrations Etudes* 92 (January–February 2000): 1–8.

Ngai, Mae N. *Impossible Subjects: Illegal Aliens and the Making of Modern America.* Princeton, NJ: Princeton University Press, 2004.

Noiriel, Gérard. "La nationalité au miroir des mots." In *De l'immigraton à l'integration en France et en Allemagne*, edited by Bernard Falga, Catherine Wihtol de Wenden, and Claus Leggewie. 21–31. Paris: Cerf, 1994.

———. *Le creuset français: Histoire de l'immigration XIXe–XXe siècle.* Paris: Seuil, 1988.

Oliveira Silva de, Edna, and Martine El Mehalawi-Nouet. "L'aspiration à l'autonomie des femmes immigrées." *Hommes et Libertés* 33 (1984): 38–41.

Omi, Michael, and Howard Winant, *Racial Formation in the United States from the 1960s to the 1980s*. New York: Routledge, 1986.

Ong, Aihwa. "The Gender and Labor Politics of Postmodernity." In *The Politics of Culture in the Shadow of Capital*, edited by Lisa Lowe and David Lloyd. 61–97. Durham, NC: Duke University Press, 1997.

———. "Cultural Citizenship as Subject-Making: Immigrants Negotiate Racial and Cultural Boundaries in the United States." *Current Anthropology* 37, no. 5 (December 1996): 737–762.

Ouali, Nouria. "Les télévisions francophones et l'image des femmes immigrées." *Annuaire de l'Afrique du Nord* 34 (1995): 971–980.

Parreñas, Rhacel Salazar. *Servants of Globalization: Women, Migration, and Domestic Work*. Stanford, CA: Stanford University Press, 2001.

Patton, Cindy. "From Nation to Family: Containing African AIDS." In *The Lesbian and Gay Studies Reader*, edited by Henri Abelove, Michele Aina Barale, and David Halperin. 127–138. New York: Routledge, 1993.

Pei-Chia, Lan. *Global Cinderellas: Migrant Domestics and Newly Rich Employers in Taiwan*. Durham, NC: Duke University Press, 2006.

Ponthieux, Sophie, and Amandine Schreiber. "Dans les couples de salariés, la répartition du travail domestique reste inégale." *Données Sociales* (2006): 43–51.

Pouliquen, Jean-Paul, and Denis Quinqueton. "Le PaCS est-il républicain?" *Le Monde* (October 15, 1999).

Quiminal, Catherine. "Le rapport colonial revisité: Les luttes des africains et des africaines en France." *Sociétés Africaines et Diaspora* 4 (December 1996): 15–26.

Quiminal, Catherine, Babacar Diouf, Babacar Fall, and Mahamet Timera. "Mobilisation associative et dynamiques d'intégration des femmes d'Afrique subsaharienne en France." *Migrations Études* 61 (October–November–December 1995): 1–12.

Rahal-Sidhoum, Saïda. "Du statut des femmes." *Quantara* 14 (January–February–March 1995): 59–61.

———. *Éléments d'analyse de statut socio-juridique des femmes immigrées en vue d'un statut pour l'autonomie des femmes immigrées en France*. Paris: Convention C.F. I./F.N.D.V.A., 1987.

Raissiguier, Catherine. "Muslim Women in France: Impossible Subjects?" Racism in the Closet: Interrogating Postcolonial Sexuality, Special Issue, *DarkMatter* (May 2008). http://www.darkmatter101.org/site/2008/05/02/muslim-women-in -france-impossible-subjects

———. "French Immigration Laws: The Sans-Papières' Perspectives." *Women and Immigration Law in Europe: New Variations of Feminist Themes*, edited by Sarah van Walsum and Thomas Spijkerboer. 204–221. New York: Routledge-Cavendish, 2007.

———. "Women from the Maghreb and Sub-Saharan Africa in France: Fighting for Health and Basic Human Rights." In *Engendering Human Rights: Cultural and*

Socioeconomic Realities in Africa, edited by Obiama Nnaemeka and Joy Ezeilo. 111–128. New York: Palgrave-Macmillan, 2005.

———. "Scattered Markets, Localized Workers: Gender and Immigration in France." In *Black Women, Globalization and Economic Justice: Studies from Africa and the African Diaspora*, edited by Filomena Steady. 180–193. Rochester, Vermont: Schenkman Books, 2002.

———. "Troubling Mothers: Immigrant Women from Africa in France." *JENdA: A Journal of Culture and African Women Studies* 4 (2003). Translated into French as "Ces mères qui dérangent." In *Genre, travail et migrations en Europe*, edited by Madeleine Hersent and Claude Zaidman. 25–43. Paris: Université Denis Diderot, 2003.

———. "Bodily Metaphors, Material Exclusions: The Sexual and Racial Politics of Domestic Partnership in France." In *Violence and the Body*, edited by Arturo Aldama. 94–112. Bloomington: Indiana University Press, 2003.

———. "The Sexual and Racial Politics of Civil Unions in France." *Radical History Review* 83 (Spring 2002): 73–93.

———. "Is Gendering Immigration Enough? The Case of France." In *Shifting Bonds, Shifting Bounds: Women's Mobility and Citizenship in Europe*, edited by Virgínia Ferreira, Teresa Tavares, and Sílvia Portugal. 139–148. Oeiras: Celta Editora, 1998.

———. "Gender, Race, and Exclusion: A New Look at the French Republican Tradition." *International Feminist Journal of Politics* 1, no. 3 (1999): 435–457.

———. *Becoming Women/Becoming Workers: Identity Formation in a French Vocational School*. Albany: SUNY Press, 1994.

RAJFIRE. *Femmes sans papiers: En lutte!* RAJFIRE (February 1997).

———. Brochure No. 2. RAJFIRE (March 2000).

———. *Sans-papières: Des papiers et tous nos droits!* Paris: Atalante Vidéo, 2001.

Reynié, Dominique. "29 Mai 2005, un paysage dynamité." Lettre no.215. Robert Schuman Foundation (June 2005). http://constitution-europeenne.info/special/france_analyse.pdf

Rodier, Claire, and Nathalie Ferré. "Visas: Le verrou de la honte." *Plein Droit* 35 (September 1997). http://www.gisti.org/doc/plein-droit/35/visas.html

Rollins, Judith. *Between Women: Domestics and Their Employers*. Philadelphia: Temple University Press, 1985.

Romero, Mary. *Maid in the U.S.A.* New York: Routledge, 1992.

Rubery, Jill, and Colette Fagan. "Does Feminization Mean a Flexible Labour Force?" In *New Frontiers in European Industrial Relations,* edited by Richard Hyman and Anthony Ferner. 140–166. Cambridge, MA: Blackwell, 1994.

Rude-Antoine, Edwige. "Des épouses soumises à des régimes particuliers." *Migrants-Formation* 105 (June 1996): 45–61.

———. "Le statut personnel en France." *ADRI Point Sur* (July 1994): 1–12.

————. "Le statut personnel: Liberté ou sujétion?" *Plein Droit* 24 (April–June 1994): 8–12.

————. "La polygamie face au droit positif français." *Migration Societé* 35 (September–October 1994): 61–68.

————. "La polygamie et le droit Français." *Regards sur l'Actualité* (December 1991): 38–49.

Salaün, Sylvain. "Régularisations: Retour sur un mouvement en devenir." *Accueillir* 214–215 (1997): 6.

Sané, Mamadi. *"Sorti de l'ombre:" Journal d'un sans-papiers.* Paris: Le Temps des Cerises, 1996.

Sassen, Saskia. "Immigration Policy in a Global Economy." *SAIS Review* 17, no. 2 (Summer–Fall 1997): 1–19.

Scales-Trent, Judy. "African Women in France: Citizenship, Family, and Work." *Brooklyn Journal of International Law* 24, no. 3 (1999): 705–737.

Schor, Ralph. *L'opinion française et les étrangers. 1919–1939.* Paris: Publications de la Sorbonne, 1985.

Schmidt, Bernard. "Verdict in 'Charlie Hebdo' Satirical Newspaper Case: When in Doubt Choose Freedom of Speech." *Quantara.de.* (May 4, 2007). Translated from the German by Ron Walker. http://www.qantara.de/webcom/show_article.php/_c-476/_nr-762/i.html

Schnapper, Dominique. "The Debate on Immigration and the Crisis on National Identity." *West European Politics* 17, no. 2 (April 1994): 127–139.

————. *La France de l'intégration: Sociologie de la nation en 1990.* Paris: Gallimard, 1991.

Schneider, Friedrich, and Dominik Enste. "Hiding in the Shadows: The Growth of the Underground Economy." *Economic Issues* 30 (March 2000). https://www.imf.org/external/pubs/ft/issues/issues30/index.htm

Sciolino, Elaine. "Unlikely Hero in Europe's Spat: The 'Polish Plumber.'" *New York Times* (June 26, 2005). http://www.nytimes.com/2005/06/26/international/europe/26poland.html

————. "Sarkozy Pledges Crackdown on Rioters." *New York Times* (November 29, 2007).

Scott, Joan Wallach. *Parité! Sexual Equality and the Crisis of French Universalism.* Chicago: University of Chicago Press, 2005.

————. *Only Paradoxes to Offer: French Feminists and the Rights of Man.* Cambridge, MA: Harvard University Press, 1996.

Shohat, Ella. "Notes on the 'Post-Colonial.'" *Social Text* 31/32 (1992): 99–113.

Silberman, Roxanne. "Regroupement familial: Ce que disent les statistiques." *Hommes et Migrations* 1141 (March 1991): 13–17.

Siméant, Johanna. *La cause des sans-papiers.* Paris: Presses de Sciences Po, 1998.

Smith, Anna Marie. *New Rights Discourse on Race and Sexuality: Britain 1968–1990.* Cambridge, UK: Cambridge University Press, 1994.

————. "The Centering of Right-Wing Extremism Through the Construction of an 'Inclusionary' Homophobia and Racism." In *Playing with Fire: Queer Politics, Queer Theories,* edited by Shane Phelan. 113–165. New York: Routledge, 1997.

Soysal, Yasemin N. *Limits of Citizenship: Migrants and Postnational Membership in Europe.* Chicago: University of Chicago Press, 1994.

Stoler, Ann Laura. *Race and the Education of Desire: Foucault's History of Sexuality and the Colonial Order of Things.* Durham, SC: Duke University Press, 1995.

Tapinos, Georges. "Immigration féminine et statut des femmes étrangères en France." *Revue Française des Affaires Sociales* Hors Série (1992): 29–60.

Terray, Emmanuel. "Le travail des étrangers en situation irrégulière ou la délocalisation sur place." In *Sans-papiers: L'archaïsme fatal,* edited by Etienne Balibar, Monique Chemillier-Gendreau, Jacqueline Costa-Lascoux, and Emmanuel Terray. 9–34. Paris: La Découverte, 1999.

Terry, Jennifer, and Jacqueline Urla, eds. *Deviant Bodies: Critical Perspectives on Difference in Science and Popular Culture.* Bloomington: Indiana University Press, 1995.

Tévanian, Pierre. *Le racisme républicain: Réflexions sur le modèle français de discrimination.* Paris: L'Esprit Frappeur, 2001.

Tévanian, Pierre, and Sylvie Tissot. "La lepénisation des esprits: Éléments pour une grille d'analyse du racisme en France." *Les Mots Sont Important* (June 2006). http://lmsi.net/spip.php?article555

Thiery, Xavier. "Les entrées d'étrangers en France. Evolutions statistiques et bilan de l'opération de régularisation exceptionnelle de 1997." *Population* 55, no. 3 (2000): 423–450.

Thomas, Brigitte. "La gestion quotidienne des problèmes générés par des questions de statut personnel." In *Les droits personnels des femmes étrangères en France: Le cas des femmes algériennes, marocaines, tunisiennes et turques et leurs conséquences juridiques et sociales,* edited by Saïda Rahal-Sidhoum. 9–23. Paris: Actes de la rencontre, June 25, 1992.

Tribalat, Michèle. *De l'immigration à l'assimilation. Enquête sur les populations etrangères en France,* Paris: La Découverte/Ined, 1999.

Vetter, Maddy. *Situation juridique et sociale des femmes âgées étrangères (en région P. A. C. A.).* Bureau Régional de Ressources Juridiques Internationales (1997): 1–21.

Viennot, Élianne. "Les femmes d'Etat de l'Ancien Régime." In *La démocratie 'à la française' ou les femmes indésirables,* edited by Élianne Viennot. 51–62. Paris: Publications de l'Université Paris 7-Denis Diderot, 1996.

Viet, Vincent. *La France immigrée: Construction d'une politique 1914–1997.* Paris: Fayard, 1998.

Wahnich, Sophie. *L'impossible citoyen: L'étranger dans le discours de la révolution française*. Paris: Albin Michel, 1997.

Weil, Patrick. *Qu'est-ce qu'un français? Histoire de la nationalité française depuis la révolution*. Paris: Grasset, 2002.

———. *La France et ses étrangers: L'aventure d'une politique de l'immigration de 1938 à nos jours*. Paris: Gallimard, 1991.

Wieviorka, Michel. *Une société fragmentée? Le multiculturalisme en débat*. Paris: La Découverte, 1997.

Wihtol de Wenden, Catherine, and Margo Corona DeLey, "French Immigration Policy Reform and the Female Migrant." In *International Immigration and the Female Experience*, edited by Rita James Simon and Caroline B. Brettell. 197–212. Totowa, NJ: Rowman and Littlefield, 1986.

Yuval-Davis, Nira, and Floya Anthias, eds. *Women-Nation-State*. London: Macmillan, 1989.

Yuval-Davis, Nira. *Gender and Nation*. London and New York: Sage, 1997.

INDEX

Italic page numbers refer to illustrations.

Abdallah, Samir, 148n24
abstract individualism, 4, 6
Accoyer, Bernard, 89, 124, 171n55
ACT UP, 24, 116
adoption, homosexual, 122, 127, 128, 131, 169n23, 170n30
affaire du foulard (headscarf case), 33, 74, 78
African immigrants, 72–90; changing image of the immigrant, 157n9; families among, 18; family reunification for, 96; proportion of total immigrants increases, 96; women as locked within tradition and domestic sphere, 10–11, 12, 72–73, 76–79; women's labor-force participation, 97–98; young men in violent outbursts of 2005, 89; young women seen as victims or revolting against their families, 77, 78. *See also* Maghrebian immigrants; sub-Saharan African immigrants
"African mother" image, 12, 72, 76, 79, 88
Agence pour le développement des relations interculturelles (ADRI), 35
Aïcha (interviewee), 68–69
AIDS: Africa associated with, 116; *Islam=SIDA*, 113, 115–19; PaCS law associated with, 123; used to represent queers, 113, 116
Algerian immigrants, *see* Maghrebian immigrants
Allaux, Jean-Pierre, 23

allocations familliales (family allowances), 76, 89
Amara, Fadela, 161n37
Aminata (interviewee), 99–101, 164n29
Aminata D. (interviewee), 101–2, 103
antiracist organizations, 23
application receipts (*récipicés*), 61–62, 84
arranged (forced) marriages, 33, 74, 78
Asian immigrants: proportion of total immigrants increases, 96, 164n22. *See also* Chinese immigrants
assimilation (integration): in dual approach to immigration, 59; failed integration of young Maghrebi men, 34, 58; headscarf case focuses attention on, 33, 78; immigrant women as vectors of integration, 76; immigrant women seen as unable to assimilate, 73, 95; "integration contracts," 140; Islam seen as roadblock to, 78, 115, 124, 158n16; North and sub-Saharan Africans seen as unassimilable, 33; "republican integration," 139; subversive nature of resistance to, 150n5
Association for the Support of Democratic Algerian Women (*Association de solidarité avec les femmes algériennes démocrates*; ASFAD), 30
asylum, 16, 26, 87, 139, 146n9, 160n34

Balibar, Étienne, 118, 147n23
La ballade des sans-papiers (Abdallah and Ventura), 148n24

of forced, 137; *sans-papiers* as de facto nondeportable, 15
deregulation, 110
derivative rights, 60, 61, 69
difference: biological versus cultural explanations of, 118; limits of focusing on, 6; organizing around lack rather than, 40; postcolonial immigrants' radical, 80; *sans-papiers* avoid language of, 10; sex difference, 6–7; women come to symbolize immigrant, 78. *See also* gender
divorce, 63
DNA testing, 131
Doligé, Eric, 122
Dord, Dominique, 122
Dufoix, Georgina, 137, 155n27

Eastern European immigrants: Polish plumbers, 91–95; in *sans-papiers* collectives, 16
economy: deindustrialization, 80. *See also* employment; globalization
employment, 91–111; changing face of labor immigration, 96–98; contingent, 108, 110; domestic work and care giving, 94, 101–2, 105; exploitative employers, 102–3, 166n41; feminization of labor, 110; full-time jobs with benefits, 108, 110; immigrant women as working women, 95, 98; immigrant women's employment before emigrating, 17–18; immigrant women's legal barriers to, 60–61; labor-force participation of women in France, 164n25; part-time work, 98, 164n27, 165n30; as requirement for family reunification, 62; *sans-papières* as working women, 12, 98–108; temporary, 108, 110; temporary male migrant workers (*travailleurs immigrés*), 33, 57, 59; underemployment, 98; work immigration ceases, 59, 96, 97, 137; work permits, 61, 137, 140, 154n21. *See also* black market (underground) employment; sex workers; unemployment
equality: abstract universal, 5, 7, 10; in French political tradition, 1; gender inequalities in polygamous families, 80, 82; parity movement on gender parity, 5–7; rights claims based on corrective treatment or universal, 130
ethnic ranking, 57–58, 153n7

European immigrants: after World War II, 57–58; favored over non-European, 88, 94, 153n5; Portuguese immigrants, 61, 92, 97, 154n12; steady decline in numbers, 96; women's labor-force participation, 97. *See also* Eastern European immigrants
European Union: European Community lobbied on behalf of immigrant women, 69–70; French national identity affected by, 120; Polish plumbers in debate on constitution, 91, 92, 161n6, 162n7, 162n9; Turkey's proposed membership, 94; women in part-time work in, 98
Évian accords, 138, 152n2
exclusion: as constitutive of French republican citizenship, 5; as gendered and classed, 5; processes change over time, 5; racial, 5; *sans-papiers* challenge their, 133; transnational economic forces implement dual process for immigrant women, 109; women excluded from French republican citizenship, 4, 5–7

Fagan, Colette, 110
families: broadening definition of, 128; centrality in *sans-papières*' lives, 56; familial ties in obtaining change in status, 47, 48; homosexuality seen as threat to, 119, 120–24; increasing presence of, 18; in news stories on *sans-papiers*, 35; PaCS does not create, 128, 169n23; PaCS seen as threat to, 119, 120–24; in Saint-Bernard struggle, 18–19; *sans-papières* with children at national demonstration, 19; *sans-papiers* activities orchestrated around, 30, 70, 150n49; *sans-papiers* as de facto nondeportable due to, 15; used to deny legalization to those without links to France, 70. *See also* family reunification; polygamous families
family allowances (*allocations familliales*), 76, 89
family reunification, 56–64; for African immigrants, 96; changes, 1974–1998, 59–64, 138, 152n3; in Clairette's case, 86; Collective of Immigrant Women denounces, 69; conditions required for initiating, 62; defined, 56; historical context, 56–59; in Karina's case, 55; as more acceptable than work immigration, 97; near impossibility of, 65, 66, 67, 90;

hijab: headscarf case (*l'affaire du foulard*), 33, 74, 78; law prohibiting in schools, 158n15
Hommes et Libertés, 69
homophobia, 112–28; anti-gay and anti-immigrant rhetoric as connected, 112–15; of Boutin, 169n24; in PaCS law debate, 120, 122, 169n28; and racism and sexism as connected, 112–15, 120, 124–25, 127
homosexuality, *see* gays and lesbians
honor killings, 78
Hortefeux Law, 131–32, 172n3
hosting certificates, 24, 138, 139, 148n31
housing: as requirement for family reunification, 62, 65; for single men, 65; for women leaving polygamous families, 64, 82, 160n28
L'Humanité, 35
human rights: abuse in Saint-Bernard debacle, 38; Debré's proposal removes immigrants', 148n31; Hortefeux Law and, 131; *Ligue des droits de l'homme*, 69; Pasqua laws seen as reducing, 63; *sans-papiers* raise questions of, 2, 24; *sans-papiers* unsettle logic of, 20
hunger strikes: Saint-Bernard *sans-papiers* engage in, 22, 36, 42; *sans-papières* engage in, 18, 27, 35, 42, 149n44; *sans-papiers* engage in, 147n13

identity of lack, 10, 37–43, 130–31
illegal aliens: in United States, 3. *See also sans-papiers*
immigrant support groups, 23
immigrant women: African women begin to massively enter France, 16; autonomous feminine immigration, 163n19; changes in family reunification affect, 59–64; "commonsense ideas" about, 79; constructed as perpetual minors, 88; employment before emigrating, 17–18; employment hierarchies of, 109; family reunification's women-and-children-will-follow-scenario of, 58–59, 60; feminization of immigration, 59, 96–98, 108, 110; framing immigrant femininities, 33–34; heterogeneity of backgrounds and lived experience, 78; hypervisibility of, 76–77; labor-force participation, 97; labor-market locations, 108–9; legal barrier to employment, 60–61; as locked within tradition and domestic sphere, 10–11, 12, 72–73, 76–79, 95; as percentage of total immigrant population, 96; in racialization and politicization of immigration, 90, 95, 97; reductive constructions of, 78–79; in regularization process, 17; *sans-papiers'* engagement with issues of collective decision making raises question of participation of, 24, 25; social services and programs for, 79; used to represent threat of immigration, 32, 33, 34, 76; as vectors of integration, 76; as working women, 95, 98. *See also sans-papières*
immigration: AIDS associated with immigrants, 116; anti-gay and anti-immigrant rhetoric as connected, 112–15; arbitrariness of decision-making, 47, 63, 67; changing face of labor, 96–98; chosen, 131; "commonsense ideas" about, 79, 125; *contrôles au faciés*, 118, 168n20; criminalization of immigrants, 2, 125–26; demonization of postcolonial immigrants, 127; disingenuous reasons for denying change in status, 46; dual approach to, 59; feminization of, 59, 96–98, 108, 110; framing as security issue, 81; gendered underpinnings and effects of French law, 58, 59, 65, 68–69, 73, 77, 129–30, 132; immigrant as defined in France, 145n2; immigrants as impossible subjects, 2–4; *immigré*, 166n51; inside/outside dichotomy, 9; as "invasion," 34, 37, 74, 88, 110, 122, 126, 161n35; Islam represents postcolonial immigrants, 113, 115; juridico-administrative matrix for regulating, 57; Order of November 2, 1945, 57–58, 146n7; in PaCS law debate, 124; politicization of, 81, 88, 90; quasi-impossibility of legal, 65–69; restrictive policies since 1970s, 54, 58, 65, 129; riots of 2005, 89, 110, 129, 131; as scapegoat for France's problems, 129; slowness of review process, 67; supranational forces influencing, 2; temporary male migrant workers (*travailleurs immigrés*), 33, 57, 59; unemployment linked with, 60, 125, 162n9; work immigration ceases, 59, 96, 97, 137. *See also* family reunification; immigrant women; Pasqua laws; racialization of immigration; *sans-papiers*; visas

impossible subjects, 6, 40; labor-force participation in France, 164n25; parity movement on gender parity, 5–7, 30; in part-time work, 98, 165n30; sexism, racism, and homophobia as connected, 112–15, 120, 124–25, 127; unemployment of, 110. *See also* feminism; immigrant women

Women of the Sans-Papiers Coordinating Committee (*Les femmes de la coordination des sans-papiers*), 30
Women's Center (*La maison des femmes*) (Paris), 25–26, 30
work permits, 61, 137, 140, 154n21

Yamina (interviewee), 51